Methodos Series

Methodological Prospects in the Social Sciences

Volume 18

This Book Series is devoted to examining and solving the major methodological problems social sciences are facing. Take for example the gap between empirical and theoretical research, the explanatory power of models, the relevance of multilevel analysis, the weakness of cumulative knowledge, the role of ordinary knowledge in the research process, or the place which should be reserved to "time, change and history" when explaining social facts. These problems are well known and yet they are seldom treated in depth in scientific literature because of their general nature. So that these problems may be examined and solutions found, the series prompts and fosters the setting-up of international multidisciplinary research teams, and it is work by these teams that appears in the Book Series. The series can also host books produced by a single author which follow the same objectives. Proposals for manuscripts and plans for collective books will be carefully examined. The epistemological scope of these methodological problems is obvious and resorting to Philosophy of Science becomes a necessity. The main objective of the Series remains however the methodological solutions that can be applied to the problems in hand. Therefore the books of the Series are closely connected to the research practices.

Michèle Indira Friend

The Institutional Compass: Method, Use and Scope

Springer

Michèle Indira Friend
Univ. Artois, UMR 8181, UCCS – Unité
de Catalyse et Chimie du Solide
Univ. Lille, CNRS
Lille, France

I-SITE (Lille)

ISSN 1572-7750 ISSN 2542-9892 (electronic)
Methodos Series
ISBN 978-3-031-05452-5 ISBN 978-3-031-05453-2 (eBook)
https://doi.org/10.1007/978-3-031-05453-2

This Springer imprint is published by the registered company Springer Nature Switzerland AG
The registered company address is: Gewerbestrasse 11, 6330 Cham, Switzerland

This book is dedicated to wisdom – the wisdom developed by plants, animals and ecosystems, the wisdom of humans, developed and fostered in all cultures, the wisdom that will manage to persist and maybe spread.

Preface

People ask me how I came up with the idea for the compass. To answer honestly, I cannot say that there was an "ah ha" moment or that I had a sudden inspiration. It was under duress that I developed the idea over several years, making changes, adjustments and extensions.

The compass started with the convergence of four ideas: the conception of a non-linear, entropy-based accounting system, multi-criteria decision aides, institutional economics and the three *gunas* of Oriental philosophy. The first is an idea that my father has been working on since I was born, so it was on my father's knee that I learned about it. For him, accounting is not only monetary but is also based on entropy production – an idea he acquired by studying Nicholas Georgescu-Roegen's book: *The Entropy Law and the Economic Process*. I learnt the second when taking Stanislav Shmelev's summer school on ecological economics. I learnt the third from conference presentations by Arild Vatn and Peter Söderbaum, and by teaching from their books. They are the inspiration for the concept of institution. I learned the fourth from Satish Kumar's book: *Spiritual Compass*. The idea of a compass was meant in the sense of qualitative direction.

Elaborating further, my father taught me that economics is not money based, and that entropy is what we should really keep track of if we want to measure the wealth of a nation (or the fate of our planet). He also made me aware of the philosophical issues that surround statistics, of ecological economics, of the notion of ecosystem health – as it was developed by his colleague David Rapport. Shmelev taught me how several multi-criteria decision aides work and some of the philosophical questions that accompany them. Vatn and Söderbaum, through their conference presentations and writing, taught me to think in terms of institutions and that while institutions influence, us, we influence them back. Institutions change and the change can be directed. In particular, I appreciate Söderbaum's conception of political economic person as an actor in an institution and share his distaste for relying on expert advisors for making decisions. The distaste is due to excluding public participation in decision-making in what are partly political problems, and so cannot be really solved with a technical solution. Kumar's book introduced me to the idea of the three *gunas* of Jain, Hindu and Buddhist philosophies.

Bringing these four conceptions together and realising that policy decisions are made in complex situations where there is a lot of uncertainty, I thought decision makers needed a tool that was multi-dimensional (non-linear), comprehensive, ideologically malleable, holistic and qualitative but based on "hard facts" that are quantitative, democratically inclusive and very simple in the representation so that policy decisions can be easily communicated, understood and justified. This is what I provide here.

I anticipate resistance to the ideas. First, it seems impossible to design such a tool. How can a decision aide be qualitative and objective? This question has followed me throughout the process of developing the compass methodology. My background in philosophy of mathematics makes me acutely attuned to questions of objectivity. But there is a more psychological form of resistance from policymakers. Making decisions democratic and inclusive threatens the policymaker and their experts with loss of power. However, this threat is illusory. Wide participation in decision-making has the advantage of significantly reducing responsibility, since it is now shared, and of promoting the longevity of policy decisions – paradoxically bringing favourable historical acclaim and respect to the policymaker.

The rest of the working out of the methodology had to do with data and representation. I had to work out what to include and how to analyse it. It then had to be represented in a completely intuitive and simple form. This came together in the form of a compass with colours representing qualities. The data is drawn together with a little mathematics. The mathematics was worked out with sleeves rolled up, scribbling with a pen on paper.

Lille, France Michèle Indira Friend

Acknowledgements

This project received funding from the RECABIO project which is supported by the French government through Le Programme d'Investissements d'Avenir (I-SITE ULNE/ANR-16-IDEX-0004 ULNE) managed by the Agence Nationale de la Recherche.

Despite COVID-19 restrictions being implemented a month after my arrival in France, I received a warm welcome in the UCCS laboratory to join the pilot project: Science for a Changing Planet. Two sub-projects with which I collaborate are: RECABIO and VAALBIO. It is the latter that has funded the open access for this publication, and the professional illustrator Thierry Ayoun. I share the laboratory's values in making this book open access.

As for the illustrations, without Thierry Ayoun's help, they would have been a collection of distorted messes. Ayoun's careful observations and meticulous work have set a high standard. We had long discussions about colours, effects and possibilities. He also suggested the idea of the two charts at the end of the book. In the case studies, we see slightly different compass colours and a different effect. This is because the case-study illustrations were made by my students: Ahmed Yaman Abdin and Ana Mulió Álvarez. I thank them for their careful work. It is important to show the difference here since it helps us to understand that the colours are a choice. The illustrations are important for the material in the book since the representation of data is powerful.

On a more personal level, in France, I have been very well supported and welcomed, particularly by Sébastien Paul, Franck Dumeignil and Veronique Lecourtois.

The Philosophy Department at George Washington University has supported my absence in my status of taking leave without pay. They have graciously taken over my teaching and kept a place for me to return when my contract in France ends.

I would like to offer special thanks to Peter Seglow who read two versions of the manuscript and offered important suggestions for alterations. The text is more concise and direct as a result. Ulrich Koch provided encouraging feedback on an early version. This was particularly pertinent for me, since both Peter and Ulrich are not members of my usual readership. The anonymous reviewer for the manuscript offered praise and helpful suggestions for improvement.

I have taught previous versions of the compass to students at George Washington University and at Centrale Lille. Students are good listeners and, of course, ask questions when they run into trouble. Every time they asked a question, it indicated to me that either I had not thought things through enough or that I needed to explain with greater care or more precision. I thank them for their attention and questions. An ex-student of mine, Quinn Samouilidis, did all of the data analysis for the product labels for a shop. See Section 9.1 and case study II. This was a long exercise. I thank him for his tireless work and interest in doing this project.

I have made presentations of the compass at international conferences with my father and selected students: Ana Mulió Álvarez, Lilith Don, Anthony Friend, Emilie Ghaffari and Nicole McLernon. On two occasions we ran workshops together. They were good experiences for the students, and the audiences at the conferences asked helpful questions and offered encouragement. Ana wrote the first case study in this book. Her candid and precise discussion are invaluable for reflecting on the data analysis. I would also like to thank Ahmed Yaman Abdin – my collaborator on the case study of Hauts-de-France. His interest, enthusiasm and friendship have been encouraging. He did the figures for case study I and III.

I received encouragement from members of the systems science community. In particular, they include: Bill Smith, Stuart Umpleby, Peter Tuddenham, Kerry Turner, Marc Pierson, Robert Johannson, Dennis Finlayson, Gary R. Smith and George Mobus.

Abstract

An institutional compass is used to holistically and comprehensively *evaluate* an institution. The adoption of the word "institution" is inspired by institutional economists. For the purposes here, an institution is an organisation with rules. It could be a political or geographical region on any scale, a transportation network, a factory or even a household. The primary audience for this methodology is policymakers: politicians who have to make difficult decisions in an uncertain environment, where it is unclear how to compare, for example, job security to environmental protection.

The evaluation of the institution is *represented* as a direction on a coloured circle. The direction is a degree on a circle with 0° starting at the top, increasing in a clockwise direction. The simplicity of the representation makes it a good tool for communication, and therefore, for making policy decisions more participative. There are three general compass sectors, each identified with a general quality. The three are: harmony, discipline and excitement. These are general qualities that are identified with institutions *and* data points. Like a normal compass, the direction can have any degree, showing nuance between the qualities. Unlike a normal compass, in the representation, the arrow has a length, and this indicates the strength (momentum/intensity) with which it is heading in that direction.

Any organisation can develop an institutional compass to examine the discrepancy between where the institution would like to see itself (suggested in its mandate) and the actual situation it finds itself in. The latter is determined through an aggregation of statistical data and facts entered on a table. The evaluation can be used to inform policy decisions, to guide and justify policy, to negotiate policy or by someone outside to launch a detailed critique. Several compasses can be constructed and used to compare the same institution over time or to compare similar institutions to each other.

The methodology is novel in at least five respects: in the representation of the data, in the aggregation technique, in the way in which objectivity is sought, in the technique of data analysis and in the scope of the compass to serve different purposes. The scope includes adjusting the description to align with a particular

Fig. 1 An institutional compass

worldview. This allows us to anticipate where tensions will arise between communities with different worldviews and find a point of negotiation. The scope further includes: detecting feedback loops, a qualitative accounting system and as a normative signal added to systems thinking (Fig. 6.3).

In this book, the explanation of the methodology for constructing a basic institutional compass is followed by the several adaptations. One adaptation is treated in detail. This is the adaptation to make what I call an "institutional ecological economics compass". The ecological compass works according to the central ideas of ecological economics. This adaptation is given detailed treatment since it is this thinking that accompanies our transition towards a greener economy and towards strong sustainability.

Actual case studies are then considered. The first is a compass of The World Health Organisation. The second is to use the compass to label products in a shop. The Third concers biomass conversion on an industrial scale in a particular geopolitical region: Hauts-de-France.

The compass is most directly inspired by the work of David Barkin, Salvador Peniche Camps, Anthony Friend, Rob Hoffman, Satish Kumar, David Rapport, Georgescu-Roegen, Stanislav Shmelev, Peter Söderbaum, Stuart Umpleby and Arild Vatn.

Keywords Institutional compass; Policy decisions; Qualitative accounting; Ecological economics; Environment; Sustainability; Data analysis; Complexity

Contents

List of Figures

List of Tables

Part I
Introduction

I introduce the institutional compass to the reader. We make a first acquaintance with some key concepts. We learn about the importance of the compass, how it can be used and when it replaces and outstrips existing multi-criteria decision aides.

Chapter 1
General Introduction

This book is primarily aimed at people occupying the rank of policy maker, policy advisor or decision maker: those in charge of an institution such as a bank, a shop, a company, a university, a government, members of a decision committee or an international organisation. It is not meant to serve as a course textbook. Rather, it is meant as a handbook, used by anyone who finds making decisions difficult. Since the readership is diverse in background and expertise the reader should read chapters and parts selectively, as and when questions or concerns surface. More guidance about the parts of the book is found in this chapter. The crux of the book is the method outlined in Chap. 5.

The reason for making the effort to understand how to construct an institutional compass is that politicians and other decision makers increasingly find themselves in complex situations where there are many incomparable tensions – between promoting jobs in a region *versus* preserving an ecological zone in its greater integrity *versus* encouraging investment *versus* maintaining infrastructure *versus* deciding on repressive measures on one part of the population to ensure protection of another part *versus* ensuring power or long-term peace. It is too easy to be caught in the moment, to react to the latest information to which we have been exposed. A good decision maker corrects for his, or her, spontaneity and emotion, has a clear view of the issues at play and makes a judicious and balanced decision. An indication of a good decision is its long-term effects. Another is in the confidence inspired in others by the decision maker. A third is in the resulting health of the economy, society or ecology of a region. In an effort to ensure good decisions in large organisations, we institute decision making processes that take time. The time and cumbersome quality of some of these decision-making institutions is a safeguard against poor spontaneous and emotional decisions. But for all that, it is not always the best decisions that are made, even given the information available. This is because even with the most sophisticated decision aides to date, important information is missing or is not weighted appropriately.

By using an institutional compass to make or modify policy decisions, policy makers are equipped with a comprehensive and balanced picture of their institution

M. I. Friend, *The Institutional Compass: Method, Use and Scope*, Methodos Series 18, https://doi.org/10.1007/978-3-031-05453-2_1

and its context. They have a sense of the direction in which their institution is heading and whether this is the right direction. They have a means of communicating decisions intuitively, explaining them at length and justifying them in depth, and modifying them in the light of new evidence or changes in the environment without losing track of the final aim. Decision makers can watch over time the steadiness of the direction of their institution, or watch it change as a result of policy, and so they can adjust policy quickly to regain the desired direction.

For an institutional compass, the direction is qualitative and quantitative. The quality is associated with an adjective, the quantity is the intensity with which the institution is heading in that qualitative direction. Instead of the qualities: "good, bad", "good, neutral, bad" or "like, dislike", which we might call "scalar" or "ranking" qualities, we use others that are each good in the right place and in the right proportion. They are not scalar, but descriptive in a broader sense. Considering decisions in terms of general, non-ranking, qualities, gives us a sense of rational remove because it is not the way in which we usually think, or are too often conditioned to think. The qualities are not in themselves ranked, but we can, of course, have a preference for one over another. This will depend in part on our own psychology and, more broadly, on our culture. See Fig. 10.1. It is important to notice this. The ranking of a quality is not internal to the quality. It is a separate (meta-) step to decide to rank them or to prefer one to another. The thinking in terms of in-and-of-themselves neutral qualities, and a separate (optional) raking of the qualities affords rational remove, because it distances us from our gut reactions. Rational remove increases objectivity. It makes for clear justifications for policy decisions.

The advantage for policy makers of having a deep and strong justification for their policy decisions is that it reduces risk. Better, they will be equipped with a tool of communication that supports the justification and can be used for mediation between opposing factions. The latter, ensure the longevity of policy direction.

When we have to make decisions in a complex situation, when there are tensions, and uncertainties, we cannot rely on tools that are too simplistic or reductionist. We cannot afford to ignore information that is important to people affected by our decisions. This is why we need a *comprehensive* tool of analysis and evaluation, adapted to the particularities of the situation: the culture, the history of the region, the infrastructure and the geography. There is an increasing recognition that reductionist monetary evaluations alone are not enough for many decisions. Money-only based evaluations miss the qualitative element, and more importantly, they miss the plurality of values that accompany decisions. Even our personal decisions such as whether or not to accept a job, whether to move to a different geographical region, whether to conform or act against a political system are not made on the basis on money alone, but depend on other values such as political, moral, cultural or more personal values. They are informed by our sense of identity and our place in society. Such decisions are made on the basis of thinking in terms of the quality of life, maybe in the long term, for future generations. It is this element of quality and pluralism in values that is incorporated into an institutional compass.

1.1 Parts and Chapters of the Book

In Part I, I give some of the general ideas behind the compass. I discuss the three compass points – the three general qualities, where they come from and what they mean. I introduce a number of important ideas that contribute to the compass and its uses. I compare the compass to alternative decision aides. Each has its place, and each has been inspirational for the compass. The place of the institutional compass is when we are faced with complex decisions where there are many considerations that are not easy to compare to each other, that we dare not weigh using one measure for fear of making too poor a decision. There is a place in the construction of the compass to make the decisions inclusively, and to air differences in worldview and philosophy. The places for inclusion and philosophical question are the right places in the decision-making process, and are measured against the stark reality of facts.

In Part II, I present the methodology for constructing an institutional compass. This is the heart of the book. The method is original and novel, and therefore, each step is scrutinised and justified. The introduction, Part II and the conclusion are conceptual. Part III deepens the conceptions.

In Part III, I show some extensions and adaptations of the compass. I consider one particular extension in some detail: how to construct an ecological economics institutional compass. This extends the method for constructing an institutional compass by combining three compasses, or equivalently, by normalising the data using a normative normalisation technique. That is, a technique for aligning data to a norm or world view. In the case of ecological economics, the norm is to weight ecological data more strongly than social data, and the latter more strongly than economic data. We can reverse the preferences to align with other norms.

The full scope of the compass is not yet known. Working with it becomes a way of seeing.

In Part IV we look at case studies. These are actual compasses that have been constructed and used for various purposes. At the end we draw some philosophical conclusions for the entire book.

The book is written to be tolerant of a selective reader. That is, since the readership has a wide range of experience, concerns, education and norms; sections of the book are not appropriate for some readers but are for others. Unfortunately, such tolerance comes at a price – there is some repetition. The reader is invited to discover the compass for himself or herself. The index and chapter headings will help with navigation.

Chapter 2
Vocabulary

We begin by introducing the key words: "institution", "institutional *compass*" and "ideological orientation" as they will be used here. We then briefly discuss how the book is organised and finally introduce some arguments to the effect that existing methods for decision making are inadequate, and therefore it is worth considering a stronger alternative. Lastly, the purpose of this introductory part of the book is to air the concepts of the compass in a flowing manner to give a first impression. The concepts will be refined in the following parts.

2.1 Institutions

An *institution* is any of: a habit or custom, an ethical norm or standard, or a formal institution (Vatn, 2005, 6–7). A habit is something we change as an individual. A custom is something we change as a group, for example we might change from an imperial to a metric system of measurement, or change our custom of watching the television in a group to watching small screens individually. An ethical norm or standard is a social construct, and so an individual who breaks it, risks social condemnation. To change it we have to change our collective norms of behaviour. What is considered to be rude or provocative at one time becomes accepted and banal at another time. A formal institution has explicit rules and these can be enforced. To change it, we have to change the rules or measures of enforcement. Examples of formal institutions are legal systems, schools, governments or factories.

In this book, we shall be mostly concerned with formal institutions.

M. I. Friend, *The Institutional Compass: Method, Use and Scope*, Methodos Series 18, https://doi.org/10.1007/978-3-031-05453-2_2

2.2 Institutional *Compass*

An institutional compass is used to holistically and comprehensively *evaluate* an institution by assigning a quality to the institution, represented as a direction. The purpose of the evaluation is to guide policy decisions. If an institution is going in the wrong direction, decision makers and policy makers are given guidance by the compass construction as to how to make or modify policy.

The evaluation is *represented* as a direction on a coloured circle. Unlike a normal compass with four compass points, here there are three: harmony, discipline and excitement. These are general qualities that are identified with institutions and data points, and are represented by a suggestive colour on the compass.

The three compass points come from the idea of the three *gunas* of Jain, Hindu and Buddhist philosophies. In these philosophies they are spiritual virtues. Each person exhibits one more than another, and might be unhappy about the particular *guna* that he, or she, exhibits. A *guru* will assess a person spiritually in terms of the three *gunas*.

A *guru* will have a meta-attitude towards the *gunas*. Some think that what *guna* is beneficial will depend on each person and on his, or her, stage in life. Another *guru* will favour, say, harmony over the others. Depending on the *guru's* assessment and his, or her, meta-attitude, he, or she, will then guide the disciple towards the *guna* that is best for that person.

Kumar treats the *gunas* more as simple general qualities than as virtues, although each is virtuous and good in the right quantity and in the right balance. Kumar's insight is that when we think of them as general qualities, we are conceptually free to attribute them to objects, organisations and institutions as well as persons with a spirit. They are demoted from virtue to quality in order to extend the scope of the *guna* concept. In this book, we adopt Kumar's insight.

This concept of the three *gunas* was chosen for the compass for four reasons. One is that it belongs to several old philosophical and religious traditions and so has stood the test of time. A second, is that it discourages our dichotomous and scalar thinking in terms of good and bad. Too often this is all that we are asked to do – to rate something, an experience, in terms of: good, bad; like, dislike, ☺, ☹ and so on. To rate something in this way, we hardly have to think. We re-act intuitively, instinctively and immediately. Again, this is to be avoided. The *gunas* are *not*: good, bad, and neutral. They are three different qualities that are important, necessary and have their place. We might at times in our lives favour one over another, but this reflects *our* meta-attitude, maybe our ideological orientation, or our particular situation and not the descriptive state of the institution under question. Each of the *gunas* is good. We need each. In Oriental thinking, if they are in perfect balance we have stagnation, a type of death. The slight or dramatic predominance of one *guna* over the others is what brings movement and change. The most general, philosophical question that arises from the compass is to decide what balance or imbalance we need or want, and what general quality is desirable. To sum up, being asked to think a little differently i.e., in terms of three general qualities that are not arranged on a scale, affords us a little conceptual distance, and this enforces a reasoned, more rational thought, as opposed to a mere gut reaction.

A third reason is related and this has to do with how our brain works. The numbers one, two and three are primitive numbers for our brains. Even infants and many animals grasp these numbers. Four or higher numbers require more parts of the human brain for us to work with them. So, three is neither dichotomous nor does is require more abstract or language-based parts of our brain. It is still intuitive.

Related to this is the fourth reason to choose three qualities. Three is good for a two-dimensional representation. If we had only two qualities: good and bad, say, then we would have a linear representation, a simple scale. The representation we use in the compass is simple, but not quite as simple as a scale. It is a compass direction. The very slight complexity of the representation gives pause for thought. The simplicity makes it a good tool for communication and negotiation. The balance of complexity and simplicity elicits good philosophical reflection.

Why do we need ancient wisdom, a slight change in thinking (reasons two and three) and a quite but not completely simple representation? This will be answered at length throughout the book, but briefly: the policy decisions that the compass is designed to help with are taken in complex situations where it is not obvious that one choice is better than another *tout court*. They are better according to some measure or some consideration, and which consideration is pertinent depends quite often on ideology. We are also making decisions in situations where there are increasing amounts of uncertainty.[1] Uncertainty can be compensated for by sharing responsibility for decisions and by consulting widely to ensure that we – policy makers or experts – have not overlooked something important.

Like a normal compass, the direction of an institutional compass can have any degree, showing nuance between the three compass sectors. That is, the direction represents degrees of a quality with respect to another secondary quality. Unlike a normal compass, the direction-arrow can vary in length, and this indicates the strength, momentum or intensity with which the institution is heading in that direction.

We construct an institutional compass by aggregating a table of data to give us a unique and comprehensive reading (given the data) of where an institution lies in terms of the three general qualities. We can then say that overall, and given the data we have, our institution displays the general quality of excitement, for example. We can say more: it might show the quality of excitement, but tend towards discipline, for example. We can comment on the length of the arrow, that it is very exciting, or closer to being in balance with the other two qualities.

[1] This is what people say, and maybe it is true. It might be more accurate to say that we are explicitly aware of more "unknowns", or are able to express a greater number of relevant possible inaccuracies in our data. However, to measure uncertainty or how to count the number of unknown facts is no simple matter to resolve meaningfully, since a little reflection will reveal that under a lot of measures, there is an infinite amount of uncertainty, and an infinite number of unknown facts.

2.2.1 Uses of the Institutional Compass

In the first instance, an institutional compass can be *used for*: making policy decisions, critiquing policy, communicating policy choices and justifying policy. It's uses can be extended to: compare different present institutions, compare the same institution over time – thus testing past policy decisions. It can be extended to compare future policy options or function as a qualitative accounting system. It can be extended and adapted to evaluate an institution or several institutions according to particular ideological orientations. These are explicitly *normative* extensions. They depend on an ideological orientation.

2.3 Ideological Orientation

An *ideological orientation* is a tendency towards a worldview.[2] It is less precise than a theory or particular ideology. It might be more or less scientific. Either way, it is recognised to be *politically* important. Formal institutions are set up to play a political role. They are also subject to internal politics. Evaluators, consultants and policy makers have political ambitions and worldviews. It is possible to make compasses for the same institution according to *different*, or opposing, ideological orientations.

Ideologies are sometimes distrusted as belonging to idealists or dreamers; or worse, they might be associated with extremists who are willing to sacrifice lives to realise the ideal – be it a political organisation of society or a religion.

Here, 'ideology' is contrasted to ideological orientation. An ideological orientation is more banal than an ideology. We all have some values that are shaped by our education, culture, upbringing and experiences – whether we accept them or rebel against them. We might value: scientific research, modern painting, comfort, family, community, honesty, logic, order, our historical identity... all sorts of things. Our values are also shaped by our beliefs. Some of these are well supported, others are just "common sense", yet others are just intuitive. We cannot always convince others to share our values. An ideological orientation, as the term is used here, is just a default way of orienting oneself in the world. It includes, emotions, values and beliefs. To compare the two: an ideology is a complete, or well thought through system, whereas an ideological orientation is a tendency towards an ideology, but it

[2] I take the term from Söderbaum. He warns us that the term "ideology" has fallen into disfavour. It is associated either with fanatics or with people with their heads in the clouds – the idealists. The term is meant in neither sense. It is meant in the sense of *weltanschauung*, a worldview or set of beliefs that shape our common sense and our way of seeing, where it is understood that not everyone shares the same worldview, and what is common sense to one person might be quite exotic to another. Common sense varies with communities and cultures.

might have gaps, be only partly thought through, and is likely to change as we experience and as we are exposed to alternative ideological orientations. Most of us have an ideological orientation and not an ideology.

Chapter 3
The State of the Art in Decision Making

We compare the institutional compass to other decision aides.

The institutional compass is not suitable for all decisions. However, its best use is when we find ourselves trying to make policy in complex situations with a lot of uncertainty. We shall see that the institutional compass makes an important contribution to the suite of existing decision aides. In its right place, it is a significant improvement on the existing aides.

3.1 Why Is the Institutional Compass Important?

At present, policy decisions are largely made in terms of money – for maximising profit. We are told that this is the bottom line, or at least an important constraint, but it usually ends up being the top line too, and so, the only real consideration. Such policy decisions can be made out of greed, because monetary calculations are thought to provide an objective measure or because it is thought that making more profit increases the well-being of the investors or the people involved in the institution. Making decisions to maximise profit is *appropriate* when maximising profit in the short term is the highest, or unique, consideration. At best, it is suitable for share-holder investment, for profit-only businesses, or for institutions in financial crisis, although even this is disputable (Varoufakis, 2017). Making decisions this way is *inappropriate* on other occasions. Unfortunately, policy decisions are still, too often, made on a profit-making basis despite the fact that what goes into this sort of calculation is precariously superficial.

While I hesitate to offer a diagnosis, I suspect that when we are not merely motivated by greed for money, we nevertheless, make policy decisions in this way because we have one numerical figure: a money amount. This gives our policy choice a justification in terms of a number. Money functions as a "common yardstick" as Söderbaum puts it (Söderbaum, 2000, 53). The valuation in terms of money has a levelling effect, so that everything on the market can be compared with

M. I. Friend, *The Institutional Compass: Method, Use and Scope*, Methodos Series 18, https://doi.org/10.1007/978-3-031-05453-2_3

everything else. Monetary calculations are usually mathematically simple. We think that they are objective and we believe we understand them. Because this method of making decisions is too often the bottom line, the top line and the only line, or the real basis upon which policy decisions are made, let us call it into question.

3.1.1 *Objectivity of Price*

> . . .But a price is a curious kind of fact, that differs starkly from the type of [objective] fact that seventeenth-century experts [or scientists] were seeking to defend. . . .It provides little certainty or common ground, and always offers an advantage to the person who detects it and reacts fastest. (Davies, 2018, 157)

Let us ponder. In philosophy, 'objectivity' refers to mind-independence. The mind independence is rooted either in there being some object independent of us, the object is just there presented to us as reality, or the objectivity is rooted in there being some truth of the matter that we discover (as opposed to create). Now let us think of the supposed objectivity of prices. For most of us in the "developed world", our overwhelmingly most frequent experience with prices is when we go to purchase processed and packaged goods. We are confronted by copies of interchangeable products,[1] and we compare them to other copies of interchangeable products that are similar. We compare them by price, size, presumed quality, packaging, maybe country of origin or reputation of the company. In the modern free market supermarket, each product is marked with a price. As a consumer, or customer, we can decide whether or not to purchase the product, but we feel that we cannot negotiate the price, as we would have done in a more traditional market. We have the illusion that the price of the good is not something that any particular person directly controls. It is, after all, marked on the product[2] and comes from a calculation balancing supply and demand. It is calculated by some experts. The psychological effect of marking the price on a product is to *dissuade* bargaining. The prices are objective, in the sense that we have very little control over them. It is for psychological reasons that we relinquish our control over them.

Occasionally, we have other experiences, when we can negotiate price. On these occasions we have partial control over the price. When we negotiate price, both

---

[1] I mean this in the sense that it is rare to only have one item of a given sort on the supermarket shelves. For example, there will be four of five jars of tomato sauce with basil differing according to size and company name. This is then next to five jars of the same company's tomato sauce without basil, but with lower salt, and this is next to five jars of another company's tomato sauce with garlic etc.

[2] Usually, the mark is produced by a machine: using a machine font on a standardised sticky label. This adds to the illusion of objectivity of the price. The standardised sticky label price is scanned by a machine – so there will be no errors. The price signals, the semiotics, give the impression that the price is fixed and almost independent of human intervention. All that the individual can do is "shop around".

parties have to agree. In larger groups, collectively, we also have partial control. We can boycott a product, and so, reduce demand, and thereby, we lower the price. But by-and-large our *experience* of price is as of something outside our control, so as something objective. Mathematical calculations are also objective. Adding the prices of several goods together determines a set price for the goods. We can add correctly or incorrectly, we cannot choose to change the outcome of the addition.

Our individual helplessness tells us of our market dependence. Collectively, it is an illusion. In the world of finance and price determination, there is a lot of choice. There are several formulas to choose from. As experts, we can calculate in order to have the company make a profit, a loss or to break even. It might be *unusual* to calculate how to make a loss deliberately.[3] But such a choice being *unusual* does not, in itself, mean that it cannot be made. The choice could be made to try to maximise profit in the long term, as opposed to making a small but steady profit or instead of taking a risk to make a large profit. We anticipate demand and correct our supply to meet it. In the name of making a profit, we encourage demand through packaging and advertising, based on the choice to maximise profit in the short term.

We also believe that we understand prices. And we do, in the sense of having a rough idea of whether or not we can afford to purchase a product on a particular occasion, or what privations will ensue. We sometimes think we can work out what range of debt we can overcome. We also know roughly that prices are calculated on the basis of supply, demand and profit making. But if we compare prices of similar or quite different items or services, sometimes we meet with absurd surprises.

We all have our favourite examples, but here are three. Airline tickets can vary considerably. Yet the service is very much the same. House prices are also very different one from the other, and vary more with location than the quality of the building. Artwork varies considerably in price, and while in some artist communities, some conventions might be decided upon such as: larger pieces are priced higher, oil paintings cost more than water-colour, more time or attention to detail might be priced higher and so on; it remains that these are conventions that are decided upon. So, once someone explains the reasons or conventions for the varying prices, then we "understand" why this airline ticket costs more than that, why this house is priced higher than that or why this painting is priced higher than that. With far-from-identical items we can think we understand price variation. There is a rational for each price, and we are, after all, free to forgo the purchase of inessential items. But it remains unclear what it really means for a painting to be the same price as an airline ticket and a thirtieth the price of a house.

For such reasons, it is not so very clear that price is objective as such, that we understand it or that it is justified. Consider the obverse. We do not understand debt very well, especially large debt. Keen (2000) shows how an economy can halt under too heavy a debt, and cannot be re-started without a debt moratorium. We are also not clear about debt when we cross a threshold of there being too many people in

[3]For a humorous novel based on the deliberate calculation to make a loss, I refer the reader to The Death of Reginald Perrin by David Nobbs.

debt. Debt by one person in many thousand is very different from debt of one person in ten. Scale can disturb our sense of understanding; large scale of an individual debt or scale in terms of percentage of people.

Since prices and money amounts are not so very objective, nor so very well understood, making policy decisions purely on the basis of them is unwise.

Worse, in a complex setting, using only one quantity is subject to very large error margins. For example, the epidemiology model used by the Institute for Health Metrics and Evaluation in the effort to predict the number of deaths from the COVID-19 virus in the United States of America was based only on *past numbers of deaths*. The prediction was between 80,000 and 170,000 (Larousserie, 2020, 2). The margin is too large to be significant. Six months after the article was written, even the highest extreme was known to be a woeful under-estimation. The reason for the significant error margin is that in this particular method, not enough factors are considered. We even got the mathematics wrong, thinking that the progression was more-or-less linear (as it was in the past pattern of increase) whereas it was (to become more obviously) exponential. We have a less error-prone predicting tool when we consider many more criteria, such as when we use a multi-criteria decision aide or a multi-compartment decision aide. They add comprehensiveness. This reduces the error margin. Adding more dimensions, adds accuracy to the model, and this makes multi-criteria decision aides more useful for policy decision making.

Before we move from one-dimensional decision making to multi-dimension decision making, let us examine another important claim in defence of cost-benefit analysis[4] or life-cycle analysis.[5] It is claimed that money-based decision making is objective because it is independent of our subjective values. This is an important claim because it brings to the fore the concept of objectivity, that is so dear to science, and also brings to the fore the more general theory from which the money-based cost-benefit calculation comes from: neoclassical economic theory. For some readers, it will not be necessary to emphasise this point. Therefore, the detailed version of the argument is relegated to the appendix. In it, we give a stark version of the theory to expose the skeleton, so that we can question it, without being distracted by its flesh of marginal calculations. It is a fact that neoclassical economic theory

[4]Cost-benefit analysis is traditionally done in terms of money. Even non-monetary variables, such as time, transactions "costs", environmental damage are given a monetary price. Of course, it is conceptually possible to include time as a *temporal* measure, and damage to the environment in terms of species loss, *without* expressing either as a price. For example, we could acknowledge that we can benefit by x amount of money against the loss of three insect species. The problem with this, it is argued, is that we are then comparing unlike to unlike, and there is no clear resolution to the problem of whether the benefit is *worth* the cost. For this reason, cost-benefit analysis with clear resolutions is done by assigning a monetary number of both costs and benefits, using various sophisticated techniques such as willingness to pay or hoteling.

[5]"Life-cycle analysis" is an oxymoron. It is the calculation of the price changes of a product. When a product goes on the market it is "born". It peaks when it reaches its highest profitability (price margin between cost of production and exchange value), and declines as competitors enter the market. It "dies" when the marginal gain is zero or close to zero. The "life-cycle" follows a bell-curve. There is no life in a price fluctuation.

holds the monopoly in economics departments at universities, and so many of us are not given much of a chance to know about alternative theories. So, we think that economics *is* neoclassical economics. As we can see from the appendix, the supposed objectivity or the value-neutrality of neoclassical economics is pre-supposed and false.

3.1.2 Return to Policy Decision Making

When we do not make policy decisions purely with the end of maximising profit, or because we think our decisions are somehow objective and understood if we make them on the basis of profit increasing, then we might make them in the belief that we, who participate in the institution, even very marginally, shall be better off. That is, we think that income is an indicator of well-being.

In 1995, statistically this was correct as a rough assumption up to a disposable income (purchasing power parity) of $US 13,000 on average per person in a country (Jackson, 2009, 42). See Fig. 3.1. The dots in the graph represent countries. The actual cut off might have changed since the graph was first made. The calculation is one of purchasing power parity calculated in terms of gross domestic product, henceforth: GDP per person in a country *versus* the mean in the population of the people who consider themselves to be happy or satisfied with their situation in life. Ignoring the "mean" part of the calculation – which might include very high disparity of income, what we find statistically, is that after this threshold, there is not much difference. Another way of putting this is that the regression curve for showing the match between mean income and mean satisfaction is not a straight line,

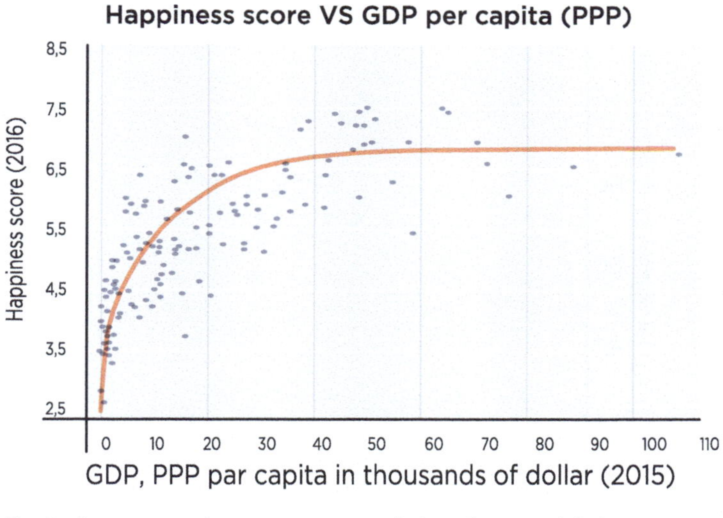

Fig. 3.1 Purchasing power parity *versus* mean population who are satisfied

but a curve. This shows us that there are diminishing returns on growth of GDP after a purchasing power parity of $US 13,000 on average, per person in a country. If we look at other indicators of "well-being" such as health indicators or education, we find similar results (Jackson, 2009, 56–59). See Fig. 3.2. There the dots represent countries. There is a threshold in income beyond which mean purchase parity does not track well-being. Therefore, for those countries that enjoy a higher mean purchase power than the threshold, or for those sub-cultures who enjoy a higher mean purchase power than the threshold, it is appropriate to pay closer attention to the other indicators.

There is another reason we might use to defend using monetary calculations at the expense of other indicators to guide policy. Sometimes we make policy decisions purely on the basis of money, for purposes of expediency. In an apologetic mood, when we are aware of the superficiality of the calculation, we might think that if our institution has surplus money later, then we cut ourselves the slack to execute the real purpose of the institution better. In other words, we *defer* trying to realise the mandate of our institution *directly* under two sorts of pressure, one is that it is too subjective or too complicated to explain or understand the implications of non-monetary policy, the other is that at a later date, when we have the cash, we can think at greater leisure how to better realise our true mandate. I suppose that we hope that the complications will be erased in time. So, even when the mandate is clearly not put in monetary terms, policy decisions are nevertheless still made in these terms.

This is no accident. In the modern world, our acceptance of finance-based decisions is systemic. It is for this reason that I labour the point so very much. We should be aware of how prevalent such thinking is, even if we do not believe that we

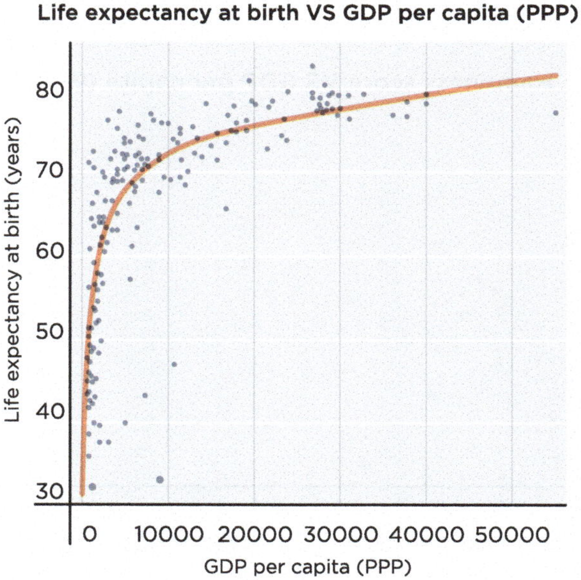

Fig. 3.2 Purchasing power parity *versus* longevity

ourselves share it. In the modern, so called "developed" world, we are taught from a very young age to behave as *homo-economicus*, and that institutions are 'better off' if we make similar sorts of decision for them. We are taught to want money. As mentioned at the end of the last section, universities increasingly teach neoclassical economic theory to the exclusion of alternatives (Söderbaum, 2017, 26). We also think that we understand credit and debit, which we do to some extent, but as a 'value' it is highly abstract and only reflects value in exchange. It follows that in many instances making policy decisions based the idea of maximising profit is inadequate.

So how do we make decisions now, when we want to try to realise the purpose of the institution directly and at present?

3.2 Existing Multi-criteria Decision Aides

As a policy maker, we might be aware of the limitations of money-only decisions. Once aware, we can choose to make decisions in another way. For example, we *could* use some of the many lovely tools for making policy decisions: have recourse to multi-criteria decision aides as found in Shmelev (2012), or multi-compartment decisions aides.[6] Fitoussi, Sen and Stiglitz, propose a 'dash-board' of such decision aides (Fitoussi et al., 2010). See Fig. 3.3. These are a much better option than money-based decisions because we have the opportunity to bring more values to the fore, such as long-term profits, social values and environmental values. We do not convert them into a monetary value. They are measured in non-monetary terms. Social values will include at least: health, education, culture and security. Environmental values are intrinsic. We recognise the value of an ecosystem just by its existence. We value the integrity of the ecosystem. This includes biodiversity and health of the ecosystem. We know that human activity affects the health of ecosystems, and so we might be interested in indicators such as: CO_2 emissions, soil retention/erosion, extent of natural spaces actually managed by indigenous peoples, energy use, water purity and so on.

Using multi-criteria decision aides or multi-compartment decision aides brings values other than profit into our decision making. There are circumstances when these are appropriate.

[6]The difference between multi-criteria and multi-compartment decision aides is that the first takes individual objects, persons, countries or institutions as the basis for comparison. We then tabulate and represent the basic units in terms of several criteria. Examples of representations can be seen in Fig. 3.1. With multi-compartment decision aides, we compartmentalise in terms of one or a group of criteria. "Any of those who have {x, y, z}", where x, y, z are characteristics. We then make other compartments of, say, "any of those who have {x, v, w}" and "any of those who have {w, s, t, z}". We then simulate interactions between compartments. Because we run dynamic simulations, there is no frozen two-dimensional picture. Instead, there are numerical outcomes in a time series. Because the calculations are dynamic, they could be represented in a film (Larousserie, 2020).

a

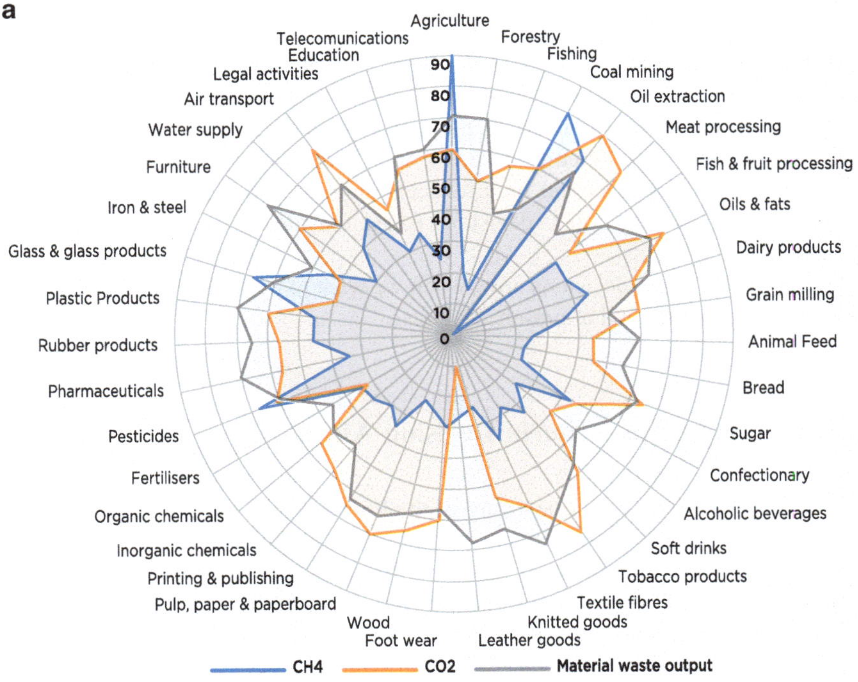

b

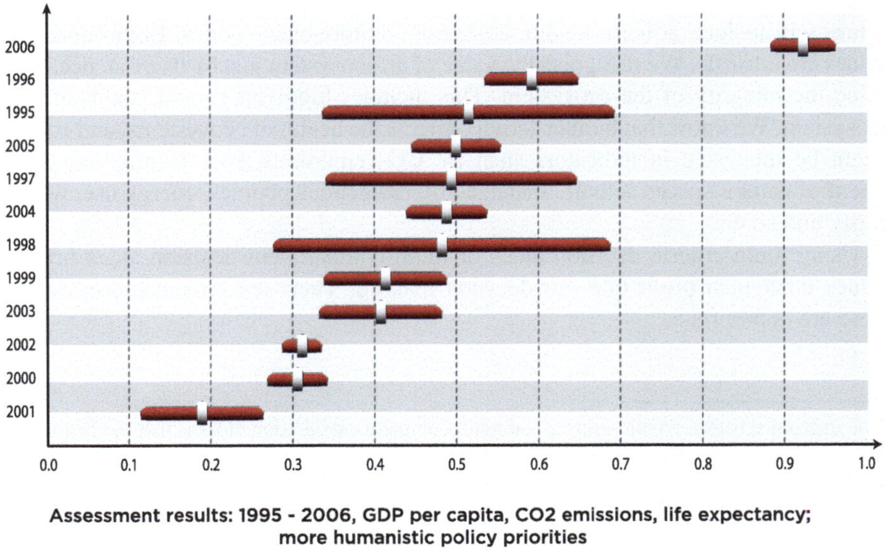

Fig. 3.3 (**a**) A multi-criteria decision aide. (**b**) Another multi-criteria decision aide. (**c**) A third multi-criteria decision aide. (Source: Shmelev (2012), p. 124, Shmelev & Powell (2006))

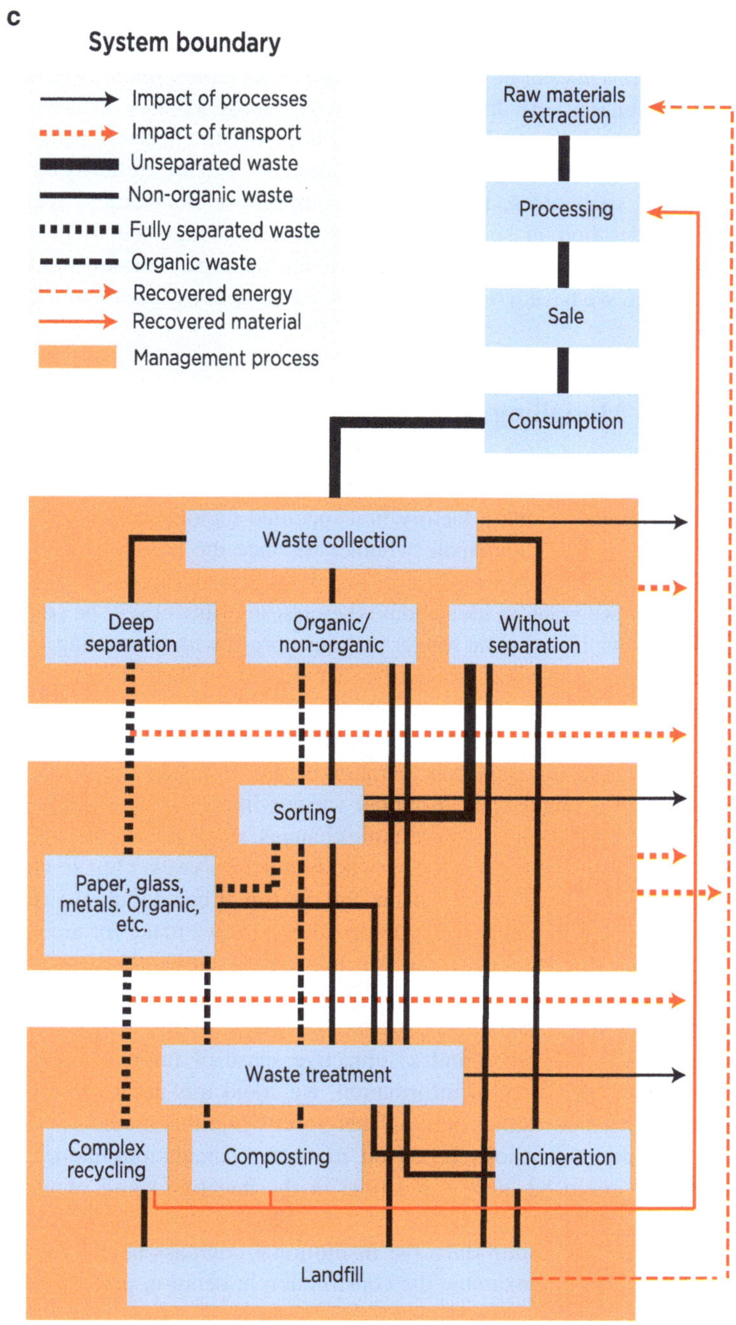

Fig. 3.3 (continued)

One of the problems with the existing tools, exacerbated in the case of the "dashboard" approach is that the representation of the data is difficult to read. It has to be done by an expert. Unless one is trained to read these representations of data, or to read a table of data, it is very difficult to use them to make a policy decision based on the represented data. It is equally complicated to justify the decision using the aide, to people who lack the training. In reply, one could defer to the authority of an expert trained in using such aides, but then we compromise democracy, which is an important consideration in some institutions, and is recognised to be important when making decisions that affect society or the natural environment. When we defer to an expert, we have a technocracy, not a democracy (Söderbaum, 2017, 35).

3.3 Futures Modelling

Another popular sophisticated means of reaching decisions is futures modelling. Here we take a scenario, say, a factory in a specified region. As a factory decision maker, we might want to anticipate whether we face the possibility of making a profit, staying steady with our income or making a loss and having to close down. Before we invest, we want an idea about when our investment will be paid off, and we can make profits. If we are no longer making a profit with an existing factory, we have options to try to increase production, decrease it or diversify. We use futures modelling to predict possible outcomes and time-scales. We can shift the contextual parameters on the outcomes depending on what we think is likely.

The important non-monetary consideration is that we realise that our factory sits in a context. So, we might want to model various likely futures of the monetary, social or environmental context: interest rate changes, stock-market crashes, political unrest, crime, war, drought, natural disasters, bumper harvests, climate change and so on, since these influence supply chains and consumer behaviour. We run models based on future scenarios under different decisions that we make for the production in the factory. We come to a decision, depending on what we think is likely in the future, our parameters for variation, our tolerance of risk and our understanding of the modelling and its limitations.

This too, requires expertise and a subjective sense of future possibilities. We could be ignoring quite a lot of information, we could mis-judge it and we could mis-understand the models themselves. Therefore, while this method is very much preferable to making decisions based on monetary calculations alone, it is still technocratic and could be quite subjective, in the negative sense of missing too much information.

We can do better. We introduce the institutional compass here, merely for the sake of contrast. We shall examine the construction in detail in part II.

3.4 The Institutional Compass as a Better Multi-criteria Decision Aide

In this book, I propose a *new* tool for policy analysis, justification, development and change. I call it 'the institutional compass'. It can be used by any institution for creating, modifying, justifying or critiquing policies.

In contrast to the tools depicted in Fig. 3.3a–c, *visually*, the institutional compass is something very simple and intuitive. See Fig. 3.4. The simplicity of representation meets the demands of policy makers (Söderbaum, 2000, 54). The compass has three sectors: harmony, discipline and excitement. There is one arrow that represents the summation of a large table of data. The constructed arrow indicates the *direction* in which the institution is heading *de facto* according to the data.

The final arrow lies in one of sectors. This reflects the fact that the statistical data, when aggregated, show that, *overall*, the institution displays this quality more than the others. The degree of the arrow *within* the quality sector indicates the degree to which it approaches, or tends away from, the other two qualities. The length indicates the strength with which it sits in that quality. A shorter arrow would indicate more balance between the three qualities, but also that it is easy to shift into another sector, albeit in a mild or balanced way.

We make a conscious philosophical or ideological choice about where it is that we would like the arrow to be, and how long we would like it to be. Some ideological positions are reflected by a preference for one sector over another, some prefer a balance – represented by a short arrow close to the centre. A society that follows Confucius will prefer institutions that lie in the harmony sector and will encourage institutions to move in that direction. A society based on principles of competition will prefer excitement. A society based on principles of stoicism and order will prefer discipline.

Behind the simple final representation lies a culturally sensitive, statistically robust and holistic construction.

Fig. 3.4 An institutional compass

3.4.1 The Three Qualities

Following Kumar (2007), the general qualities are inspired by the three *gunas* of Hindu, Jain and Buddhist philosophy: *sattva, raja* and *tamas.*[7] I translate these as: harmony, excitement and discipline, respectively. These are general, in the sense that other qualities fall under them. If properly written, i.e., not completely made up of empty verbiage, institutional mandates will indicate which of the three qualities is desired by members of the institution, *qua* members.

Policy decisions for an institution are then made on the basis of the 'final arrow', as depicted in Fig. 3.4. How we create a new policy, how we adapt or change a policy, how we analyse or criticise a policy, how we justify a policy will then depend on the data table. We look to the data points that re-enforce the quality sought in the mandate, and those that pull away from the desired quality. Through policy we promote the data that points in the desired direction, and try to impede or discourage the data that points in the opposite direction.

3.4.2 The Institutional Compass Compared to the Ecological Footprint Measure

The compass is not better in *all respects* than the ecological footprint. They do different things. The ecological footprint is a *measure* (in terms of acres of arable land) of the energy and resources needed to maintain a life-style. Because of the common denominator: arable land; people's life-styles, and to some extent institutions, can be compared by a score. This makes comparison numeric rather than purely qualitative. This is helpful for more reductionist and linear thinkers. It is better for computer aided decision making.

Apart from missing some important things to measure in evaluating a life-style, the ecological footprint measure is *indirect*. There is a conversion from an activity to the amount of arable land needed for that activity. This makes the measure (proportionately) hostage to agricultural technology and practices. As farming technology changes, so will the measure. This is not too bad, since, presumably, the measure decreases for everyone uniformly as the technology improves efficiency. But of course, in the practice of agriculture, this is not the case. Not everyone has the same access to the same technology instantaneously, and different crops use different

[7]The idea of contrasting these qualities is present in several deep religious traditions. I am *not* engaging the traditions as such. I distance myself from particular religious conceptions of when and how to apply them and how they interact with each other. I simply follow Kumar and make use of three *qualities* suggested by the *gunas* that can be applied to any institution. The meta-analysis of what to do when a particular quality is present and dominating will depend on the institution and it's cultural setting.

technology. So as a measure, the ecological footprint cannot be realistic, even in terms of arable land.

In contrast to this indirect (converted) measurement, the compass takes into account directly what is happening in and around an institution. The types of activity or material goods or energy used are *not converted*. They are noted and entered in a data table. They are then compared to each other in terms of the three general qualities. The common denominator is qualitative and quantitative.

This is an important and subtle point. Any independent quantitative data can be entered in the compass table. So, anything thought to be relevant is included. Each data point is treated and analysed separately as possessing a quality, and a strength in that quality. As we accumulate data showing the same quality, the strength and degree of the quality in that institution stabilises. Eventual stability is an indicator of objectivity, since it shows that we are only re-enforcing the same quality point or that new data is not significant. Stability in a sector arrow is a type of convergence. It is similar to, but more abstract than, Bayesian statistical convergence. When we have sector stability, we can be quite objective in saying that the institution enjoys that quality to this extent, and added data will no longer change the result. This is what we mean by stability. It is a meta-statistical conception of stability and objectivity.

To explain: begin with the concept of statistical convergence or stability. When trying to determine what the percentage distribution is in a population, say for a preference for x over y, we ensure that our sample is representative. We then ask members of the population until the percentage distribution stabilises. At that point, there is no reason to interview more people. The result will no longer change. Manuals for statistics give us a rough number that is usual for reaching stability. This is the number used to mark sufficiency. That is, when we have reached this number in a representative population, we know that we have asked a sufficient number of people such that the statistic is accurate within a reasonable error margin.

When we seek sector objectivity in the compass, we look for stability one level of generality up – at the level of the quality: how harmonious, exciting and disciplined is our institution? The answer will stabilise. Once stabilised, there is no point in adding more data from that sector. It is as objective as the data we use.

In summary, if we wanted to use the compass to tell us of the quality of our lifestyle, and our toll on the natural environment, we would measure this directly. How much land is actually used, how many chickens are actually raised and slaughtered, how many tons of fish are actually caught, what volume of waste is generated and so on. All the data would be entered on a table and analysed.

After, we have the option to add an explicitly normative dimension to our analysis – in terms of what it means to live "sustainably" or what it means to run over the limits of the planet if all eight billion of us were to live in the same life-style. The limits in waste absorption, arable land, fishing stocks are each different and are not converted to a common measure. We might find that a certain life-style is not bad in terms of biodiversity loss, but it is in terms of a particular sort of pollution in a very restricted area of soil. What mix of lifestyles the planet can support is an interesting question. It is better treated with the compass than with the ecological footprint measure.

3.4.3 The Institutional Compass Compared to Cradle to Grave Analysis

The cradle to grave analysis of a product or even of an institution, takes into account the resources and waste of production, the use value and how use affects the environment. It also takes into account the type and resources needed for waste management at the "end" of the life of a product. In particular, when we do a cradle to grave analysis, we look at volume of land-fill and pollution that seeps into the soil, water or air if it is incinerated.

When constructing a compass, all of this information is relevant. So, the institutional compass uses all of this information but adds more, such as the social costs and benefits. Furthermore, the intension behind the two methods is a little different. Cradle to grave analysis is used for conforming to regulations (about pollution, for example). We make a separate analysis for each product. It can be used for certifying a company as "responsible" for the product even when it becomes waste because the company is then in charge of making available some form of treatment of the product at the end of its use by the consumer. Cradle to grave analysis could be used to compare functionally interchangeable products, say, an electrical scooter to a diesel operated scooter. In this way, in some very limited situations, it could be used to help with policy decision making, critiquing or policy justification, but only in the limited cases of supporting functionally comparable products. In contrast, the institutional compass can be used to compare very different products to each other, whole institutions or regions.

We have made a comparison of the institutional compass with several alternative tools that help in decision making. Each has its place and merits. Each has its purpose and its limitations. The limitations of the existing decision aides are overcome or better treated by the institutional compass.

3.5 Objectivity, Superficiality and Depth of Analysis

We looked at the question of objectivity in Sects. 3.1.1 and 3.4.2. In Sect. 3.1.1 we were interested in the supposed objectivity of price, and saw there that price is often determined independent of the consumer, but that this is not enough to make it mind-independent. It is the latter that is needed to make something objective, and price is not objective in this sense. In Sect. 3.4.2, we discussed a different sort of objectivity, that of sector stability. This is reached when adding more independent data makes no difference to the compass reading of the extent to which an institution shows one of the general qualities (read from the length of the arrow) and the extent to which it sits squarely within that quality as opposed to leaning towards the others (read from the degree of the arrow). We shall see this clearly in the part II of the book.

The quality of the data is, of course, important for objectivity. This should be an obvious point. And we shall return to it. Rather than address it here, let us think of objectivity for the purpose of decision making.

As we look at the method for constructing a compass, it will become obvious that we can be less, or more, objective in our constructions. The degree of objectivity is necessary for good policy, but it is not sufficient. The degree of objectivity marks the soundness of the information we are using to make policy decisions. However, there is another very important and separate aspect to consider which is how we treat that information.

We can create, adapt, analyse, criticise or justify a policy in a *superficial* manner by gerrymandering the *representation* of the statistics that swing, lengthen or shorten the final arrow by "adjusting" the data points that influence the final arrow. We simply fudge the books by changing degree or, often more important, length of a few influential data point arrows.

We can be less superficial. We can forgo gerrymandering and leave the initial analysis of data points intact. However, we then concentrate on the influential data points and address them directly in our policy. For example, if there is significant soil erosion, we import and distribute soil. Of course, this addresses the embarrassing statistic, but it will probably aggravate another. Thus, it will not significantly change the final arrow of the construction in the long term.

Or, *more deeply*, we can look at the *underlying causes* of the influential data points.

How deep or superficial we want to be in policy decision making is a choice. But it is not a mere choice. In general, the soundness and longevity of a policy will depend on the depth of analysis. How superficial we want to be in our analysis and decisions depends on our ambitions for the longevity of the decisions.

Claim 1: The deeper the analysis of the compass reading, *ceteris paribus,* the greater the longevity of the policy.

So, we can make, analyse, justify, criticise, modify policy based on the final arrow and our ambitions for the institution. This is the primary purpose of the institutional compass. We shall see other purposes to which it can be put in Part III.

3.6 Comparing Institutions Using the Compass

If we have only one compass constructed, then this tells us holistically and qualitatively about an institution at a particular time (of data recording). The compass is more informative when used for comparisons between the same institution at different times, or between similar institutions in the same or different contexts.

Claim 2: The compass can be used as a "common measure" for comparing institutions. The comparison is qualitative, quantitative and holistic.

When the data has been aggregated into one simple piece of information: that the institution displays one quality more strongly than another, and that it does so with a certain strength, we can then use this information to compare it to other institutions. By comparing compass readings, we learn that institution x displays a different general quality than institution y, or that they share the same general quality but differ (or are the same) in strength.

The measure is different from what many of us are used to because it is not quantitative, but both quantitative and qualitative. It is also not a binary comparison in the form of good and bad, although we might *prefer* one of the general qualities over the others, and therefore, associate it with "good" by ranking our preference for that quality; a bit like preferring red to brown. Red is not better than brown *per se*, but I might have a preference for it and rank it higher especially within a chosen context. What is good and what is bad is sensitive to context and purpose of an institution. So, one quality is good in one institution, in a particular cultural setting, at a particular time-period, where another is bad in that cultural setting at that time.

Drawing this out and making it explicit is part of the turn from normative to descriptive. That is, there is a difference between making the normative claim: "people should tidy up after themselves when eating in the common room", and saying "eighty percent of employees agree that people should tidy up after themselves when eating in the common room." The first is normative, as indicated by the word "should" that sets a standard. The second is descriptive in that it just records what a percentage of people claim. In a description, no normative judgment is passed, no norm is set. Norms are clearly ideological. Descriptions are more objective since they just record a fact that can be verified. In making the turn from a norm to a description on a data point, we add objectivity to it. We remove our own judgment or feeling, and replace it with a recording of how it is that a percentage of the people feel about the fact. The turn adds ideological transparency in the sense that we now have a better sense of the ideological orientation of the population we recorded or questioned. The ideological transparency brought about by the turn elicits philosophical debate, and this is needed when making policy decisions in a complex setting where many people are affected, possibly for many generations.

Claim 3: The turn from normative to descriptive in considering our ideological orientations, has two roles. It makes the construction of the compass more objective, and it elicits philosophical debate that should not be avoided. These roles are a strength of the compass construction, not a weakness.

In the act of adding a partly ideologically informed explanation as to how or why we think an institution shows a particular quality, we turn a normative claim into a description. This is a way of adding objectivity to the eventual analysis and of helping with eventual policy recommendations. We shall discuss objectivity in many places in this book. The reason is that in policy, which is partly political and partly based on the real situation that faces us, it is important to be very careful about when we are objective, subjective and relatively objective.

Objectivity comes in degrees and types. It is important to be as objective as possible for scientific reasons. On the other hand, policy is not a pure and hard science. It is political and cultural. We should not ignore this aspect of policy in our decision aide. Instead, we should be aware of this, and keep the varying ideological, cultural, emotional reactions in their right place when making decisions. This is what we aim to do with the compass. For example, when writing up an analysis of the final reading of the compass, we should explain our own ideological orientation, since, this allows readers to correct for the inevitable bias in analysis. The correction adds to the objectivity. When we are explicit about our ideological orientation, we invite discussion. We try to persuade others, and might change our own minds in the light of rational and persuasive reasons. We then have the chance to resolve our differences, be reconciled to the compromises we are asked to make, or we might find creative solutions for resolving differences. If we hide or disregard our ideological orientation, then we miss too much important information when making policy decisions. The missing out of data in the name of objectivity is an error when making policy decisions, since decisions are political. To avoid the error, we seek a comprehensive decision aide.

3.7 Holism and Objectivity

The comparison of compasses for institutions is holistic in the following senses. First, it is comprehensive. That is, we can continue to add information to hone and make the final reading more accurate, and therefore, objective. What "more objective" means is what I referred to above as a sense of convergence in Sect. 3.4.2. Second, we can analyse the same institution from different perspectives, from inside the institution and from outside, from the point of view of anyone[8] affected by the institution. In other words, we look at the institution together with its greater context. Third, the comparison is quantitative and qualitative. A purely quantitative measure is not holistic, it is one dimensional. Fourth, we can use very different data from one compass to another, and still make an informative comparison. This makes compass construction sensitive and tailored to the context of the institution. This is an important point that will emerge as we understand the compass construction better. The objective comparison comes at the level of the qualities.

In compass construction, data is classified as belonging to one of the three sectors. Data from the same general quality-sector is aggregated to form what I call a "sector arrow". These are what pull against each other to form the final arrow – an aggregation of the three. So, it does not matter which particular data we put in a sector, what matters is that we have enough good data in each sector to (more or less, objectively) represent the degree of that general quality of the institution.

In this way we can compare things that are otherwise very unlike each other, without falling into a trap of mis-representation that happens by omission. This is a

---

[8] When we discuss the adaptation to the concerns of ecological economists, we shall also include ecosystems in what is affected by an institution.

conceptual trap we fall into when we think that we need to always use the *same* data points to make comparisons. We are caught in the trap with other multi-criteria decision aides because the choice of data points is fixed in advance, or has to be available in each institution that is compared. This means that we miss important data particular to one institution and missing in another. So, one institution is not comprehensively represented by the aide because we used what we thought was representative data, when it is not. The important difference is between representative data *available across* institutions and a comprehensive suite of data *for* an institution.

By being able to add any data relevant to that institution, we avoid the problem that we encounter with single criterion comparisons, or even with multi-criteria comparisons, when the list of points of comparison are fixed in advance. Such lists are good for *certification*, but not for holistic *evaluation* that adapts to the particularities of the institution. For the latter, I sometimes use the terms: "context", "milieu" or "cultural sensitivity".

For example, we might compare countries on their physical health statistics, and insist on all and only the following: longevity of the population, survival rate of babies through their first year, percentage of population dying from heart-attacks and obesity. Under this particular selection of data, we will get a very different results between countries' health situation than if we choose a different suite: percentage of the population that contracts a cold or flu every one or two years, longevity of people living in the lowest twenty percent of income, percentage of people who die from lung cancer and percentage of people who die from malnutrition. The lesson to learn is that what counts as representative data, say, of the health of a community, is a good general indicator but might fail in important particular instances.

The point I am trying to make is that if we choose a particular set of data points, in the name of *objective* comparison, we will sometimes get perverse results. Objectivity should not be confused with same. This is what we have learned with using gross domestic product *per capita* as a measure of the well-being of a country. The GDP (gross domesticated product) measure is objective, in the sense of being calculated roughly in the same way in each country, but as a measure of wellbeing it is not accurate. It is an indirect and quite imperfect measure of well-being after a disposable income of $10, 000–$15,000 per year per capita (Jackson, 2009, 56–59). See Figs. 3.1 and 3.2. We find the same shortcoming in carbon footprint measures, in environmental impact assessments, in cradle to grave analysis and even in the ecological footprint assessment.

With the institutional compass, I am proposing something radically different. Give me *whatever data you have*, and enough in each sector that the sector arrow stabilises and I'll generate a compass reading that is appropriately objective. The objectivity is not met at the level of "same data" but of "aggregation of data that indicates one of the three general qualities of the institution" plus "the aggregation of the three indicated qualities".

At this stage, the reader will have many questions. Remember that this introductory part is to give a general impression, not answer all of the questions. They will be answered in due course as we look at the construction in detail and as we look at the extensions and adaptations.

3.8 Originality and Contribution of the Institutional Compass

The institutional compass is original in the way in which objectivity is conceived, in the technique of data analysis, in the representation of data for purposes of communication, in the possibility of explicitly adding an ideological orientation on top – a normative view, in policy guidance and in the several adaptations.

We discussed objectivity in the last section, and the issue will re-surface. Here, let us turn our attention to the other respects in which the institutional compass is original.

The data analysis is original because it is in terms of qualities and is culturally sensitive. The mathematical algorithm used in the method of aggregation of the data is original. The representation of the aggregated data is simple and original, the interaction between the representation and the data is original – there is a feedback loop. Adding the explicit interaction between descriptive judgements and normative judgments in the context of decision aides is original. Existing multi-criteria decision aides avoid the normative in the spirit of objectivity. But users of such aides forget that we can turn any norm into a description. The policy guidance is quite explicit, we have already weighted the data in terms of importance. This is clear when we return to the original analysis. The several adaptations are also original, since the basis for the adaptations is original.

This introduction was meant to give the reader an overall impression. I gave no details on the method of construction. I hope only to have piqued your curiosity to find out how this new method is carried out. We now go into more depth, repeating some of what has been already said, but now in a focussed way, to lay out in detail how to construct an institutional compass. We start with some background concepts.

References

Davies, W. (2018). *Nervous states; Democracy and the decline of reason*. Norton and Company.

Fitoussi, Sen, & Stiglitz. (2010). *Mis-measuring our lives*. Earthspan.

Jackson, T. (2009). *Prosperity without growth; Economics for a finite planet*. Earthscan.

Keen, S. (2000). The non-linear economics of debt deflation. In W. A. Barnett et al. (Eds.), *Commerce complexity and evolution* (pp. 87–117). Cambridge University Press.

Kumar, S. (2007). *Spiritual compass; Three qualities of life*. Green Books Ltd. Foxhole.

Larousserie, D. (2020). Comment sont élaborées les modélisations épidémiologiques. *Le Monde*. Vendredi 8 au Samedi 9 mai 2020. p. 2.

Shmelev, S. (2012). *Ecological economics; Sustainability in practice*. Springer.

Shmelev, S. E., & Powell, J. R. (2006). Ecological economic modelling for strategic regional waste management systems. *Ecological Economics, 59*(1), 115–130.
Söderbaum, P. (2000). *Ecological economics*. Earthscan Publications.
Söderbaum, P. (2017). How economics can become compatible with democracy. In S. Shmelev (Ed.), *Green economy reader; Lectures in ecological economics and sustainability* (pp. 22–38). Springer.
Varoufakis, Y. (2017). *And the weak suffer what they must? Europe, austerity and the threat to global stability*. Vintage (Penguin Random House).

Part II
The Method for Constructing the Institutional Compass

In this part, I present and discuss the method for constructing the institutional compass. This is what is called the “generic” or “basic” method.

Chapter 4
The Three Qualities Again

4.1 Explanation of the General Qualities

To construct an institutional compass, it will be important to thoroughly understand the three qualities: what they are and how to think about them.

We look at the qualities more systematically. There will be some repetition of what was said before. We start with three very general qualities: harmony, discipline and excitement.[1] These are translations of: *sattva, raja* and *tamas*, respectively. They are the three *gunas* of Jain, Hindu and Buddhist philosophies. In these philosophies, they are spiritual virtues. People will exhibit one more than another. Some people are harmonious and content, others are showy and energetic, others are disciplined, serious, dark or gloomy. In these Ancient traditions, spiritual guidance is given to re-adjust a person with respect to the virtues. A meta-attitude is taken within each tradition: to seek balance between the three, to favour one over the others and to favour one to a greater or lesser extent at different phases of life.

Following Kumar (2007) we put aside the spiritual interpretation of the *gunas* and treat them simply as general qualities that can be applied to the non-spiritual: to objects or institutions. What is important for us here is that each of these general qualities has sub-qualities. Those of harmony are: pure, good, constructive, respectful, pleasant, soft, easy, light, natural and seamless. Examples of sub-qualities of discipline are: dark, destructive, harmful, serious, painful, stinky, suppressive, abrasive, constricting, despotic, putrid, diseased, depressing, morbid, violent and invasive. Examples of sub-qualities of excitement are: active, plush, lively, confused, regal, sensational, sharp, hilarious, perfumed, exotic, brassy, colourful, showy and spectacular.

[1] We might think of these as meta-qualities.

M. I. Friend, *The Institutional Compass: Method, Use and Scope*, Methodos Series 18, https://doi.org/10.1007/978-3-031-05453-2_4

For people who are not acquainted with the Oriental traditions, it takes time to become used to the three qualities, and they bear discussion. Reading Kumar's book will give a strong impression and grasp of the qualities. I recommend it highly for anyone interested in adopting the method.

Claim 4: One importance of the three general qualities is that, on considered reflection, almost every object, event, institution or society will have one that predominates.

For example, time has the three qualities. "Living in the here and now, acting spontaneously and unselfconsciously, responding to a situation as it is and seeing the present moment is sattvic" (Kumar, 27). "Dwelling on the future is rajasic [especially when] ... we become involved in exciting projects" (Kumar 28). "Living in the past is tamasic: Why did you do that? Why didn't I do that? You shouldn't have done that! We complain and moan" (Kumar 29). Food has the three qualities: sweet and light food is sattvic, spicy food is rajasic and heavy and stale food is tamasic (Kumar, 30). Buildings have these qualities. Houses are sattvic, palaces are rajasic, prisons are tamasic (Kumar, 34).

Try the following exercise: compare a plastic flower, a flower in a field and a cultivated cut flower for indoors. The plastic flower falls under 'discipline' because it is dead and cynical, is made of plastic which is made from fossil fuels, plastic flowers are often dusty. The flower in the field falls under 'harmony' since it is alive, natural, pleasant, plays a role in the local ecology, brightens the landscape, helps living organisms and so on. The cultivated cut flower falls under: 'excitement', since it is usually larger and more extravagant than natural flowers, it is cut and taken away from its natural surroundings, so no longer contributes to the ecology, but adds beauty to the household. The cultivation of flowers for cutting shows mastery over nature, an enhancement of nature.

Try another comparison; this time one that is more institutional. Compare a primary school, a prison and a world-class sports team. The primary school falls under: 'harmony'. This is because it is normal for children to receive a primary school education. This helps to unite the society, giving the students social skills and literacy in numbers and letters so that they can communicate more widely. The prison falls under: 'discipline' since prisoners are restricted in their movements, have little control over their daily routine, are punished for disobeying rules and are constantly watched. A more enlightened prison aiming at the re-integration of prisoners in society when they leave the prison will still fall under discipline, but, if the techniques used are relatively kind and constructive, it will show more of a tendency towards harmony than that of a retributive prison. The world-class sports team falls under 'excitement'. The team members show outstanding physical ability, are matched only by the best in the world, bring pride and excitement to those who follow their results and they might enjoy a high degree of publicity.

We should be careful about attributing qualities to objects. First impressions can mislead.

Claim 5: Outward appearances and first associations might be deceptive.

A person might be very wealthy and live in a rich dwelling, so we would suppose that person to be *rajasic* or lead an exciting life, but spiritually, he, or she, might be serene and modest and so *sattvic* or harmonious. In contrast, a person might appear modest and unassuming because living very modestly, so appear *sattvic* or harmonious, but on a spiritual level be full of rage and greed, and so is more *tamasic*, or disciplined (Kumar, 2007, pp. 38–40). For entering data on the table, it is better if we are sensitive beyond mere appearance.

Notice that in working through these examples, I added an explanation as to *why* I thought that the objects and institutions belonged predominantly to a particular quality. The extended qualification explains why we think that the object or institution has a particular quality that dominates. There are three lessons to learn from this. One is that:

Claim 6: We see institutions, events and statistics from a perspective.

That perspective can change, even during the very exercise of constructing a compass. This is part of the feedback loop that attends construction. We should be aware of our perspective. The perspective is subjective, but the awareness of it, means that we can "correct" for it to fit with other people's perspectives. The awareness of our biases makes it possible to think objectively about them, since it gives us some conceptual distance from the bias and highlights the different perspectives of those analysing data. Declaring one's biases or ideological orientation explicitly is one version of the turn from norm to description as mentioned in Sect. 3.6.

Second: remember claim 3. We include the norm as a description, as a fact. People hold this norm or standard with respect to this institution. This should be taken into account when making policy decisions.

This is a little different from the previous point. A norm is something we feel. We are rarely explicit about what norms we hold, since they go unnoticed, until they are challenged. Here we are explicit and transparent about the norms we hold and how they affect our analysis of data points. In being explicit, we turn the norm into a description of what it is that we hold to be true of the world, as it relates to the data point. This is sometimes referred to as "seeing as". We see one object as threatening, and another as beneficial, and this is subjective in the sense of differing from one person to another. By adding it to a description, as a justification for attributing a quality to an object, the norm is then exposed for others to criticise or react to in their turn. This adds to objectivity in the sense of turning a feeling into a fact. We declare openly: "I do not approve of your conduct." This is very different from simply ignoring it, or shunning the person without giving an open explanation. In lived situations, it is not always desirable, or necessarily a good idea, to be so open, since sometimes this is received as being offensive or aggressive. However, here, we are trying to be scientific, to add clarity. The third lesson is that:

Claim 7: One of the virtues of compass construction is to draw out debates about qualities and perspectives.

This is only healthy and democratic. It is better to have a debate than to allow misunderstanding to fulminate and lead to violence. Through such debate, we learn about other people's perspectives. We can then understand them better, and so maybe not agree, but to some extent sympathise. We can also anticipate other's reactions in novel situations, hopefully providing the means to stem emotional escalation.

Not only might outer appearances be deceptive, but institutions and people change in their general qualities. For example, a school might change over time. It might start as harmonious in its first years, then it might move into the general quality of excitement as it gains a reputation for academic success. In an attempt to protect the high reputation, the school might become more disciplined: with more rules, high standards (so failing more students) and an increase in ruthless measures taken to remove students who disrupt the flow of teaching, and mar the reputation. So:

Claim 8: The general qualities of an institution can change over time.

We can use the compass to track such changes by looking at the statistics that separately indicate the general qualities at different times. Some of the indicators will be ones we want to watch over time. The final arrow on the compass will change over time as an institution develops and changes. Comparing compasses is an instructive exercise and helps with another feedback loop – the assessment of the effectiveness of past policy decisions. With that assessment, we become more responsible for our past policy decisions. We can track the qualitative effect of policy.

4.2 Attitudes Towards the Qualities

We can take different (meta-)attitudes towards what the qualities indicate, and we can be more or less subtle in our policy decisions. In Ancient Indian philosophical thinking, *sattva*, or harmony, is the path of wisdom. So, we re-balance a person or an institution by guiding him, her, towards harmony. In Western and Modern thinking, where we seek indications of 'progress', we tend to be attracted to excitement in an institution. According to ancient thinking there is the danger that excitement falls towards discipline rather than leading back to harmony.

Return to our school example, this time as school policy makers who want our school to be exciting. In so doing, we are under the threat of the arrow moving too much towards discipline. We then can make a choice about which meta-attitude to take: to align policy with Ancient Indian Philosophy and follow the path of wisdom, or we can align it with more Modern thinking and risk having too much discipline. This is a philosophical choice that we make, and we should do so consciously, that is, conscious of our having made this choice. Having us examine and make explicit our conscious choices concerning favouring one quality over another for our institution is another strength of the compass construction exercise.

Claim 9: The arrows can rotate in both directions.

Excitement can rotate towards harmony, as the institution settles and what was taken to be exciting becomes normal and is part of that institution. The academic excellence of the school can become part of that school's identity, as opposed to the ambition of the school. This happens when the school sustains the excellence – in comparison to competing schools.

Harmony arrows can rotate towards discipline by being too boring or stultifying. When everything works too well, there is the danger that we become under-stimulated. We can become dull, unimaginative and slovenly. We then slip into rigid routine and discipline, especially when we protect our inactivity, or become physically more limited - less flexible and adaptive. We then have a rigidity of institution based on inertia.

Similarly, discipline arrows can rotate towards excitement or harmony by supporting or emphasising what brings those qualities to the institution and by removing or dampening the effect of what it is that brings discipline to the institution. To deepen one's understanding of the three qualities as they are being considered here, and to better grasp the meta-attitudes, again, I highly recommend Kumar's *Spiritual Compass* as an accompanying book to this. It is a pleasant and easy read.

Institutions are dynamic. When the internal inertial forces are not strong, they change from within. When the inertial forces are strong, change has to come from outside.

Claim 10: Keeping an institutional arrow in the same place on the compass requires vigilance and constant adaptation.

This is because the context of an institution changes. It changes in alignment with, or in reaction to, an institution, or it might change quite independently of the institution. Climate change affects the context of institutions, the responsibility for climate change is shared by many institutions and distributed amongst them.

Since we can take different attitudes towards the qualities, favouring one over others, or favouring balance, and since we are advocating ideological transparency, we can represent the attitude on a compass. We construct a "wish spot".

Chapter 5
Constructing an Institutional Compass: Methodology

5.1 Introduction

We can divide the methodology into six parts. One is to construct a wish compass. This is a meditative, philosophical exercise. The second is the collection and analysis of data. The third is to represent the whole of the data on the compass. The fourth is to use the compass and data table to make policy recommendations. We can do this based on one compass, but it is more interesting and more informative if we have several. In the fifth part, we make the exercise more participative. We invite members of the institution or people affected by the institution to suggest data or help with the analysis. The last part is to declare one's ideological orientation. This last step is important for several reasons. We shall discuss them in due course.

Once a compass has been constructed, we can up-date the compass reading as we become aware of changes in the data. So, we can watch how a policy decision changes an institution over time. Policy failure is indicated by the final arrow of the compass moving away from the wish spot. Policy success is indicated when the compass arrow moves towards or is situated in the wish spot. This simple reading is warranted provided the surrounding context is relatively stable, or changes are reasonably anticipated. Compasses comparing institutions help us to choose between competing institutions, or competing policies. We can use the compass to model future scenarios, to anticipate how the data will change, and how the compass reading will change with different policies.

Of course, there might be outside factors that change the data too. For this reason, we should not judge the success or failure of a policy decision without taking into account the changing context of the institution. We might also want to compare similar institutions to each other. If they, too, are changing because of a changing outside context, then we have a better explanation as to why it is that policy is not working – it is not working because the outside context is changing. For example, there might be political upheaval, an earthquake, a drought, the spread of a contagious disease through the surrounding population. Each of these might lie outside the

M. I. Friend, *The Institutional Compass: Method, Use and Scope*, Methodos Series 18, https://doi.org/10.1007/978-3-031-05453-2_5

immediate influence of the institution and affect the placement of the actual arrow, *despite* policy. This helps us to re-adjust policy expectations.

The enriching philosophical questions that arise during compass construction become sharpened when we look at extensions and adaptations of the compass to fit particular ideological orientations. Another sort of adaptation is to operationalise the compass. That is, to align policy making with the areas over which an institution has direct control. We shall explore extensions and adaptations in part III, after going through the three stages of the basic construction methodology.

5.2 Constructing a Compass with a Wish Spot

We now have enough information to construct a compass with a "wish spot". See Fig. 5.1. The wish spot is an oval we draw on the compass. This sets a norm for the institution in terms of the compass. The oval marks the place on the compass where we would like the institution to be. We make a wish spot before we look for data. We simply look at the mandate for the institution, or ask the head of the institution, or the decision makers in the institution, and study the impressions we receive in terms of the three qualities. This is an impressionistic exercise. The goal of policy is to ensure that the actual arrow ends somewhere in the wish spot.

When we *construct* an "actual" compass, we do so on the basis of real data. A constructed compass gives a description of where an institution actually is given the data. In our initial analysis for making policy recommendations, we compare the final arrow in the actual compass to the wish spot. This is how we guide policy using the compass. We look to the data to work out which data points will help the final arrow of the actual compass to shift towards the wish spot. If it is already there, then we are vigilant to ensure that it stays. Or we could change our norm, become more ambitious for the institution. These choices are important and worth making explicit when making policy decisions.

Choosing a wish spot is a philosophical exercise. It is a good one for introducing an audience to the three qualities and acquainting them with the representation. It is a meditative exercise. We ask not only about the qualities themselves, but also about what differences in degree mean. What does it mean for an institution to be in

Fig. 5.1 A wish compass

excitement towards discipline, for example. We should discuss all of these nuances as an exercise in learning about the three qualities and our institution.

The wish spot might sit squarely within one sector, or it might overlap with another or all three – so being placed somewhere in the centre of the circle. All of these wishes are possible.

The wish spot has a size. A larger wish spot is less policy-ambitious. We are content with falling vaguely in this qualitative area. A small wish spot is more specific and ambitious. We really want a particular quality to predominate – where that particular quality might not be one of the three words as such, but might be identified with another word. For example, some institutions strive towards excellence, and we glean this by reading the mandate of the institution. If the institution is after excellence, then the wish spot will be somewhere in excitement. It will probably also be more towards discipline, since there will be competition and strife to achieve excellence. If this is the attitude that clearly predominates, then the wish spot can be quite small.

A wish spot far away from the centre of the circle indicates that we are not after balance between the qualities. With a few exceptions, achieving such wish will make the institution less stable. On the other hand, according to the Ancient traditions, a perfect balance between the qualities is interpreted as complete stagnation of an institution. There is no movement. This might be good in some traditions since it might indicate enlightenment. A slight imbalance in the qualities makes a perturbation. The perturbation is enough to bring change. The further away the wish spot is from the centre the more unstable and the institution becomes. Again, there might be exceptional reasons for wishing for such instability. The wish spot should be considered carefully for these reasons.

5.3 Collection and Analysis of Data, the Indicator Arrows

The final actual arrow of the compass is the result of aggregating statistical data. It represents the totality of the data in terms of the three qualities. Before making the aggregation, each data point is also represented on the compass, that is, in terms of its general quality, its tendency towards another quality and the strength with which it shows this quality. Each data point is represented by what we shall call "indicator arrows" because data points are indicators of some aspect of an institution. We shall see the mathematical method of aggregation in the next section. For now, let us concentrate on the statistical data. We have several initial steps.

As per any policy decision, we want to choose data that is available, accurate (recent, representative and sufficient) and which we can safely assume will be available in the future (if we are interested in comparing the success of the policy of institution over time) or is available for comparative institutions (if we want to compare institutions to each other). Thus,

Step 1: Our first task is to find some quantitative data on the institution.

Step 2: Verify that the quality of the data is reasonably high.

There are two types of quantitative data: cardinal and ordinal. Cardinal data is an absolute measure, such as "$US 30,000 were spent on equipment last year". Ordinal data is relative, for example, "factory x used twice as much water as factory y", or "sub-region x has the highest unemployment in the larger region". Both give us information, and each shows its importance with respect to the context of the institution. The first is sensitive to absolute limits, the second to comparison and competition.

Finding data and verifying the accuracy are not meant to be controversial, at least in the 'Western'/'Northern' world, but might be much more challenging to carry out in some communities or for some institutions. The ease of data collection depends on the formality and context of the institution. That is, more casual, impromptu "institutions" will have less data, or the quantities might not be known. A spontaneous protest movement, a sports celebration or the loss of a tradition are ethereal. They do not last long, and there is usually not much in the way of a formal record. A more stable and formal institution, such as a government, a well-established industry or a university will all have relatively high-quality data available for analysis. In making a note concerning the quality of data, we add another dimension to our analysis.

Claim 11: High quality data with sensitive analysis makes for a more objective indicator arrow.

"Objectivity" is meant in the sense of accuracy. And this is why sensitivity is important. If we are unsure about the accuracy-quality, then part of our policy might be to address the quality. We allot some funds or energy towards gathering better data.

5.4 Data Analysis

Data analysis takes thought and discussion. We determine what the data means. It is a philosophical endeavour. We classify data according to the three qualities, but then we decide on a degree within the quality and a length. Each data point receives careful analysis. Because of the degree and length, each data point can be represented as an indicator arrow on a circle.

5.4.1 Classifying Data in Terms of the General Qualities

Step 3a[1]: Classify the data in terms of the three general qualities.

This third step is not all that mysterious, but there are some complications to be seen soon. Starting with the banality of the step: when someone informs us of a statistic, he, or she, does so to indicate a general quality to which we are supposed to react emotionally. The person might elicit the general sensation: that by-and-large everything is running smoothly and 'normally' (harmony), or that we should be on our guard, feel angry, frustrated or want to take political action (discipline) or that we should feel excited, proud/jealous or passionate (excitement). A borderline feeling such as 'alarm' might be thought of as part of discipline and tend more-or-less towards excitement. Data is sorted as representing one of the three qualities.[2]

This reflection on the qualitative and emotional reaction to the data draws a *normative* and *culturally sensitive* aspect to the analysis. This is deliberate, and is considered to be another *strength* of the analysis: that we can now be quite explicit as to where and in what sense our policy is normative, and that different cultures might react in different ways to the 'same' statistic, and might change their reaction over time. For example, what were felt to be alarming rates of death by motor car accident forty years ago are not felt to be as alarming today. We very quickly adapt to new unpleasant situations by "normalising" them. We should be aware of this. Part of the compass construction exercise is sociological and psychological in this sense. This does not quite mean that the arrow is subjective. We can be objective about the particular psychology by measuring the degree to which an emotion is shared by a culture. Culture specific is not the same as subjective since there is an objective description of a culture in the sense that we can measure, by questionnaire or behaviour, the percentage of reactions of people belonging to a culture. For example, "x percent of the population use the public transportation system at least eight times a week." We can then assume that "at least x percent of the population endorse the

[1]The reason we call it 3a is that there will be a step 3b in Sect. 8.2 when we construct a more elaborate compass.

[2]There lurks a possible source of confusion. To construct the compass, we want to develop indicators or consider statistics that each *positively* indicate *one* of the three general qualities. By 'positively' I mean that the statistic indicates the *presence* of the general quality, not its absence. This is a bit confusing with discipline, since it is often thought to be a 'negative quality'. The confusion lies in our attributing a meta-attitude to a quality that is not good or bad in and of itself.

To dispel the confusion, distinguish between the numerical conception of 'positive' and the emotional or normative conception of 'positive'. For the indicator arrows we choose statistics that *numerically* positively represent discipline. If they very strongly represent discipline then they will have *greater* length. For example, negative (in our feeling) national statistics that will positively (in the numerical sense) show discipline is the number of: suicides, fatal accidents, crime, natural disasters or percentage of prisoners. If these are small, negligible or not alarming, then we still place the indicator in discipline, but we shorten the length of the arrow that represents the statistic on our compass.

public transportation system." More might endorse it, even if they do not use it, since it means less traffic, easier parking and so on.

There is the danger of a further confusion. The "same" statistic is counter balanced by itself expressed negatively. For example, say we are concerned about employment. The number of employed in the relevant part of the population eligible for employment is the inverse of the number of *un*employed in the relevant part of the population eligible for employment.

For psychological reasons of choosing a baseline, it is worth thinking of the two side-by-side. For example, we might think of the statistic: "population of malnourished humans in the world is 11%". This is the same as the "population of properly or well-nourished humans in the world is 89%". Psychologically, we could be forgiven for being alarmed by the first, but thinking of the second as quite a success story. After all, the human population on the Earth is quite high. It took the green revolution, an efficient transportation system and some degree of world peace and refugee management to feed so many people. The latter is the result of new (industrial) agricultural practices, transportation technology, logistical organisation, infrastructure, moral intolerance of famine better distribution of money and food, careful politics and a more global free market. The qualifications should be added to the data table. They can help us with policy recommendations, especially since all of these considerations should also figure in the table of data as separate indicators. So, we re-express the 11% in different terms. For example, "20% of farmers in country x suffer from malnutrition." Or, "5% fewer people than last year living under the poverty threshold suffer from malnutrition." We want to be sensitive about our emotional reaction to statistics, and correct for it by reading the inverses and becoming aware of our reactions. Of course, we do not add both, since this would be double-counting. It is in the consideration of the one statistic, represented in inverse ways that we chose one and enter the data once.

Deciding on the general quality, and eventually the degree within the quality sector, should not be done by one person. It should be a democratic matter. Different people have different reactions to the same statistic. This is normal. Again, it is a *strength* of the compass construction that such disagreements are aired and recognised. Indeed, if there is too much disagreement in a group of people about which general quality a statistic belongs to, then either drop that statistic and look for another, or split it into two statistics by adding and stating the key details that make it clear which general quality it exemplifies *for whom*.

For example, we might have to be explicit about the perspective from which a statistic is viewed: from this perspective the statistic exhibits discipline, but from that perspective it indicates excitement. We now have two indicators. The sub-culture sensitivity is then made explicit. This serves as a warning that one part of the population might take offense if the situation is exacerbated by policy.

Let us look at more examples. National statistics are fairly accurate and available (now, in the future and in several nations). Statistics that indicate harmony in a nation might include: literacy rate over ninety percent, over sixty percent participation in an electoral process, life expectancy of the population is seventy or higher. Statistics that numerically positively indicate the emotionally negative quality of discipline might include: percentage of people in prison, a significant financial gap, more than one cubic meter of waste per person per week. Statistics that indicate excitement might include: twenty percent of the population or more have a graduate university degree, four or more Olympic medals won by a country, at least one Nobel prize won every twenty years, the country includes at least three UNESCO sites, and at least three "natural wonders", and so on. Which statistics fall under which general quality varies with cultures and sub-cultures. More details can be found in Sect. 5.4.2 where economic, social and environmental data are discussed in terms of the three qualities.

Nevertheless, let me offer more guidance here. Economic data can be sorted as follows: fixed fees, prices, steady costs, maintenance – anything that repeats itself more-or-less from one economic period to another is classified as belonging to harmony. Financial failure, bankruptcy, debt, are all classified as belonging to discipline. Investments, new money, new expenses, unstable money flows are classified in excitement. Environmental indicators can also be easily classified, although we might have reasons to deviate from the recommendations here. Natural spaces, or spaces lightly managed, or better, managed or kept by indigenous people, are classified as belonging to harmony. Discipline in nature is indicated by extinction of species – loss of bio-diversity, pollution, since it stresses the environment, invasive species (not intentionally introduced by humans), soil erosion, the loss of the planet's stock of low entropy – the extraction of oil for fuel, of minerals in mines, the spread of disease, the covering of soil with buildings, roads, the blocking of river flows by building hydro-electrical dams, the extraction of water for irrigation are all part of discipline. Any time we show our dominance over nature we classify this as excitement. Our dominance includes agriculture, aquaculture, hunting, fishing and gathering, new species, specialised breeds of animals, hybrid plants, clones, genetically modified plants and animals, the introducing of a new species of insect to an area to curtail the population of an existing species, the moving of fertile soil and so one.

Socio-political and cultural indicators are a little messier. Let us consider three types: health, education/ culture and security. Health-harmony indicators concern what is normal in a human population: birth rates, fertility, longevity, general fitness and stable, healthy diet, knowledge about health... Health-discipline indicators include disease, impairments to functioning normally, such as loss of hearing or loss of a limb, and we should include mental illness such as depression. Health-excitement include new medical practices or procedures, new drugs, improvements in health infrastructure or distribution, gadgets that improve health and so on.

Education and culture indicators that fall under harmony include: primary school education, the smooth functioning of society, politeness, consideration, modesty, in dress, for example. Those that fall under discipline include school failures, or percentages of illiterate or innumerate population, loss of a language or way of life, loss of cultural knowledge, failed attempts to promote education or culture, maybe a shift towards violence in a culture. Those that fall under excitement include: festivals, art performances, large celebrations, higher education statistics, education prizes, competitive sporting achievements and so on.

Security-harmony indicators include: safety in transportation, feeling safe, being able to go out alone, protection from natural disasters such as earthquakes, or protection from human based disasters such as wars or the spread of human-transmitted disease. Security-discipline include: death or injury due to human attack, sub-cultures that physically attack other parts of the population, war, death or injury due to natural disasters such as flooding, earthquakes, fires and so on. Security-excitement include new techniques or technologies to ensure security or protection, either against other humans or from nature.

It is a skill, developed by experience, to classify data in terms of the predominant quality. For emotional or psychological reasons, many statistics that are cited in the media, and so are readily available, are more naturally placed in the excitement and discipline sectors. That is because we pay attention to them because excitement and discipline elicit higher emotions than harmony. Since media is created to draw attention, we tend to only find high emotion statistics in the media, and leave out the "boring" harmony ones. This includes a lot of data that is available on the internet, since people who contribute information to the internet want a readership. Moreover, increasingly, the different media institutions are run as a business for profit; they cannot 'sell' the media without eliciting strong emotional reactions. More systemically, as 'consumers' of media, we have been conditioned to *expect* to have an emotional reaction when reading the newspaper, watching the news on the television and so on. Under the "media as business" model, media has become confused with entertainment. And that has become our (not very good) reason for purchasing that form of media. For this reason, finding harmony data can only be carried out if we look beyond the media, at serious reports. As noted above, many formal institutions have a suite of internal data. There are, of course, good sources of data gathered by reputable scientific or government agencies.

The insistence here on three qualities prevents us from falling into the trap of only considering data that elicits the emotion "good" or the emotion "bad". This is a serious error committed by some analysts, who, for example, might only look at the discipline data. For example, Raworth (2017, 295–299) represents data according to limits: shortfall in the socio-economic sphere and overshoot in the eco-sphere.[3] It is a trap because we cannot have a balanced conception of the whole situation if we only consider such data. The data of harmony is as important as the discipline and excitement data. See Fig. 5.2.

To summarise, we counter-balance the stronger emotions associated with discipline or excitement by citing the less publicised (because emotionally boring) statistics that indicate harmony. Institutional memos and records are the source of harmony statistics. Moreover, paying attention to the emotional quality of a statistic is part of the exercise. We are aware that the emotional quality varies with culture, individual psychology and individual past history, including being recently psychologically 'primed'. Finding statistics that indicate harmony might be more difficult.

Let us examine the cultural element more closely. How we react emotionally to some statistics, depends on our culture. Thus, one culture might view a statistic as

[3] For a critical comparison of the compass to doughnut economics see Abdin & Friend, forthcoming.

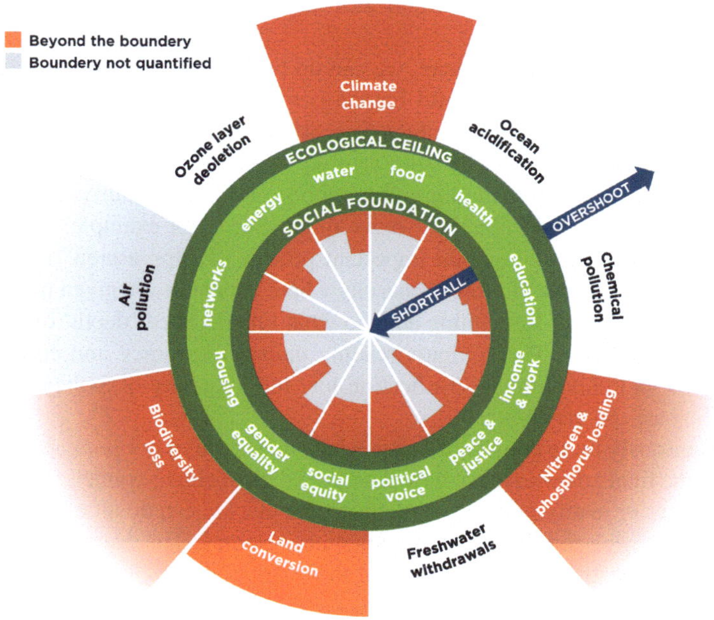

Fig. 5.2 Raworth's representation of doughnut economics

indicative of the general quality of harmony while another might view it as discipline. Take for example, the number of peaceful protests in a given city. Say we locate this in excitement because they are political but peaceful. The degree will be close to discipline, since protests are indicators of confrontation. Now, say the number is low compared to other similar cities. *Prima facie*, this should indicate that the arrow is closer to harmony and is short. But, in a country, where the president has given the police the right to shoot protestors with impunity (Lambert, p. 8),[4] we might want to indicate it with a long arrow and classify it as discipline, closer to harmony, since there is "order" on the streets due to brutality or the threat of brutality. Better yet, we could class countries in terms of their laws concerning protests – no tolerance, low tolerance, high tolerance. We then think of the statistic for that country compared to the other counties with the same tolerance measure. This is what I mean by being "sensitive". It also means being creative or thoughtful about the meaning, significance or importance of the statistic. There is no need to ignore important information when constructing a compass.

Therefore, the proffered name for the statistic is not always enough to tell us which third the statistic belongs to or what degree it should have. It's significance (that the number is low or high) and its context are also important. Which general

[4]The example is Rio de Janeiro in May 2020, under the presidency of Bolsonaro.

quality the low number of protests indicates has to do with a wider context and general cultural values.

If we still encounter difficulty here, we can do two things. One option is to drop the statistic. The latter is less helpful for the compass construction for reasons of accuracy, and therefore, robustness of the final arrow.[5] The alternative is to be more specific about the name for the statistic, splitting it into two or more, to reflect the different contexts or ways of thinking about the statistic. We qualify the name, or give it a longer more nuanced name. So, we might call it, for example, "number of protests where the police are given important powers of suppression" is different from the statistic: "number of protests in a city where the police are given little power to act against protesters." Re-naming adds to what I have called 'depth' of analysis, and regional specificity. The compass reading gains in accuracy and comprehensiveness. This will play into the justification for, and longevity of, policy decisions made on the basis of the compass.

Taking seriously these complications is what adds depth to our *policies*. Remember, we use the final arrow to make new policies, adapt or change policies, analyse or criticise policies or justify policies. And remember that we can do all of these things in a more or less *superficial* manner. But remember claim 1: The deeper the analysis, *ceteris paribus,* the greater the longevity of the policy.

Summarising: this aspect of the analysis is delicate but also adds sensitivity and depth.

Continuing with the method, we want to represent each statistic as an indicator arrow on the circle. The first step is sufficient for us to draw arrows at all. The second step ensures reliability. The third step situates each indicator arrow in one of the sectors. We draw a table with one column for general quality, a second column for the name and any qualifiers. What of direction and length? See Table 5.1.

5.4.2 The Degree Within the General Quality Sector

We now have to be even more sensitive to culture and pay close attention to the nuance surrounding the qualitative measure of the indicator arrow. Some statistics will fall in the middle of the third, and some will tend towards one of the other thirds, in limit cases an indicator arrow might sit right on the border between two qualities. In such a case, I recommend that we choose another statistic, for reasons concerning the aggregation formula in Sect. 5.5.1.

The degree, or direction of the indicator arrow within the third, will be represented by degree. If a statistic by-an-large indicates harmony, it is located in the harmony sector. But the arrow does not have to be placed in the middle of the sector. It might tend towards excitement or towards discipline. As we wrote before, a

[5] Robustness will be addressed when we have constructed our sector arrow in the next section.

Table 5.1 An example of a table for plotting indicator arrows

EXAMPLE OF A TABLE FOR PLOTTING INDICATOR ARROWS				
General Quality	**Name of Indicator and Notes**	**Degree**	**length**	**Corrected length**
Harmony	Wages stay within three percent from year to year for at least ninety percent of the employees.	100	.7	.7/3 = .23
Harmony	Ninety percent of employees take fewer than four days of sick-leave.	30	.9	.9/3 = .3
Harmony	For every one hundred square meters of office space there is at least five meters of garden space.	110	.3	.3/3 = .1
Excitement	At least eighty percent of the employees participate in festivities.	140	.75	.75/4 = .18
Excitement	A money earning charity drive exceeded the goal of raising ten thousand Pesos.	140	.3	.3/4 = .07
Excitement	The local media published three articles on the art show.	240	.3	.3/4 = .07
Excitement	A third or more of the garden space mentioned above is indoors.	150	.1	.1/4 = .02
Discipline	More than one thousand Pesos were spent to buy equipment that is not used.	320	.75	.75/3 = .25
Discipline	More than two percent of the company were fired in the last year.	270	.75	.75/3 = .25
Discipline	The building uses more than xx megawatts per month.	280	.45	.45/3 = .15

harmony indicator can tend towards discipline if it is boring, since boring can slip into dull and insensitive, or the harmony might be too light and ethereal, so tend towards excitement.

Similarly, excitement can tend towards harmony or discipline. It will tend towards harmony if it is pleasant and easy – a striking melody played on light wind instruments and at the right speed, might be exciting towards harmony. It could become oppressive if played very loudly with pounding drums. Then it is classed as exciting, but tend towards discipline. Excitement is associated with new things, as they become normalised, they rotate into harmony.

Discipline indicators can tend towards harmony or excitement. A certain brutal architecture might become normalised enough that it is expected, so closer to harmony. Or, it could be seen as very avant-garde and modern, and so be considered to be exciting. An invasive species will be classified as falling under discipline for the environment, since it is disruptive and indicates a vacuum. But eventually, it will be integrated. When it becomes integrated into the new eco-system (the population of the invasive species stabilises), the presence of the species becomes a harmony indicator.

Now we turn to a discussion about protocol to determine the degree. The importance of this step is that it allows the data analysis to be partly inclusive of the wider population.

Step 4: Assign a precise *degree* to each indicator arrow.

One easy protocol is to use visual feedback with a group of people representing the population affected by the institution. We display an indicator arrow on the circle that is half the radius (to make the length neutral) and see how people feel it represents what they think about the quality of the indicator. We move it around, change its length, discuss the changes until we reach consensus.[6] It is surprising how quickly this can be done, and how easy it actually is. The inconvenience is to bring the people together to voice their opinions.

An alternative protocol is to vote. Say, a large group decides on an indicator arrow for the discipline third. We then vote on whether the arrow should then swing towards harmony or excitement. If 20% would swing the arrow towards harmony, and 80% would swing it towards excitement, then since degrees are ordered clockwise, and start with 0 at the top, and there are 120 degrees allotted to discipline sector, the arrow will be 96° towards excitement, within that sector, so have a degree of 120 + 96 = 216.

We might want to do something more sophisticated than straight voting, and have weighted votes, so people say whether they feel strongly, medium or lightly about their choice. Or we might accord different weights to votes by different people:

[6]If consensus is impossible, this shows us that there are two or more very different reactions to the statistic. This means we should split it up, and make several data entries on the table – each specifying either a perspective or a sub-culture. Do not worry about small splinter groups. We assign a weighting later.

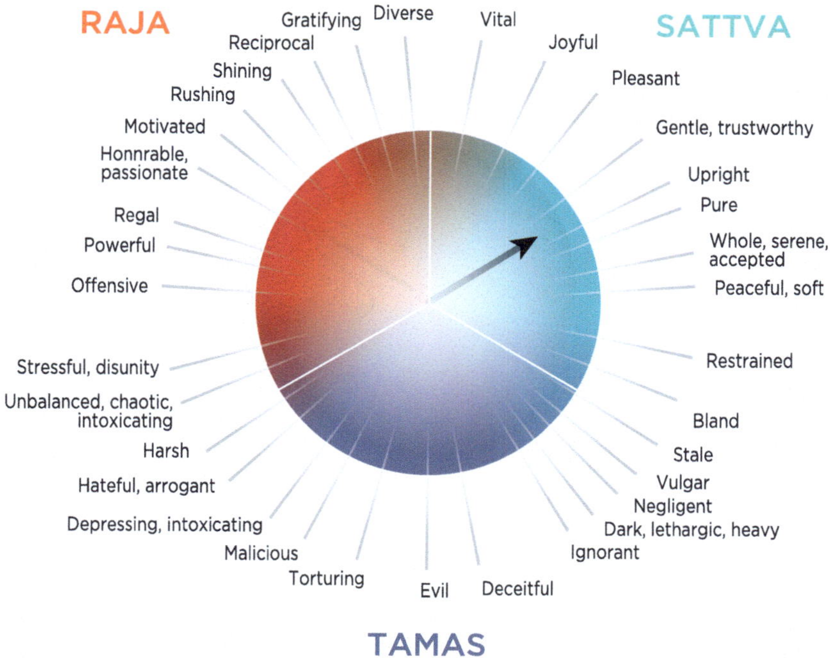

Fig. 5.3 A compass with adjectives assigned to degrees

people more or less affected by the institution, or people with greater knowledge, for example. These are all parameters *worth* discussing and considering carefully, since they indirectly answer to claims 1, 5 and 7. Eliciting these discussions is a deliberate part of the exercise of constructing the compass. These questions are political, philosophical and important. But they also answer to robustness considerations which we shall see shortly.

Another exercise that is related is to consider adjectives other than "harmony", "discipline" and "excitement", such as: "plush", "regal", "boring", "useful", "challenging" and so on, and decide on a sector for each and a specific degree within the sector. See Fig. 5.3. What degree we decide upon and which adjective belongs next to which is sensitive work, but not impossible. A good linguist and a bit of trial and error or linguistic analysis should make the task of degree assignment easier.

This exercise is useful, but might be time consuming. It is quite possible to make a mistake in degree assignment. For example, when designing questionnaires, we might offer a suite of adjectives and ask respondents to choose one or several. We then still have to decide on a separate protocol to work out what to do when the adjective is not unanimous, but this is not too difficult, if 20% choose the adjective given the degree 30, and 10% choose the adjective given the degree 90, 40% choose the adjective with degree 40 and so on, then we have interesting information. First, we check on our assignment of degrees to adjectives, there should either be a bell-curve or a wave. See Fig. 5.3. If not, then we have probably not made a very judicious

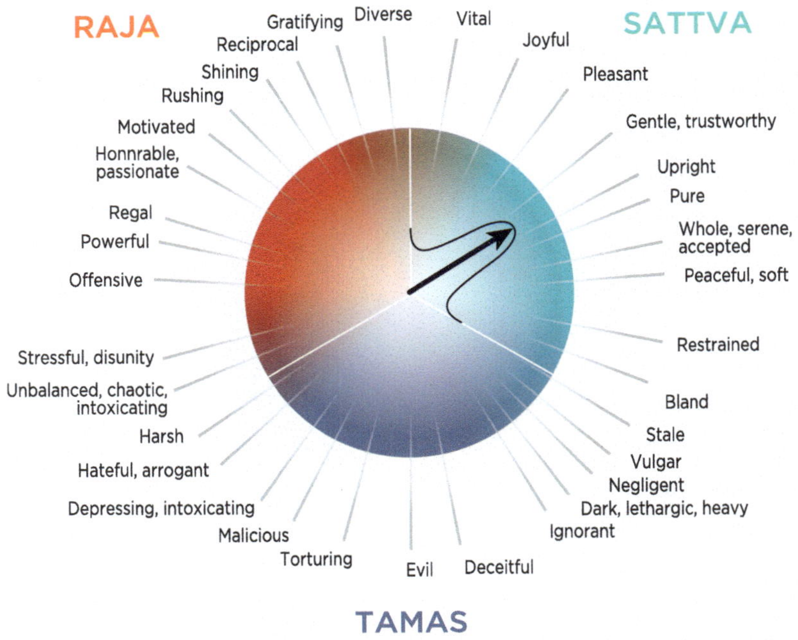

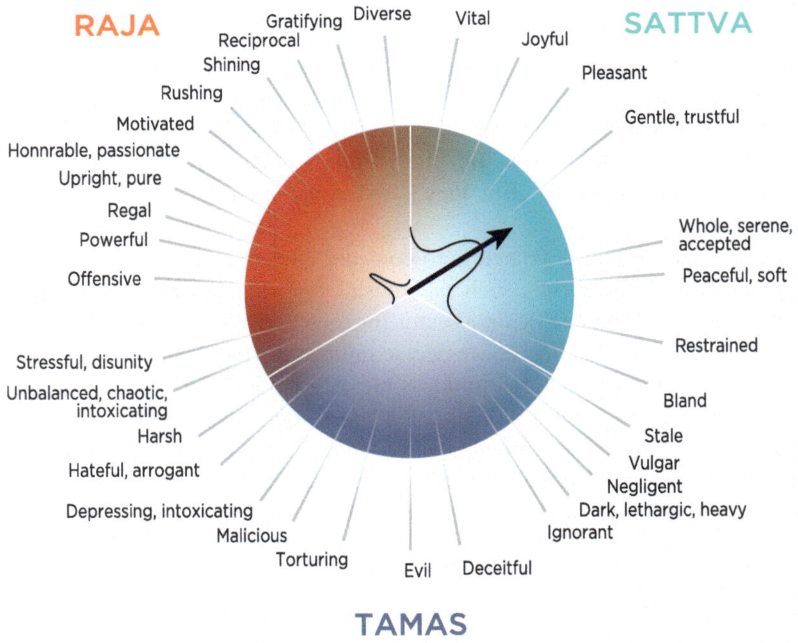

Fig. 5.4 Bell curve and dis-joint curve for adjectives on the compass: what happens if we get the order of adjectives wrong

assignment, and might want to re-assign degrees to the adjectives to make smoother curves or start again. If we have several peaks, then this indicates that we need to split the indicator, while noting the different sizes of the peaks. Once we have a single curve, we choose the top of the curve as the degree for the indicator arrow (Fig. 5.4).

When making policies, based on statistical findings, it is highly relevant and important to have discussions about what it is that a statistic indicates in general, and not be afraid to change the name to reflect further subtleties. Such discussion might be long and frustrating for some people, but it will save time in the long run, due to the stability of the policy. The stability is promoted by understanding how others see the statistic. We incorporate public insights and reactions to help to design policy that anticipates future disagreement. Robustness will be further promoted by the sheer number, and variety of types of people consulted. At the end of the day, the degree of the arrow is the most subjective, culturally sensitive and changeable aspect of the construction. We should not fear or ignore this, but acknowledge it to understand it.

5.4.3 Length of Indicator Arrows

Step 5: Assign a length to each indicator arrow.

This is just as important as degree, but in some sense, it is less subjective and volatile. Length of arrow is a numerical measure that is used for comparison of that statistic with others of the same sort. It is a matter of deciding upon the "normal" parameters within which the statistic lies. "Normal" is our "baseline". If the statistic falls in "normal", then the length of the indicator arrow should be half the radius of the circle. If the statistic is above normal then it should be more than half the radius. If it is below the threshold of normal then is it less than half of the radius. How much more or how much less depends on the maximum and the minimum.

Length will be nothing more mysterious than a function of scale, what we think are reasonable parameters and where other comparable statistics lie. Think of our usual representation of statistics. We start by stating a fact. For example: the average longevity of the population is seventy years. This bald statement will elicit *no* emotional reaction *without* some context which might be known already or which might need to be articulated. Say that this is the statistic today, and that it was higher twenty years ago, when average longevity was seventy-six. To represent the relationship between the two statistics we draw a graph with a bottom line labelled with a progression from left to right to indicate time, and another vertical line at the left labelled bottom to top to indicate measures of longevity. We usually will miss out the possibility that longevity of a population on average is equal to 0–15 years. The maximum would be, say, 90 years. The dates will not start with the beginning of mankind, but might track longevity over the last 50 years. We then plot the two

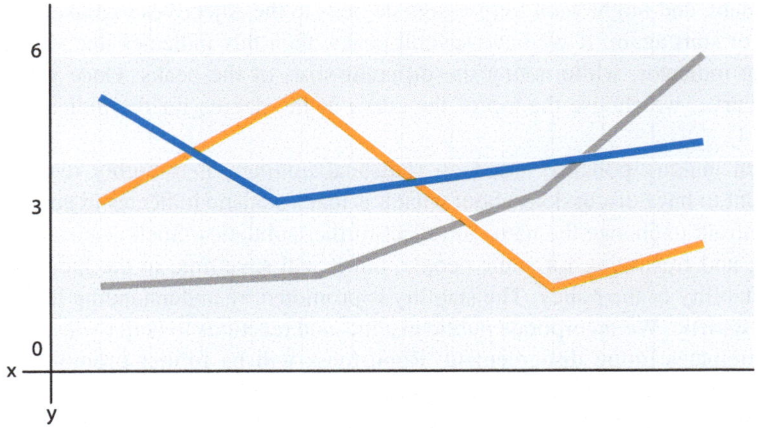

Fig. 5.5 A graph with properly chosen parameters along the vertical axis

measures on the graph. See Fig. 5.5. Experts decide on the scale and parameters of representation almost without thinking.

Deciding on the length of an indicator arrow for the compass is similar, although we shall be asked to think. In fact, this was already more-or-less implicit in the name given to the statistics in Table 5.1. We decided that a number indicates harmony provided it is between certain parameters. The parameters are part of the name. If we are really *developing* indicators, then it is important to be aware of this background activity and the presuppositions that determine the final representation.

There is a subtlety we should address immediately. We should not confuse (a) the exercise of fitting the representation aesthetically on a graph with (b) our gerrymandering the representation in such a way as to elicit or increase/decrease an emotional reaction to the representation. Whether the representation elicits alarm or not will depend on choice of scale. See Fig. 5.5. On the left side, we have a small scale of zero to six, and the differences between the lines looks large. Had we chosen a scale of minus twenty to fifty, the three graph lines would flatten out and look much the same. Now consider the aesthetics: that (a) we have to make the representation on a page of a book, article or screen (so this determines something of the parameters of possible scales fitted to a page) and we might think of future or past measures of longevity, not bothering with longevity below 15, since this is 'unimaginable'. These are features of representation with which we work every day. And this is just how we determine scale and length of indicator arrow.

In the case of our indicator arrow on the circle, its length is then determined in the same way but adapted to a circle. *Ab initio*, the maximum length is the radius of the circle for an individual indicator arrow. For just one indicator arrow, we would fix the parameters according to what is reasonably imaginable. In other words, the vertical axis on the graph of Fig. 5.5 corresponds to the radius of the circle; the mean being half the radius. The statistic is then very high if the number reaches the edge of the circle (top of the graph) but is low if it is close to the centre (at the bottom of the graph).

(b) We might want to work backwards and 'down-play' the emotion elicited. We then change the scale. This is not recommended for reasons of robustness, or objectivity, which in turn depends on honesty in representation and affects longevity of policy.

Claim 12: The representation of statistics can be objective if we sensibly decide on a baseline and the extremes, or it can be political.

Now note: say longevity of a population belongs in harmony. A high longevity is more harmonious, say, than a low longevity, subject to considerations about what it is that is influencing the statistic. For example, it might be high for discipline-related reasons (no laws allowing people to terminate their lives, so the quality of life is very low at the end of life) or for exciting reasons (the quality of health is very good even at the end of life). To re-enforce the quality of harmony, the arrow will be longer. A longer average longevity brings the arrow closer to the edge of the circle.

Step 6: Enter the statistics on a table with four columns: the general quality, the name and any qualifiers, the degree and the length.

Having chosen and developed the indicator arrows, we enter these in a table. Each arrow has a general quality, a name, a degree and a length. See Table 5.1.

Step 7: Normalise the length for the purposes of aggregation.

Note that in Table 5.1 there are three indicator arrows for each sector, except for excitement that has four. This is a very small number, and we would want more for reasons of objectivity, having an idea from different points of view (data points) of the quality of the institution. Examples of real tables are given in Sects. 11.6 and 13.3.

Eventually, we are going to add the indicator arrows together to form "sector arrows", one for each general quality. If we just add them, as they are entered on the table, then we might encounter several problems with the representation. The sector arrows could well outstrip the circumference of the circle. This would make the representation aesthetically unpleasing and unintuitive to interpret. This is the same as when we read a normal graph where the lines go beyond the vertical scale. See Fig. 5.6. The likelihood of this decreases with a lot of short arrows, but increases with more arrows in a sector. Therefore, for reasons of *final* arrow *representation* which mathematically ties together the three sector arrows, we have to adjust the length of the indicator arrows. So, before we add them, we make a mechanical normalisation on the length of each indicator arrow in two steps.

The first step is to accommodate the fact that we might be grasping at straws in an effort to include as much data as possible, in an effort to be as accurate as possible

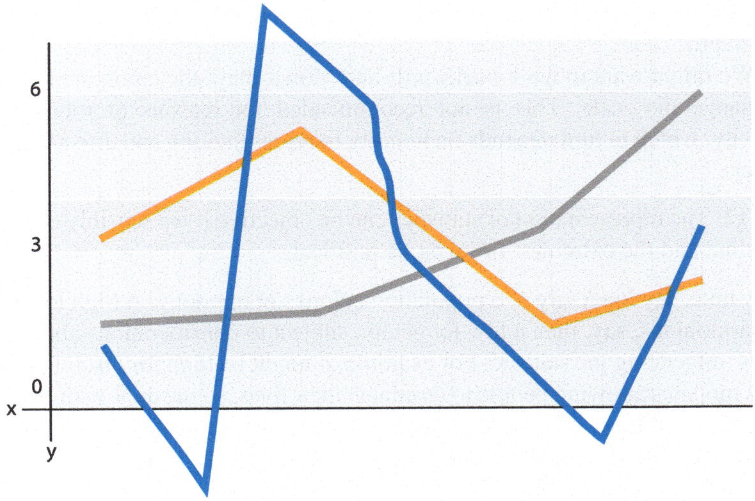

Fig. 5.6 A graph where the curve is "off the graph"

and objective as possible. *Prima facie* more data is more accurate than a little data, but we can go too far, and include insignificant data.

Not all data is as important as all other data, just from a fairly objective point of view. Later we shall add a more explicitly normative aspect to this, but we should consider one thing at a time.

Since some data is not so important – as shown by a short length. We cross out data that has an indicator arrow shorter than one third the radius. The number one third is a bit arbitrary. We could have chosen one fifth or a quarter, and so on, but it will not matter, provided we treat all of the data on the table in the same way, and that *we still have enough data* to start making meaningful calculations that eventually stabilise the sector arrows.[7] Because the length of an insignificant indicator arrow might change, we only cross it out. We keep an eye on it, if we suspect it might change and become important. At that point we remove the crossing out, and it is added to the sector arrow. Sometimes, a small number statistic turns out to be important politically or environmentally because it triggers a shift in the larger system. The system has reached a tipping point, and the change is unexpected and looks dramatic. The snarling dog "suddenly" attacks.

We learn from Thom[8] that what looks sudden can be re-described, mathematically, as inevitable. For us, the lesson is that if we do not have a good balanced

[7]What we mean by this is that if we have enough data, the sector arrow length and degree should converge, in the same way as a statistic converges as we gather more data – provided it is representative.

[8]René Thom was the founder of the catastrophe theory – a mathematical rationalisation of sudden change. He is responsible for concepts such as tipping point and attractors. Thom is one of the most brilliant mathematicians of the twentieth century.

picture, because we are missing information, then we will be surprised by some changes. If we have enough information, then we will be aware that, say, a group of people is being pushed to their limit, or an eco-system is on the brink of collapse. Even with a lot of information, it is impossible to know exactly when the "surprise" will come, but we can be vigilant or try to appease the situation in anticipation of noticeable change. It is a question of having enough information, and knowing how to interpret it. Several insignificant indicators together show volatility. For this reason, it might make sense to look at the crossed-out data, or sections of the crossed-out data together, and combine them into one arrow (that, now is significant enough, not to be crossed out). This will take experience and foresight. The advantage is that we anticipate changes that would otherwise look sudden or dramatic, since we knew all along that the social or ecological system was approaching the edge of change.

The second normalisation step is to allow for a *different number* of statistics in each quality-sector, and to prevent the sector arrows from going beyond the circumference of the circle. To meet these two requirements, we divide the length of each not-crossed-out indicator arrow by the number of not-crossed out indicators *in that sector*. This is the second step in the mechanical, or descriptive, normalisation calculation. We enter the normalised length in a new column.

To summarise the mechanical normalisation: the reason for making the correction is this. We want a nice representation for our final arrow. We recognise that, on the one hand, more data is more accurate than less, but on the other hand, not all data is equally important. The shorter indicators weight less for our institution, and might be added for reasons of robustness or because we think that they might change significantly because of, or independent of, policy. These should not carry much weight in the compass reading. So, we disregard the short arrows for the purpose of construction. But we keep them in the table. We just cross them out. To accommodate the possibility of there being different numbers of arrows in the sectors, and to ensure that one sector is not over-emphasised, we divide each length by the number of arrows in that sector. If we want to be very sophisticated, we could also cluster similar arrows, that in conjunction with each other turn out to be significant. The two-step normalisation ensures an intuitively readable final compass representation of the data table.

The normalisation also contributes to robustness of the reading. When we find that adding more arrows or indicators, does not change the overall sector arrow we have meta-convergence, and so stability in that sector. This is one of our robustness or "objectivity" checks.

We now have our table of data, analysed in a qualitative and quantitative way – in terms of length and degree (quantities) to represent qualities of an institution. We shall look back at the data table to guide policy decisions, once the data is mathematically aggregated, because it is in terms of the representation of the mathematically aggregated data that we want to make policy decisions, not in terms of individual data points.

This is what is missing in existing multi-criteria decision aides: the formal comparison of the particular to the whole. Experts using multi-criteria decision

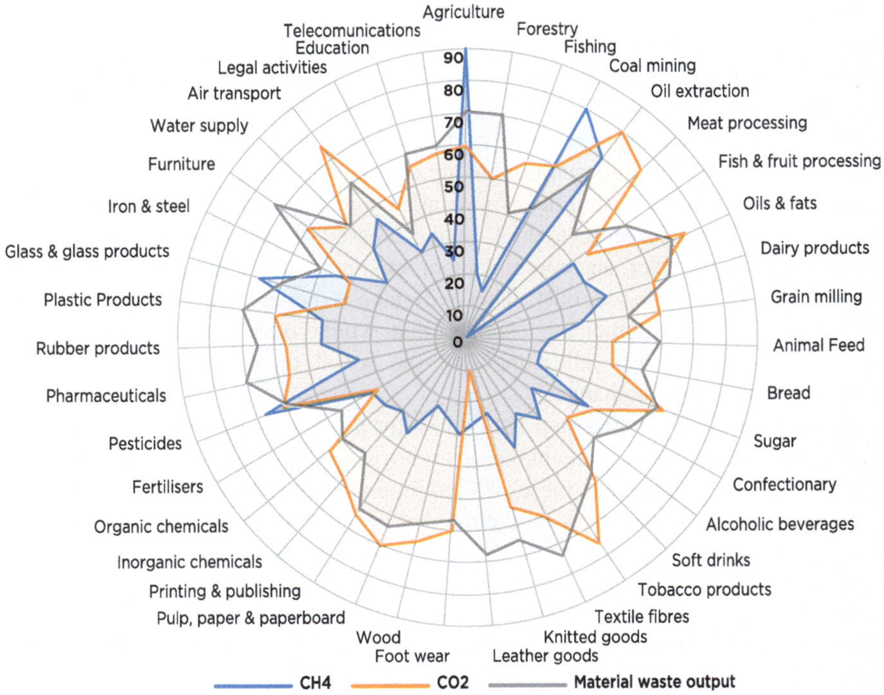

Fig. 5.7 Data represented in a multi-criteria decision aide

aides make the comparison informally, after the representation of the data separately has been constructed, such as in Fig. 5.7. In their analysis of such a diagram, they bring in a lot of informal (missing from the diagram) considerations to bear. They might consider the history of the institution, common or external factors that influence the particular data points. They bring the data together in an analysis by telling a story that ties the data. The story telling takes skill, knowledge and experience. The experts deserve our full respect.

In contrast, the compass asks us to make a more holistic analysis in terms of general qualities, relying less on skill, knowledge and experience. The compass makes the policy more intuitively understandable, and therefore, the construction and resulting policy can be done in a participative manner.

5.5 The Mathematics for Aggregating the Indicator Arrows

We aggregate the arrows in the sense of adding them up and tying them together. This gives us an overall idea of the data table. We do the aggregation on the compass-representation. The compass represents the data in an intuitive way.

The mathematical aggregation has eight steps: numbers 8–15. We go through it in detail in order to convince the reader that the mathematics used makes sense. That is, it fits the purpose of the exercise of representing a collection of data. A computer application will be developed that will carry out these steps.

Before we start, a little vocabulary should be introduced. We have four sorts of arrow on the compass: indicator arrows, sector arrows, final institutional arrows and sphere arrows. Indicator arrows each belong to a data point on a data table. The length is the "corrected length" or mechanically normalised length. Sector arrows are made by adding the indicators arrows in a sector. There are three sectors: harmony, discipline and excitement. A final institutional arrow is made by aggregating the sector arrows and re-normalising in a simple institutional compass or by adding the sphere arrows in an ecological economics compass or any compass composed by superimposing spheres. We shall see these in Sect. 7.3 on the ecological economics compass. Further ideological manipulations are explored in Sect. 8.2.

Let us now construct a final arrow for an institutional compass based upon a data table using the compass aggregation formula.

5.5.1 The Aggregation Formula

The formula is presented as a recipe or algorithm. It is part of the methodology.

Step 8: Plot each not-crossed out indicator arrow in its particular sector with the corrected/mechanically normalised length. Plot them head to tail. The first has its tail at the centre of the circle. The second has its tail at the head of the first and so on. The order does not matter. See Fig. 5.8.

Step 9: Within each sector, draw a 'sector arrow' from the centre of the circle to the head of the last arrow in that sector. A sector arrow gives us an overall-reading of that general quality for the institution. See Fig. 5.9.

Fig. 5.8 Indicator arrows plotted tail to head within each sector

Fig. 5.9 Sector arrows

Sector arrows are important for policy analysis. It is also important to ensure *robustness of sector arrows* as much as possible. Robustness means that the arrows do not change anymore. They are only re-enforced by adding information. The robustness is necessary for the policies to stand up under scrutiny and for them to be effective over time. There are two independent robustness checks.

(a) One way to ensure robustness, is re-examine our choices of indicators add more statistics, and make the length correction. Assuming that good statistics are available, or that the poor quality of the data will be overcome by adding more, we can continue to *add* statistics, until we discover that the length and direction of the sector arrows *stabilise*. They will do so under the *corrected* length, provided they are independent of each other.

This is a meta-statistical step in the method, and is inspired by the notion of convergence in Bayesian statistics. Assuming the luxury of reliable and somewhat independent statistics, we should find relative stability in the sector arrows after the corrections in length to the indicator arrows have been made. Independence of data is only relative. What we find as we add more statistics is that they start to re-enforce each other. They give us the "same" qualitative message, after we have included all of the "outliers", that is, the unusual statistics. The relative stability is what brings robustness to policy in a very real mathematical and statistical sense. Stability indicates objectivity. Moreover, this is another reason for adding the arrows not all together, but adding the indicator arrows *within* each third separately. We thereby treat each general quality independently of the others. An advantage of thinking in terms of convergence and stability is that we can stop collecting statistics in a sector when we have stability. When we have stability in a sector arrow, we have a good statistical reason to think that we have collected enough statistics to show the degree of the general quality as it is manifested by the institution. This is also an assurance of weak objectivity: "(weak) objectivity … is weakened or re-enforced through cross-checking or interaction…" (Molinini 2–3). "Cross-checking" is the idea that we find independent confirmation – the "same" idea in "different" discourses [Friend, ch. 9, 151–174]. What this means is that it is not an objectivity that stands on its own and is internally justified.[9] It is something for which we seek independent confirmation, and this adds further increments of objectivity to it. When we say that a sector arrow has weak objectivity, we mean that we have enough confirmation of the degree and intensity of the sector arrow by means of the several indicator arrows, which represent various data that fall within that sector.

Claim 13: When we have stability in a sector arrow in terms of length and degree, we have weak objectivity. This is desired and "best possible" because this is a qualitative and culturally sensitive analysis.

We should be careful here about the word "stability". "Stability" does not mean fixed over time. As already mentioned, institutions change, both for internal reasons and because of the changes in the surrounding context. We can up-date the statistics individually, and watch the sector (and final) arrow change. What is important is that *before* we do that, we have reached a stable/robust arrow at a given time. "Robustness" means that it does not fluctuate much with added *contemporary*[10] information. This stability implies an objectivity with respect to how the sectors of society think of the suite of statistics in general with respect to the institution in question.

We have to be careful for another reason. There might be something that we overlooked, that would de-stabilise the arrow, i.e., pull the sector arrow significantly in direction or alter its length. To fend from overlooking something important in our table of statistics, we have a second robustness check.

(b) The second way to ensure robustness is to consult a wider audience to decide on the sector, degree and length of the indicator arrows and to solicit for new data and indicators. Thus, we consult not only people in the administration of an institution, but also others involved *in* the institution, or those affected *by* the institution. This might force us to re-consider the naming of the statistic, and might require that we make two or more indicator arrows out of one. This careful work increases the stability and strengthens the weak-objectivity of a sector arrow.

If we meet the two robustness checks, this will ensure longevity of policy in the sense of having fewer surprises. There is always the possibility of error. All we can do is reasonably minimize it. But there is another benefit, in the form of a feed-back loop.

---

[9] Strongly objective truths are stand-alone truths – that do not require further justification, such as "The planet Mars is identical to the planet Mars". Weakly objective truths are re-enforced through cross-checking, that is, by being verified independently. The indicator arrows are independent of each other *prima facie* – although some pairs might have a common cause. They have different degrees and different lengths. The addition of them together eventually stabilises the sector arrow. This means that we have not missed anything out in that sector that is significant.

[10] "Contemporary" is not meant in the sense of "at present" but in the sense of contemporary to – at the same time as – the other statistics.

Fig. 5.10 Triangle tying the heads of the sector arrows

Fig. 5.11 The triangle without sector arrows

Consider the political aspect of consulting widely. If they have the time, and if they care about an institution or its effects, then people *like* to be consulted in the policy decision process. They feel then that their voice has been heard, and that their opinion counts. Having had their say, and by witnessing the concerns of others, they will understand and accept the final policy better.

Claim 14: Consultation, inclusiveness and participation increase the objectivity of the compass and longevity of policy based on the compass.

We have our three weakly objective sector arrows. We now need to see how they relate to each other.

Step 10: Draw a triangle linking the three heads of the sector arrows as in Fig. 5.10.

This ties the three sectors together by straight lines – the tightest tie.

Step 11: Erase the sector arrows. See Fig. 5.11.

Step 12: Find the centroid of the triangle. See Fig. 5.12.

In Euclidean geometry, there are four different centres of triangles. The relevant one for us is the centroid, the one that picks out the average of the mean vertices in the triangle. To find this, draw a line from the mid-point of each line to its opposite angle. The centre is where the three lines intersect.

Fig. 5.12 Finding the centroid of the triangle

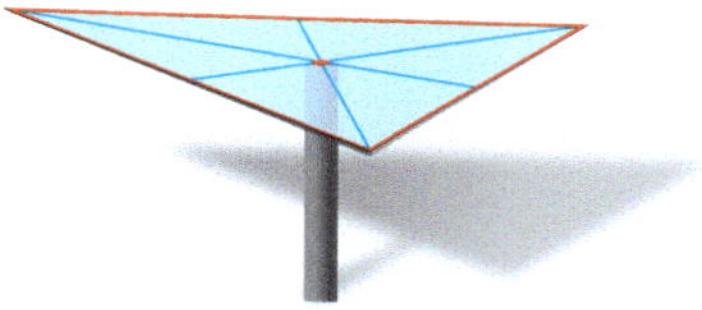

Fig. 5.13 A triangle balanced on its centroid

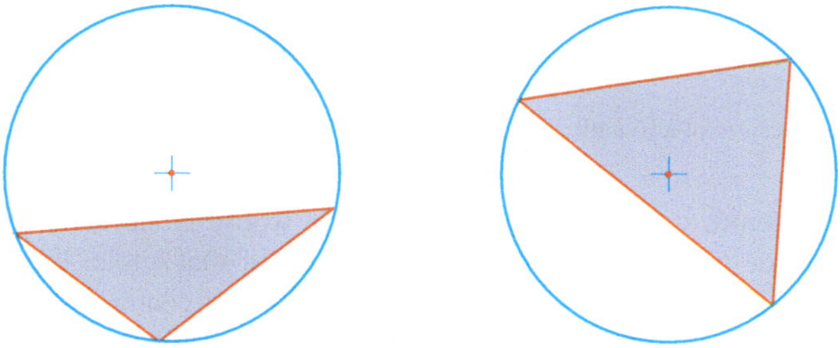

Fig. 5.14 Two circumcentres of triangles

The choice of the centroid-centre of triangle is meaningful. The triangle ties the three sector arrows together in the tightest way – by straight lines, i.e., the shortest distance between the points. The idea of finding the point that gives the average of the three vertices within the triangle, represents the placement and weight of this triangular shape. In more mechanical, or engineering, terms, the centroid, of the triangle is also the centre of balance, or gravity, of the triangle. That is, if one were to cut out a triangle made of uniform, flat material, and not too thick, and one were to balance the triangle on a spike using this centre as the point of contact of the triangle and the spike, it would remain in equilibrium, and could even spin on the top of the spike, in a locally uniform gravitational field. See Fig. 5.13.

Choosing the centroid over the circumcentre (Fig. 5.14), the orthocentre (Fig. 5.15) or the incentre (Fig. 5.16) makes sense. Let us look at the other choices to see why.

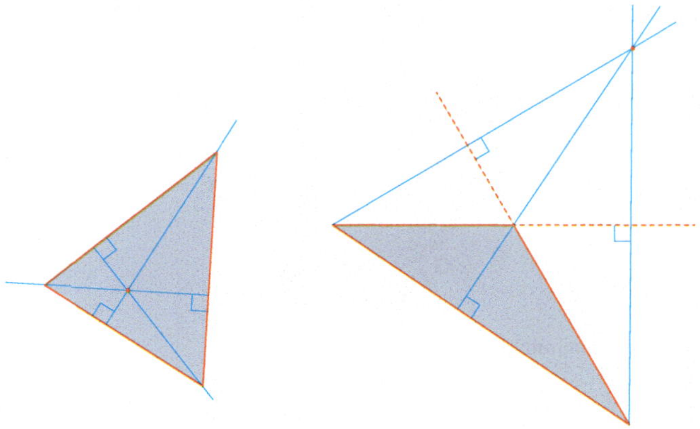

Fig. 5.15 Two orthocentres of triangles

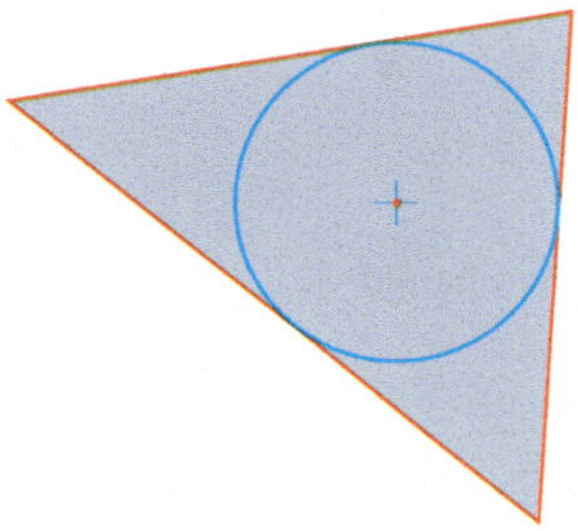

Fig. 5.16 The incentre of a triangle

The circumcentre is found by drawing a circle whose circumference intersects each point of the triangle. We then find the centre of that circle, and that is the circumcentre of the triangle. This is not a good choice of centre of triangle for us because the circumcentre might lie outside the triangle. It really represents the centre of another circle, not of the triangle directly (the circle is constructed on the basis of the triangle). The circle is a different way of tying the three points that are the tips of the sector arrows. Because it bulges out, being a circle, it represents something *more* than the qualities of the institution. Since we are trying to represent where the institution finds itself with respect to the data collected and analysed with respect to the three qualities, if we were to find a "centre" outside the triangle, this would not make sense for what we are trying to do. That is, the step of drawing yet another circle is not meaningful for amalgamating data. However, we shall see a re-consideration of this point in step 15.

The orthocentre is found by drawing a line from each point of the triangle to its opposite edge such that it intersects the edge, or extension of the edge, at a right angle. The three lines will intersect. That point of intersection is the orthocentre of the triangle. The insistence on the right angle is to give the height of the triangle with each edge as a base. It is the meeting of the three heights. In an obtuse triangle, the orthocentre might lie outside the triangle. Again, this is disingenuous with respect to the task here. The concept of the height of the triangle is not relevant to the three qualities and their resolution, given the data.

The incentre is found by drawing a circle within the triangle such that the circumference meets the edges of the triangle (as opposed to the points, as we did for the circumcentre). This incentre point is always within the triangle. But, again, it is not a suitable centre because of the added construction of a circle. The new circle represents, at best, the *tying* of the *relation between* the three qualities – tying their edges, not the end points. It is not clear to me that anything of significance is added by the *circle* inside the triangle with respect to the three qualities or the data; it makes the "centre" of the triangle indirect, since dependent on the circle and triangle construction. Nevertheless, it is preferable to the circumcentre and the orthocentre because the point will always lie within the triangle. However, the weakness of this choice lies in justifying, or making sense of this inner circle, and explaining what it is that it represents. The other drawback of choosing the incentre is that if we then draw as our final arrow an arrow from the centre of the compass circle to the incentre, it will always be very short, unless the institution only has two of the qualities, because there is no data on the third quality, and this will be quite rare.

It might be possible to justify this choice of centre of a triangle if we consider that the concept of inner circle and incentre corresponds to the "grass-transform" of the triangle. Under this conception, the centre point of the circle represents the meeting of similar waves issued from the centre to the triangle edges, as though we started a grass-fire in a field of grass at the centre and waited until they met the edges of the triangle. This might be an interesting conception, especially if we think that the three qualities are related to each other as waves, rather than as sections of a circle on a Euclidean plane. Or, if we think that data is wave-related to other data. It is not a conception I work with easily, but this is not to say that it is the wrong conception, and for some institutions it might be more suitable. I leave the choice between the centroid and the incentre up to the reader. What will be important *prima facie* will be to stay with one triangle centre when setting up comparisons between compasses.

The reason for the long lesson in geometry, is to stress that the mathematical construction has to make sense with respect to what it is that we are trying to do: to find out where an institution lies with respect to the three qualities. This is something that is missing in systems diagrams, where, for example all of the arrows between boxes are of the same size, or where it is not clear what it means for one arrow to be, say, twice as thick as another. What is missing is a sense of mathematical proportionality with respect to the purpose of the diagram that represents a system. In contrast, with weighted systems diagrams (Fig. 6.2), or better, with Sankey diagrams, we do have a good sense of proportionality. See Fig. 5.17.

While proportionality is nicely represented in a Sanky diagram, what is diagrammatically implied is that we should concern ourselves with the thickest lines or that we concern ourselves with loops. The thick lines give a cardinal proportion, in this case of non-food and non-energy raw materials that enter Germany, leave Germany or come from within Germany through mining, re-use or re-cycling. The diagram is limited because restricted to materials. We cannot combine the energy Sankey diagram, with the material Sankey diagram because the units of measure are

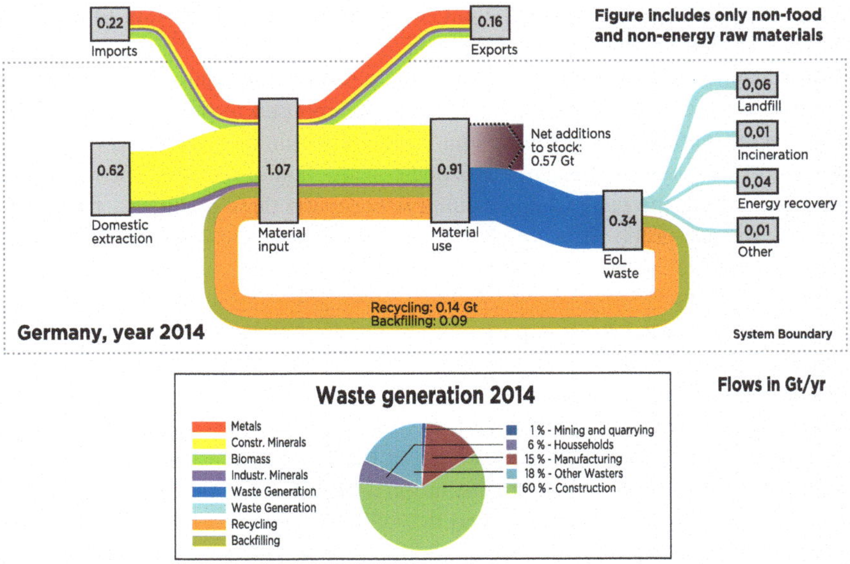

Fig. 5.17 A Sankey diagram

Fig. 5.18 Arrow from centre of the circle to the centroid of the triangle

different. How to weight energy use against material use, or air polluting versus water polluting cannot simply be a matter of looking at the thickest lines. The units are not comparible.

Step 13: Draw an arrow from the centre of the circle to the centroid of the triangle. See Fig. 5.18.

Step 14a[11]: Erase the lines used to find the centroid of the triangle. See Fig. 5.19.

Step 15: Normalise the arrow by adding 1/3 the radius to the arrow. See Fig. 5.20. This gives us our final arrow.

[11] The reason for numbering this 14a, is that 14b will appear in Sect. 8.3.

Fig. 5.19 Arrow from centre of the circle to the centroid of the triangle, erasing the triangle

Fig. 5.20 Normalise to give the final arrow

Why make this second normalisation-correction? Because the arrow would reach the edge of the circle *only* under the extreme conditions that every indicator arrow in two of the sectors has no, or negligible, length, and *all* of the indicator arrows in the remaining sector have maximal length. While this is a logical and mathematical possibility it has an extremely low probability for the sorts of institution for which the compass is designed. Such a case would be a strong meta-indicator that the identity conditions of the institution are oddly chosen, and it is inappropriate to construct a compass for that institution. For example, if one were to choose an institution with only one indicator arrow. That is, we stretch the notion of "institution" beyond the intended use of the concept here. For "institutions" that could plausibly display an extreme compass without the further correction I can suggest: the *strength* of an explosion (excitement), a massacre (discipline), a small drifting cloud (harmony). But these are not "institutions" of the sort we are usually concerned with when making policy, and we would have to be ignoring the context: the effect of the explosion, the reasons for the massacre and its effects, the reason behind there being only one cloud (since a cloud by itself is quite rare, Wordsworth notwithstanding). That is, for the overwhelming majority of institutions, the arrow from the previous step will be very short because the sector arrows balance each other. This is partly an artifact that arises from the choice of the centroid of the triangle as an insistence on the centre being located within the triangle.

To correct for the artificiality, I propose the following. Add the length of one third of the radius of the circle to the arrow. The reason I decided to make this further correction has to do with statistics and their representation as a tool of communication. As a tool of communication, the final arrow has to make an aesthetic and psychological impression. In constructing institutional compasses, my students and I used to stop at the previous stage. We were finding that, almost always, the arrows at the previous stage were very short. In fact, sometimes I would cheat and just lengthen the arrow myself more-or-less by a third of the radius, without giving a reason. But there was a reason for my instinctive reaction.

A short arrow indicates that the institution is well balanced between the three qualities, and that it does not hold the general quality with very much strength so it is easy to pull it into another sector, to overall display another quality. This does not make sense of our experience of institutions and it will not make too much sense for policy decision making either. Prisons will resemble primary schools and major international sports teams – because they will all be in balance between the three qualities, marginally favouring one over the others. It cannot be the case that almost all institutions are well balanced between the three qualities. Most show a quality significantly. If we compare a primary school to a prison and find that they are both quite well-balanced, then there is something wrong with the method.

As mentioned in Sect. 2.2 in Ancient thinking, a perfect balance between the qualities is interpreted as death or complete stagnation, maybe complete enlightenment of a person. The imbalance is what we find here on Earth, in our struggles, in our imperfections and it is these that give movement, dynamism and change.

Moreover, the representation of the data on the circle is meant to be used to give an overall intuitive impression, for comparative purposes and for communication. It cannot fulfil either function if the arrows for most institutions look almost the same – very short. I realised that we had cut the arrow short artificially with respect to the compass *radius* when I noticed that under the previous construction, before correcting the length of the then-final arrow, compass arrows were all short. The second step for correcting the length of the arrow leads to our final arrow, the one used for making decisions, for critiquing policy and for communicating policy. The policy changes, critique and communication still rest on the data entered in the tables. So, there is no danger of erring in our policy decisions because of the representation.

However, there might be reasons to make this representational correction differently, especially if our wish spot is close to the centre of the circle, since by adding a third to the arrow, it will be impossible for the actual arrow to be within the wish spot. Alternative corrections can also be considered, such as a logarithmic scale normalisation, or by choosing to use the incentre over the centroid of the triangle. So, there is a relationship between the position of the wish spot (as close to, or away from, the centre of the circle) and the choice of the centre of the triangle.

I suggest the following: if the wish spot does not include the centre point of the circle, then use the final normalisation above. In contrast, if the wish spot includes all three sectors – favouring a balance between the qualities, then do not make a final correction of length. Comparing institutions with different final normalisations will be delicate, but a solid understanding of the construction will help with the comparison which will include a discussion about the choice of wish spot – the attitude towards the qualities. See Sects. 4.2 and 5.2.

Figure 5.20 shows us the *final* arrow *given* the particular indicators we chose, together with the direction and length we thought represented that indicator. It is a compass reading, giving us an orientation in terms of the three general qualities. This is the end of the compass construction, the formula and eventual algorithm. The arrow represents what quality the institution most displays. We then use this final arrow to make an analysis. For policy recommendations we make an analysis, based on the compass.

5.6 Interpreting the Final Arrow: Making an Analysis of the Compass for Policy Decisions

To interpret the final arrow, we remark on three features: the sector it occupies, the degree within the sector and the length of the arrow. In the example of Fig. 5.20, we see that the institution in question is in the excitement sector. In particular, we can find other adjectives that more accurately mark the angle. See Fig. 5.3. The arrow has a good length, so the institution is quite exciting. We might be quite satisfied with this result, depending on our culture, the mandate of the institution and its context. In other words, we implicitly compare the final arrow to where we would like the arrow to be. Recall the "wish spot"? Put the compass with the final arrow next to the compass with the wish spot. These are what we are comparing. See Fig. 5.21.

We can now make new policies based on the final arrow, change existing policies, criticise policies and justify policies. We make the new policies, changes, criticisms and justifications based upon the discrepancy between the final arrow and the wish spot by recovering the story we told in developing the indicator arrows. We return to the data table.

Say we are satisfied. The final arrow for the institutional compass falls within the wish spot. Then we should not change policy. We might want to keep an eye on the context of the institution, since it might need to adapt to changing circumstances. We can try to anticipate these. But in general, we do not change policy, in fact we have a perfect justification to stay with present policy. Or, we could decide to be more

Fig. 5.21 Comparing the actual compass to the wish compass

ambitious, and reduce our wish spot by making it smaller. Is the arrow still inside the wish spot? If so, change nothing. If not, then we need to change policy.

When the final arrow lies outside the wish spot, as in Fig. 5.21, we can use policy to pull the arrow to the right place. We return to the data table in order to see which indicators are "pulling" the final arrow in the right direction, the ones closest to, or within, the wish spot, and see if we can promote and enforce these through policy. We also look at the arrows that are "pulling" the final arrow away from the wish spot. We think of policies to decrease these.

More precisely, we can look at indicators in the table whose degree encompasses the wish spot, and maybe lies within ten degrees of the wish spot. These are, roughly, the "good" indicator arrows that we encourage and celebrate. We want to elongate these. We then look at the "bad" arrows that pull directly away, with a margin of roughly forty degrees. These are the arrows we want to discourage and reduce in length. Working at these two extremes is enough to flip an arrow to its opposite direction. The concentration on these indicator arrows is relevant especially when the actual compass reading is more-or-less diametrically opposed, in direction, to the wish spot. These are the policy recommendations on which we focus more attention, but we do not stop here.

Now consider the other indicator arrows. These are ones we want to rotate – change the quality, if this is reasonable, or increase or decrease depending on the general direction. For a small rotation, encourage the arrows on the for side of the wish spot. Sometimes we look here for more creative solutions. See, for example the recommendations made in Sect. 13.2 concerning planting hedgerows and more ditches around fields in Hauts-de-France. We had no indicator arrows about hedgerows or about ditches, but the recommendation was to indirectly bring a solution to problems about loss of insect and bird population, flooding, water pollution, soil erosion and quality of soil. These sorts of solution are particularly relevant when the actual final arrow is not diametrically opposed to the wish spot, but rather is to the side somewhere. In this case we prioritise these solutions over the former ones discussed in the last paragraph.

As was remarked in Sect. 3.5, we can make a superficial policy analysis and recommendations or we can make a deeper analysis and recommendations.

To make a *very* superficial policy analysis, one where we do not really want to change anything, we *gerrymander the indicator arrows*. We can do this directly or indirectly. To do it directly, we change the definitions or the degree and length measurements. For example, if literacy is too low, then the very superficial recommendation is to change the definition as to what counts as literacy, so a higher percentage of people pass, and then you change that indicator arrow. Alternatively, we change the baseline, what we take to be "normal". This will shrink or elongate particular indicator arrows. This strategy is best accompanied by an education campaign to ensure that people affected by the institution agree with the baseline; we work out how to change ours and other people's *perceptions* of the particular indicators. We put a spin on the "good indicators" and the "bad indicators" so that the people affected by those indicators perceive the good ones as even better, and the bad ones as not so bad. For example, say that literacy is deemed to be too low. As a compass expert, you then recommend that we convince the population that literacy is over-rated, and is not very important. We see this in some countries where people of a certain class, minority or gender are discouraged from going to school.

The problem with the very superficial analysis and recommendation is that presumably, the definition of what was to be counted as literate, was thought through with some end in mind. That end will no longer be reached with the new definition. The weakness of the gerrymandering of the indicator arrow is that it is constant work to influence people's perceptions. We also cannot control perception in the general public, we can only try to influence it, so that sooner or later, more genuine perceptions will resurface. We cannot predict when that will be. Lastly, we are vulnerable to criticism. Nothing prevents a journalist or opposing group to construct their own compass regarding your institution. If their data analysis is very different then this will come out in the open, and the gerrymandering exposed.

A less superficial analysis leaves the lengths and degrees of the indicator arrows alone. Instead, one focuses on a suite of particular indicators, the "good" ones and the "bad" ones, where "good" and "bad" refer to the wish spot. We match policy recommendations to the indicators directly. If literacy is too low, then we find a way of making a higher percentage of the population literate.

A good and deep analysis will look at *underlying causes* for the good and bad statistics, and will target the underlying causes. For example, if the reason for the high level of illiteracy is the lack of schools for children in remote areas, then more schools need to be built, more schooling material made available in the more remote areas, more teachers trained, increased incentives for teachers to teach in the remote areas and a campaign to convince the population of the importance of schooling and literacy together with relief for the families who send their children to school, if they would otherwise work at home. Maybe two free healthy meals at school gives relief to families who otherwise find it hard to feed their children well.

So far, we have analysed the data and constructed the compass as "experts". As noted, the compass becomes more robust if we consult widely. We can use the recommendations as only that – to be put on the table for negotiation. There are three points of discussion: the location of the wish spot, the included or neglected data, and the degree and length of data arrows. Therefore, the recommendations are also an invitation for others to contribute to the analysis of the data points, or interact with the analysis, in the sense that they might disagree. They might disagree with the weighted significance of a data point that is included, because their intuitive baseline is different, i.e., what they consider to be "normal" is different. In such a case, they think that the length ought to be modified. This draws out a discussion about the baseline – what is normal statistically, what is reasonable to expect. We can split data points if agreement is impossible.

Alternatively, there might be disagreement about the degree of the included datapoint. In this case we return to the protocol used to determine the degree. Maybe another protocol should be chosen, the interaction should lead to either adopting a different protocol, and so, possibly changing the degree of the indicator arrow representing the data point, and therefore, also changing the final arrow, and it should deepen the analysis by justifying the protocols that were chosen. Another possibility is that in such an engagement or interaction we omitted a data point. In this case it should be introduced in the table, and analysed in terms of length and degree. Because of the notion of "corrected length" we can add data points without distorting the integrity of the final arrow. This is an important point that lies in contrast to existing multi-criteria decision aides where we cannot just add any data we choose. The reason for disallowing this is a very good one at face value, but it is based on a conceptual error, now that we have the compass.

5.6.1 The Point About Adding Data Points

Existing multi-criteria decision aides select *particular data points in advance*. See, for example, the labels for the spokes on the wheel in Fig. 5.7. This is thought to be important for making an *objective comparison* between competing options. But it is also a way of *silencing or obscuring* other data points that might be thought to be very important in a community or particular region. For democratic purposes it is important that voices be heard and that people who want to participate in the decision making process should be allowed to do so meaningfully. In so doing when making a compass, we do not lose the objectivity of comparison between competing options. Our common measure is not the particular data points but the qualities. This is an important point, so I'm going to repeat myself.

By including relevant data, we gain in accuracy with respect to the institution we are analysing with the compass. The accuracy is a type of objectivity. We find a *common measure of comparison* in the *three qualities*, not in choice of data points. It is general qualities that we compare, not particular facts. It is for this reason that we do not have a list of data types given in advance. It is for this reason that we insist on the weak objectivity of the sector arrows.

The compass is not a certification system, where we tick off the boxes, in the same way as being stamped "organic" or "in compliance" with such and such rules or recommendations. Instead, the compass orients us with respect to general qualities, and it remains flexible as to how those qualities are instantiated. Interaction, and disagreement over the qualities is important for objectivity, integrity and holism of the final arrow, and it is important as part of the *democratic* effort of constructing a compass. The compass, or rather the data table, is used for mediation and explanation, but here it is inclusive mediation, in the sense that we can add new information.

For mediating, we note the fact that different stakeholders or different actors might not share the same attitude towards the final compass reading or towards the analysis of particular data. In this case, we would explain to what extent and how their points of view were taken into account in the data analysis, or we change the analysis. In accordance with their views, we modify the length and/or degree of the controversial indicator arrows, or split existing data points into two. This makes explicit the political power play of the institution. It is important for various groups to be aware of this in case they want to preserve the existing power structure or change it. In power-structure debates it is important for all parties to understand what people's perceptions really are in terms of qualities and what is to count as "normal".

In other words, we return to the construction. This means that compass construction is not a finished exercise. There are feed-back loops, especially when there is major conflict. By returning to the data and refining it, we use a feedback loop to increase the objectivity of the final arrow in the form of convergence (we all finally agree, or we include disagreement by splitting data). We also implicitly use the construction exercise as a mediation exercise. This step is important if we anticipate disagreement. It will help disagreeing parties to become aware of the other's point of view, and help to somewhat dispel the disagreement by showing how, and to what extent, stakeholders and actors have participated. It is also important for reasons of using the compass honestly. It prevents superficial use of the compass, where compass constructors gerrymander the analysis of the data on the table (in terms of length and degree) in order to make the final reading align with the desires of a particular interest group – the wish spot they like. If the mediation is carefully and honestly done, then some consensus should be reached.

One more step can be made to increase objectivity of the exercise.

As an institutional economist, Söderbaum is candid about his own ideological orientation, that is, a set of ethical principles or preferences that guide his research. His candidness is far from being a weakness in the analysis. It is a strength. It gives students of his writing the ability to conceptually compensate for his preferences, when they do not share them, and gives them the ability to become aware of the preferences that they share with Söderbaum, and where they disagree with him. Awareness of our own values, or ideological orientation, is part of the science, where 'science' is not understood in the naïve way of making calculations, but in a more sophisticated way that allows for complexity, indeterminism and feed-back loops: where science is about trying to understand processes, phenomena and underlying mechanisms in an objective, honest and transparent manner. The institutional compass is meant to help with policy decisions in a complex setting, where there is indeterminism, tipping points and feed-back loops, and this, without ignoring values. We still need a common measure, to manage our efforts and resources. The common measure in the compass are the three general qualities. The values of the community are made explicit, and the values of the scientist who assists with constructing a compass are also made explicit. They might include a strong sense of democracy, and therefore, a subsuming of his, or her, own personal values in order to reflect those of the larger community.

As part of the institutional analysis, it is proper to be explicit about what aspects of one's own ideological orientation have influenced one's research. To summarise: this is important for three reasons. One is so that others reading the research can "correct" for the ideological bias. A second is that it calls on the reader to become aware of his or her own ideological orientation, and this will be important for democratic decision making. Third, it is important to be aware that carrying out research is not done from an unbiased standpoint. As scientists, we each have some sort of ideological orientation. It influences what we are sensitive to and what we ignore. Furthermore, in carrying out research, in the better cases, the research changes us. That is, we are implicated in the research. Being aware of this adds depth and tolerance for the unavoidable subjectivity and error that is included in scientific research.

Objectivity is a concern for any scientist. "Objectivity" means different things, as does subjectivity. Moreover, in this sort of scientific project, it is a relative term. What we can do is try to be *as objective as possible*. The lesson to retain is that objectivity comes in degrees. It is not an absolute in a dichotomous sense of "objective or subjective *tour court*". As we saw there are several moments in the methodology of constructing the compass where we can increase objectivity, which I sometimes call robustness, and is reflected by stability in sector arrows. Being aware of our own ideological orientation is one of the steps towards increased objectivity. As we shall see, the compass construction can be adapted to answer to a particular ideology, and we shall see examples of several such adaptations in Chaps. 7 and 8. It is only when we are aware of our own ideological orientation that we can even begin to correct for it, negotiate openly with others who hold a different ideology and make policy decisions that are sensitive to the ideologies of people affected by our institution.

5.6.2 My Ideological Orientation

I should practice what I preach and declare my own ideological orientation. It is as follows, at the time of writing. I have to mention the time because ideological orientations change, and the very act of writing this book has probably confirmed the orientation, but cannot entrench it. It will probably change as I learn, and develop my understanding of the world we live in. It will change with the changes in the world too.

For the purposes of what is being discussed here, I am most influenced by my father Anthony Friend, a statistician, ecological economist and philosopher. In this work, I am also influenced by: Söderbaum, Kumar, Rapport and Shmelev. From Söderbaum I learned institutional economics combined with ecological economics. Kumar's book taught me about the three *gunas*. Rapport taught me and my father about eco-system health and Shmelev taught me about multi-criteria decision aides. Ideologically, I think it is correct to say that I am ecological economist and an institutional economist. Following Söderbaum, I also have a strong leaning towards participative democracy. Following some of the indigenous cultures, I think in terms of seven generations into the past and into the future. The latter grounds my precautionary leanings.

Let me flesh this out in less technical language and in more detail. As an ecological economist, I believe that the health of the economy is dependent on society and that society is dependent on the natural environment. I also think that at the timescale that concerns me – three hundred years in both directions, the space-scale of the whole planet and the size-scale of: the planet down to nano-chemicals that penetrate natural biological cell membranes; we are subject to at least the first two laws of thermodynamics: that there is a fixed amount of energy in the universe and that the *availability* of the energy for doing work diminishes. More specifically, on Earth, we can distinguish between our fund of low entropy and the natural flows. The former includes all of the "non-renewable resources": oil, coal and gas, chemical potential energy, the nuclear energy found in Plutonium and Uranium. The latter are the natural flows of: heat, air, water, nutrient cycles, life and death cycles and migratory cycles. In the age of the Anthropocene, we burn off the fund of low entropy and we disrupt the natural flows.

The ideological orientation that I hold with respect to these scientific descriptive facts is that we *ought* to use up our fund of low entropy as slowly as possible and respect the natural flows as much as possible. "Possible" here is subject to cultural boundaries of acceptability. Mayumi (2001, 45) puts it nicely. He says that we ought to find a "culturally acceptable rate of entropy production". I add to this that we also want to influence the culture, as and when we can, to continue to *reduce* what is deemed *acceptable*. So, as members of institutions and as agents who can influence institutions, we try to influence people in the ambient culture to use less, especially less oil, coal and gas. Boulding (1949) writes that the role of government is to try to reduce production and consumption, whereas business tries to increase it to make profits. I roughly share this view, although the separation of government and business is not so clear today. Thus, rather than make this distinction, I prefer to think in terms of two norms that are in tension: produce and consume less, produce and consume more. Wisdom on this matter consists in resolving the tension – resisting the message of private company's advertising that tries to convince us that we are inadequate if we lack some good on the market, and that we shall be happier if we purchase it. Friend (A. Friend, 124) adds to Mayumi's formulation that government ought to measure *efficiency* in terms of a "culturally acceptable rate of entropy production per unit of consumption". Friend's ideological orientation is that it is important to keep track of the rate of entropy production, and that government should be held accountable to ensure that we respect the culturally acceptable rate that is decided upon. Moreover, we shall be better off if we increase the entropic efficiency of production.

As an ecological economist I also think that collectively, we should look after the environment first, then society, then the economy. By 'collectively' I mean at the level of international coordination and treaties at the several levels of government, and also at the level of informal communities and households. There are many tribal communities who look after the land and the ecosystem, and I take them to set the highest standard for what would count as living sustainably by the precepts of an ecological economist. They have a long tradition of living in harmony with the ecosystem that surrounds them. They live *with* nature, not *against* it or *apart from* it.

I am particularly influenced by two of their teachings. One comes from the story of the tribes' first coming to the north American continent. The story is that each tribe, as it travelled in search of a place to settle, would stop from time to time and ask nature around them – the eco-system – if they were permitted to settle there. The eco-system would either send them on or let them stay. If they were permitted to stay, then they asked nature: how do we live here? What is our responsibility to the eco-system? (Marchand et al. pp. 20–21). This is what allowed them to survive in a largely self-sufficient way for a very long time. Like all humans, and all species, they did modify the eco-systems they lived in. They planted food crops and harvested from them, but also left some of the harvest for the surrounding animals, insects and plant-life. They live in better harmony with the natural flows than we do in the modern world.

The second teaching concerns the fox character or trickster. The fox is a bit disruptive, plays jokes and gets into trouble; but the character teaches us that few situations are black or white, good or bad *tout court*. There is a bit of both. He teaches us subtlety and nuance. This is why I thought it a nice idea to have three general non-scalar qualities, and not two. The two would naturally be 'good' and 'bad'. But, as part of my ideological orientation, I do not believe that things, people, institutions, systems or situations are good or bad, as such. Rather they are good in some respects and bad in others, like the fox. Analysing data in terms of the three qualities of harmony, discipline and excitement shifts us away from the dichotomy of good and bad. It takes a little extra mental effort. The effort has the advantage of giving us a bit of emotional distance and provides a fresh perspective. Both of these contribute to objectivity in the analysis.

We can learn from ancient thinking how to live in better harmony with the environment. If we are looking after the environment well, then we concern ourselves with society, and we do this along four clusters of concern: health, security, education and culture. To promote these, we pay attention to informational and material infrastructure. When society is doing well according to indicators in the clusters, then we look after the economy. Of course, thinking like the fox, it is not as though we complete one level of concern and then cleanly start the next. Rather, in temporal terms we do all three at the same time. The three areas of collective responsibility (environment, society and economy) share a dependence relationship, and our collective efforts should align with that dependence.

As an institutional economist, following Söderbaum (2000, 2016) and Vatn (2005), I believe that institutions influence our decisions. This is not to say that we always make decisions that agree with institutions, since we can disagree and go against an institution. Doing so incurs a risk of penalty in the case of formal institutions. I also think that we can change institutions. We can do so from within and from the outside. Individuals and institutions influence each other. Moreover, we cannot escape being so influenced or of influencing them in turn. When we obey or fall in alignment with the rules or precepts of an institution, we comfort and confirm those rules and precepts. When we disobey or break rules, we challenge them and sometimes start the process of changing them.

With Söderbaum, I share a commitment to democracy. By this I do not mean a system of voting. I do mean collective decisions making and taking into account the opinions and desires of people at all levels in an institution. For example, I think that the cleaning staff at a university should be consulted even for very "high up" decisions about education and merit. Why not ask them, if they are interested in the questions. That is, everyone involved in an institution should be consulted for the purposes of making policy decisions. A university does not only pay the cleaners, it should serve them. Moreover, democracy carries outside the institutional boundaries. People affected by an institution should also be consulted. This is just common sense. It is also prudential. It is only by asking people outside an institution that we can anticipate conformity or resistance. Of course, questionnaires take a lot of effort. Instead of asking people directly, we can either invite them to contribute as they wish, or observe their behaviour - as an *imperfect* indicator of preferences.

By studying institutions, we learn how to change them. To use the vocabulary introduced by Söderbaum, we are not *homo economicai*, but rather, "political economic persons" (Söderbaum, 2000, 33–6). This means that we all have a set of values. We are aware of them to varying degrees. We are made more aware of them when our values clash with those of others around us. We then are called to examine our own values. This makes us see more clearly ourselves and others since we gain a wider perspective. It is important to be aware of our values, even when we think we are, or when we are trying to be, as objective as possible. It is good scientific practice to be aware of our values. They both enlighten and hamper our sight. They make us keenly sensitive towards certain things, and help us ignore or forget other things.

I also have a strong commitment to objectivity, insofar as it can be had, and to the degree to which it can be had. In compass construction projects, we cannot have complete or absolute objectivity. Molinini distinguishes strong objectivity from weak objectivity. Strong objectivity in information for policy decisions is impossible. But weak objectivity (Molinini 2019) is possible and appropriate. It is not the same as inter-subjectivity, or group-think, because it is not *primarily* a social phenomenon. Weak objectivity of an idea or fact comes in degrees. It is increased by being re-deployed or being found to be true (or correct) in another area of knowledge (cross-checking). It is related to Wright's (1992) concept of "wide cosmological role" of an idea or fact. An idea or fact is objective *in respect of* playing a wide cosmological role, that is, it pops up in various discourses that are more or less independent of each other. This is unexpected, and can take time to notice. The popping up of the same idea, independently, confirms the truth of the idea and adds objectivity. *Grosso modo*, while I am committed to objectivity in science, I am not naïve about the concept of objectivity, especially in the more social sciences. We hold ourselves to the appropriate standard for objectivity, not to an absolute standard.

Lastly, with respect to this work, my ideological orientation includes an embracing of philosophical questions. Rather than thinking of them as messy and hopeless, I think that they are very important. The exercise of constructing a compass is philosophical, as well as scientific and political. It is appropriate to engage in this exercise philosophically, scientifically and politically when we are confronted with difficult questions – ones that cannot be easily solved, where we cannot please everyone and where we try to weigh incompatible and incomparable variables. I work here to offer methods for preventing tensions. My training in philosophy also allows me to always be able to find a perspective from which I see the same thing differently with a different emotion. It is a sort-of mental gymnastics exercise that philosophers practice. I think that it adds to our own objectivity when we are adept at the exercise.

References

Abdin, A. Y., & Friend, M. (Forthcoming). *Doughnuts and compasses: How to decide*.
Boulding, K. (1949). Income or wealth. *Review of Economic Studies, 17*, 77–86.
Mayumi, K. (2001). *The origins of ecological economics; The biomechanics of Georgescu-Roegen*. Routledge.
Molinini, D. (2019). The weak objectivity of mathematics and its reasonable effectiveness in science. In *Axiomathes; Where science meets philosophy*. Springer.
Raworth, K. (2017). *Doughnut economics: Seven ways to think like a 21st-century economist*. Random House.
Söderbaum, P. (2000). *Ecological economics*. Earthscan Publications.
Söderbaum, P. (2016). *Economics, ideological oreintation and democracy for sustainable development* (2nd ed.). World Economics Association, Bristol, UK.
Vatn, A. (2005). *Institutions and the environment*. Edward Elgar.
Wright, C. (1992). *Truth and objectivity*. Harvard University Press.

Part III
Scope: More Uses of the Institutional Compass and Some Extensions

In this part, we increase the scope of the compass. We merge it with systems diagrams and thereby, with systems science. We continue the method to give it an explicitly ideological bent. We discuss alternative ideologies and how they can be accommodated by the methodology. We see other adaptations and extensions. In this way we witness the flexibility of the concepts, inviting the reader to make his, or her, own extensions and adaptations. Through looking at the extensions, we entrench the lessons of thinking: in terms of qualities, comprehensiveness of analysis, inclusiveness of other points of view, holistically and objectivity.

Chapter 6
Merging the Compass with Systems Science

Consider a system's approach to identifying the vulnerable, strong and influential parts of a system. An institution can be thought of as a system. It might be explicitly organised with rules or it might be self-organising. It has an effect: internal and external to the institution/ system. Actions are performed within, by, and on, a system. It is composed of nodes roughly thought of as objects or positions, and relations between them. The characteristic of a system in the sense of systems science is that:

1. The relations matter as much as, or more than, the nodes or objects,
2. There are feed-back loops, internal re-enforcements or confirmations, or external feedback loops which are consequences felt outside the system, and that have repercussions back on the system. Loops act on the system *qua* system. The loops can spiral in any direction: outward from the system, influencing the context of the system. Loops can pull the system in on itself, causing strengthening or collapse.
3. Systems have emergent properties, (the whole is more than the sum of the parts).

   There are many definitions of what an emergent property is, but here it is enough to say that a property is emergent just in case it cannot be detected or predicted on the basis of the parts of the system. For example, the pleasing effects of a piece of music is not detectable if we list the notes and the instruments used. The colour (visible to the human eye) of, for example, a protein, cannot be determined by looking at individual proteins. Proteins are the size of between five and ten nano-metres. The wavelengths of light are 380–750 nanometers. Colour is an emergent property of proteins only detectable at a certain scale.
4. Systems are dynamic.

   Systems change internally and change as a result of influences from outside.

To make a systems analysis, we identify nodes in a system and the relations between them. Nodes might be roles, particular people, sub-organisations, projects, items,

M. I. Friend, *The Institutional Compass: Method, Use and Scope*, Methodos Series 18, https://doi.org/10.1007/978-3-031-05453-2_6

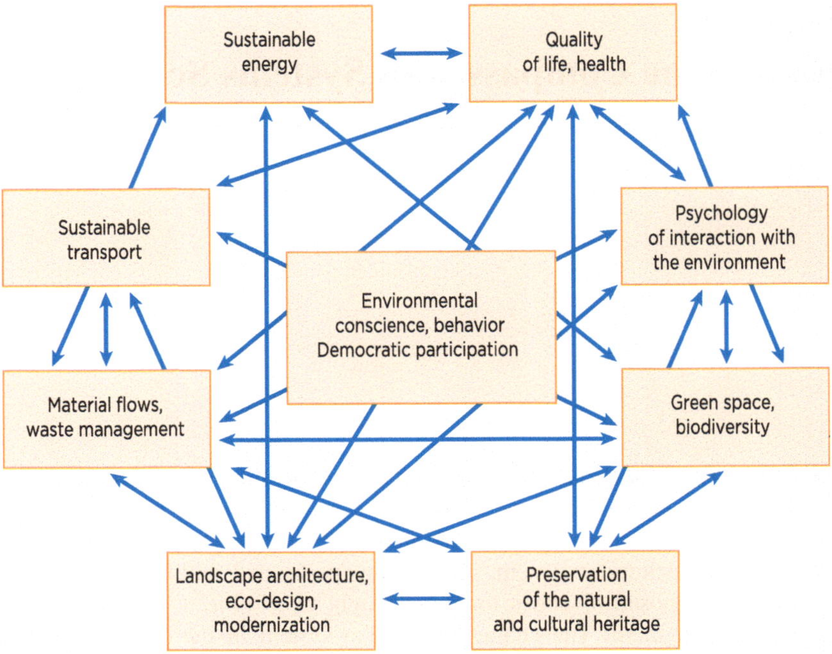

Fig. 6.1 An example systems diagram. (Source: Shmelev (2012), Shmelev & Shmeleva (2009))

cells, places, traditions and so on. A systems scientist tries to take a neutral role,[1] and maps the system using a diagram. He, or she, invites members of the system to suggest the nodes and the relations. See Fig. 6.1.

This is one simple sort of diagram. There are other much more complicated ones. This is enough to show the core idea – to identify nodes relations and directions. Feedback loops are represented by sets of arrows that cycle back to a node. We shall add a few complications here. The diagram can be expanded as more people participate in identifying nodes and relations. Each new participant notices different nodes and relations, or re-enforces existing nodes and relations. Eventually we get a sort-of convergence or stability in the diagram of nodes and relations since we start to make clusters. Of course, the stability is in the sense of stable at a time, since outside influences or internal changes will have an effect. Systems are dynamic.

Now we ask the question about the purpose of the diagram. There is always a normative element, a reason why we composed the diagram or thought it important to understand the system. In practice, if we study a failing system, we do so in order to put it right. We might also want to destroy or undermine a system. In both cases we look for important weaknesses – nodes or relations whose vulnerability threaten to collapse the system or change it significantly. To preserve the system, we

[1] Of course, to do so it might be best for the systems scientist to be explicit about his, or her, ideological orientation.

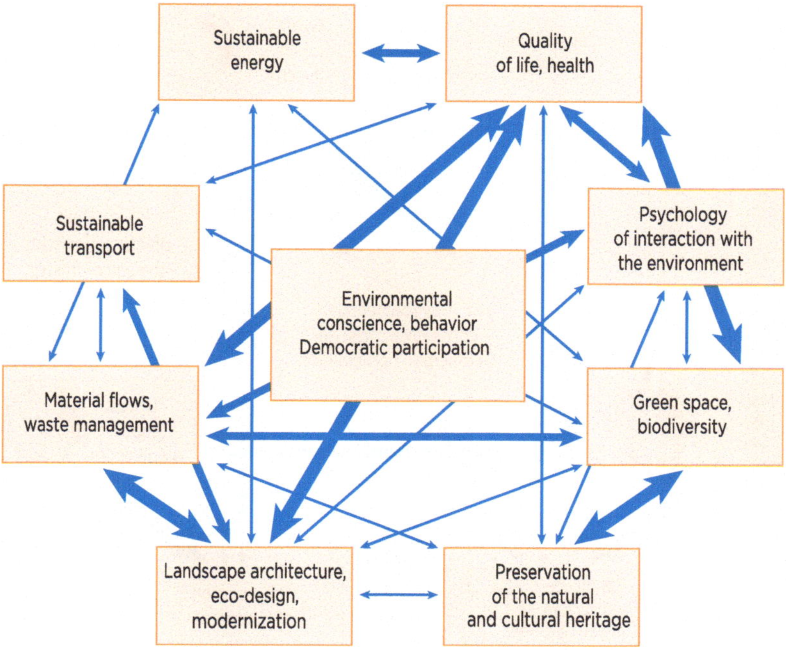

Fig. 6.2 A "weighted" systems diagram. (Adapted from Shmelev & Shmeleva (2009))

re-enforce the vulnerable nodes or relations. To destroy the system, we attack the vulnerable nodes or relations.

To deepen our analysis, let us make a three-way distinction. A system under stress, or attack, can be resilient, adaptive or change significantly. If it is resilient to that stress, then, after not too much time, it bounces back to "normal". If it adapts relative to the stress, it changes, but not in some "essential" features. If it changes significantly, it loses important or essential features that make it unrecognisable as that (its previous) system. Which of the three scenarios occurs depends entirely on our definitions of "normal" and "essential". So, we can think of a system as having a normal functioning state with an inner core of essential relations. We accord these more weight. See Fig. 6.2.

Now view the idea of system, system resilience, adaptation or significant change in terms of the compass. We might have a wish spot for the system. The compass gives us a qualitative direction. We can identify the whole system or parts of the system or relations between parts as sharing and re-enforcing the qualitative direction, or moving the system away from the qualitative direction. Some parts of the system might deliberately be designed to steer away in order to enable the other parts to pull the system in the desired direction. The qualitative direction is a quality: harmony, discipline, excitement or a combination of qualities. If we are in favour of the present direction of an institution or system, then we seek to confirm and re-enforce the essential nodes or relations, especially the ones that are the most

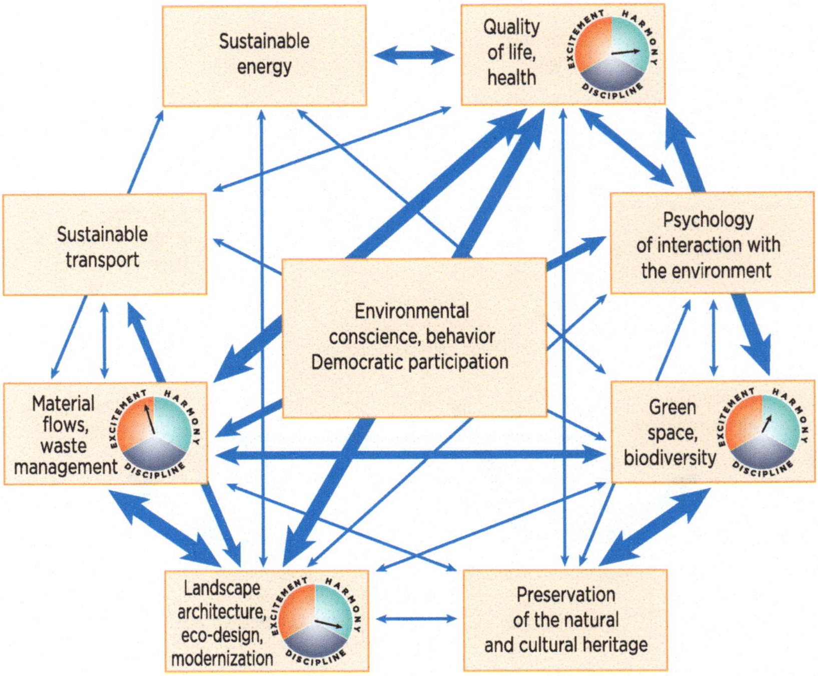

Fig. 6.3 A systems diagram with compasses at important nodes. (Adapted from Shmelev & Shmeleva (2009))

vulnerable. In terms of our table of data, the systems diagram will further help us to decide which data to enforce and which data to ignore. But now we have added the qualitative normative dimension explicitly.

The problem is that the table of data for the compass and the systems-identified vulnerable and important nodes and relations do not easily match.

A method for merging systems science diagrams, such as the one above, with the compass is to construct compasses for the systems-identified vulnerable and important nodes and relations. See Fig. 6.3. The compass table for the node or relation will guide us as to what aspect of the node or relation to enforce or attack – in order not to merely re-enforce or merely change (without direction) but to bring about the re-enforcement or change we want. This is the difference between blind re-enforcement or destruction and guided or strategic re-enforcement or destruction towards a quality.

To make such a diagram it will be necessary to have data about each node. This is also something rarely used in systems science, a table of quantitative data. We can use the table plus the compasses to efficiently target parts of systems, without forgetting to see the whole, both in terms of the wish spot, and in terms of making a generic compass for the whole system. There is no need to limit our data to data about nodes or relations between nodes. There might be data about clusters, and they might show up as emergent properties.

To summarise, we can add compasses to nodes or relations of a systems diagram in order to strategically address the system. In general, it is the vulnerable or strong nodes or relations that count. The others are less significant. What the compass construction adds is a sense of direction for change in a system. We choose that direction according to our ideological orientation, that of the institution or that of outsiders who want to change the system. To show the ideological orientation, we would accompany such a diagram by two others. A compass for the entire system and a wish compass. We then target the nodes or relations that point in the right direction or the wrong direction in order to orient the entire system towards the wish spot.

This was a simple way of merging systems diagrams with the compass. It gives us a way of thinking about the system and parts of the system qualitatively and quantitatively, of measuring the contribution of the parts towards the final arrow, while allowing for emergent properties that defy a reductionist analysis in terms of the sum of the parts.

References

Shmelev, S. (2012). *Ecological economics; Sustainability in practice*. Springer.

Shmelev, S. E., & Shmeleva, I. A. (2009). Sustainable cities: Problems of integrated interdisciplinary research. *International Journal of Sustainable Development, 12*(1), 4–24.

Chapter 7
Adapting the Compass to Align with Ecological Economics Thinking

We start with the general concepts included in ecological economics thinking. Ecological economists are normative in two respects. There is the scientific norm concerning some dependence relationships in the world and the law of entropy. There is a more ethical norm about the desire to align our life-styles with the dependence relationship and encourage others to share the desire for alignment.

7.1 General Concepts of Ecological Economics

We now consider our institution from the perspective of ecological economics. There is some controversy over what is essential and what is dispensable in ecological economics, and I shall not engage the controversy here. Instead, I offer *a* characterisation. The point is to demonstrate the adaptation of the methodology to the new thinking. This is enough to suggest alternative adaptations in line with alternative conceptions of ecological economics. The conception will influence data collection, classification and normalisation.

Here, ecological economics is thought of as essentially containing five ideas.

1. Economics is about the management of resources.
2. The monetary economy depends on society and society depends on ecology.
3. An ecosystem, a society and an economy can be thought of in terms of health.
4. The planetary natural environment is subject to the first two laws of thermodynamics.
5. There is a plurality of values that are worth accommodating in our economic thinking.

For some readers each of these is obviously true, for others some are controversial. We address them in turn. The first is slightly different from what one finds in a standard economics textbook, where economics is defined as the *allocation* of scarce resources. The reason ecological economists prefer the word "management" is that

M. I. Friend, *The Institutional Compass: Method, Use and Scope*, Methodos Series 18, https://doi.org/10.1007/978-3-031-05453-2_7

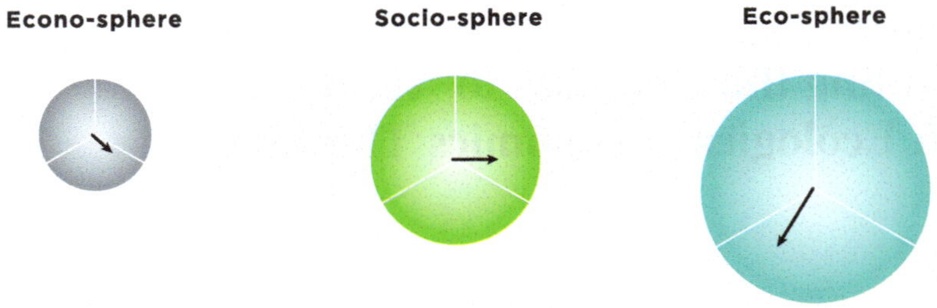

Fig. 7.1 Three compasses, one for each sphere

Fig. 7.2 Behind the scenes for an ecological economics compass

"allocation" suggests immediate distribution, whereas "management" is more amenable to the idea of keeping in reserve.

For the second, we think in terms of three spheres: the econo-sphere, the socio-sphere and the eco-sphere (Friend, 2017, 123). The econo-sphere is contained in, is a subset of, the socio-sphere. The socio-sphere is contained in, is a subset of, the eco-sphere. See Figs. 7.1 and 7.2. The relationship is one of existential dependence. That is, there is no economic activity without society, and there is no society without the natural environment to provide breathable air, potable water, nutritious food and material for shelter and clothing.

The relationship between the three spheres is also one of health. A healthy economy depends on a healthy society,[1] and the health of society depends on the health of the environment. Thus, the figure is meant to be suggestive of three types of relationship between the spheres: mathematical (relative size), existential and one of flourishing or health.

The metaphor of health is taken seriously, and we collect, or develop, indicators of health for the eco-sphere, the socio-sphere and the econo-sphere. It is a metaphor

[1] Arguably, a society at war or in revolution, is not "healthy". Nevertheless, depending on our measures, we might think that the economy of a society can be healthy during wartime. Following this train of thought, we would conclude that the health of the economy does not depend on the health of the society. This is a defendable argument. It is subject to agreeing to the measures of health and time scale. Here, we are simply going to deny this since the point of the exercise is to explore the adaptation of the compass to this thinking, not to defend it, since it amounts to deciding that war or revolution are healthy. They might be in some measure, just as stress is healthy in some measure.

taken from the idea of human health. A human is born, lives for a while and dies. During the human's life, he, or she, might be healthy, thriving or ill. "Healthy" means being free from disease, resilient against stress – being able to bounce back. "Thriving" means being able to use stress to generate something new, to learn productively, to construct, and affirm oneself even under quite severe stress. "Ill" means succumbing to stress, allowing disease to enter the body and compromise it's functioning.

Likewise, an economy can be healthy, thriving or ill. A healthy economy can survive some stress. There is some slack and opportunity. A mild economic downturn can be overcome. It is in a steady state. A thriving economy is one where, even under severe stress, such as an economic crisis, economic resources are used to re-construct and re-invent the society. Crisis is used as a propulsive force for innovation and positive change. An ill economy is one where it is impossible, very difficult or takes a long time, to get out of a downward spiral of debt and poverty. An economic crisis turns the economy in this downward spiral.

A society is healthy if it can return to normal after some stress. Social stressors might be mild or extreme. They come in at least four general categories: political (organization, power changes, legal…), educational, human health and security. The following list of stressors might fall into several of the broad categories. Societal stressors include: change of government or government policy, re-drawing of political boundaries, wars, revolution, invasion, occupation by another culture, change in education system, changes in media technology, epidemics, pandemics, significant disparity in health, or longevity, between different social groups, high criminality and violence. These are debatable and worth debating. The list is not meant to be exhaustive or even necessarily correct. What a decision maker decides is worth counting as an indicator of social health will depend in part on a wider philosophical attitude. Discussing what counts as a social stressor is part of the compass construction exercise. The discussion is revealing and explanatory, and therefore becomes part of the justification for policy. It is what makes compasses tailored to regions and cultures, so that suitable and effective policies are developed.

A society is thriving if it changes positively after succumbing to stress, and it is ill if it cannot, and degrades. Moreover, there is a matter of degree. Some societies are healthier than others, and some are healthier in particular respects than others, for example, one society might be able to overcome stress caused by a pandemic more easily than another, but might find another stressor such as cultural invasion more difficult to overcome. Also note that the time scale for social change is usually longer than for economic stress and response.

An ecosystem can be healthy, thriving or ill. The person who developed the concept of ecological health is David Rapport. I'll quote him directly and suggest some quality interpretations.

> Healthy ecosystems are characterized by three fundamental properties: organization, vitality, and resilience. Organization refers to the architecture of the ecosystem, that is, an ecosystem's characteristic diversity of species (biodiversity) and relationships of species with one another and with the abiotic environment. Vitality refers to the metabolism of the ecosystem, that is, the energy and nutrient flows characteristic of each type of ecosystem. A key measure

> of vitality is primary productivity, or the amount of plant biomass produced per unit area per unit of time. Resilience refers to the capacity of ecosystems to rebound after natural disturbances such as floods, droughts, or insect infestations. These features characterize all ecosystems, be they natural or human-constructed and maintained (e.g., agroecosystems or urban ecosystems). (Rapport, 2013, 251)

Let us now elaborate the concept to distinguish a healthy ecosystem from a thriving one. A healthy one has good bio-diversity, that is in general equilibrium, or a sort-of steady state, varying with seasons and longer cycles, such as forest fires. The time scale for ecosystems is much longer than for society or the economy. A thriving ecosystem is measured by what Rapport calls vitality. After stress, there will be an increase in biodiversity per unit area and high production of biomass – growth and reproduction, in the same area per same unit of time.

It is possible that there are no longer any thriving ecosystems on Earth since the rate of extinction is 1000 times greater than that of speciation. Thriving ecosystems might be a thing of the past, at least for the foreseeable future.

However, we want to be a little careful here, especially with climate change since it changes the abiotic and geographical boundaries of ecosystems, pushing the boundaries of hot desserts to occupy larger areas, and shrinking cooler ecosystems. Violent weather in any ecosystem causes stress.

It follows that *prima facie*, some areas of Earth are just too hostile to life to have a thriving ecosystem compared to others: because of temperatures, because of weather conditions, especially rainfall patterns, or because of human activity such as industrial agriculture that compromises biodiversity or when we impose a built-up infrastructure that changes or disrupts the natural flows of water or soil nutrient replenishment. However, *secondo facie*, it is clear that we could not hope for, or expect, the degree of biodiversity of a tropical rainforest in the arctic tundra. So, for the purposes of detecting and measuring the health of an ecosystem, we decide on a "baseline" relative to that ecosystem and climactic zone. This will be an ecosystem state that has proven to be steady over the long term with its usual cycles. Thus, it would be perfectly appropriate to decide that in Europe the biodiversity found before the use of artificial or imported fertilisers constitutes the baseline, and this is healthy, that is, we could count traditional agriculture is part of a healthy ecosystem. We could be more radical and insist that the baseline is how Europe was before agriculture was practiced. Or we could be quite complicit and accept industrial agriculture as "normal", and count that as what we mean by a healthy eco-system. Therefore, the concept of health of an ecosystem is relative to a baseline, and this has to be debated and decided upon. Whatever the decision, what we are after is some stability. A dying eco-system is not healthy. The decision will inform our conception of "sustainability". See Sect. 7.4.

A healthy ecosystem, then, is one that can recover from some stress, be it natural or manmade. A thriving one can recover from much greater stress, and an ill ecosystem cannot fully recover. It will change irreparably. Overfishing, pollution and human urban development decreases the expanse of healthy ecosystems. Climate change will increase the size of ill ones. Violent weather destroys human infrastructures allowing nature to step in, but it also destroys plants and animals and stresses ecosystems.

> The loss of ecosystem health, or ecosystem pathology, is signalled by substantial changes in one or more of these fundamental aspects [organization, vitality and resilience]. Ecosystems under stress show highly similar patterns, which have been described in terms of "ecosystem distress syndrome." Generally, organization is compromised and biodiversity is lost. Productivity of terrestrial ecosystems tends to decline, as nutrient cycling becomes less efficient and nutrients are leached out of the system. Aquatic ecosystems tend to become nutrient-enriched, and thus, initially, productivity rises. But in this case, the [short-term] increase in productivity is a sign of [long-term] ecosystem degradation, as the nutrients fuel excessive algal blooms, and the ecosystem becomes clogged with the growth of reeds, macrophytes, and other aquatic plants that would normally be kept in check. Ecosystems under repeated episodes of stress tend to lose resilience, taking a longer time to recover or achieving less complete recovery. (Rapport, 2013, 252)

When an ecosystem collapses, nature comes back but in a different and less healthy form. It is then philosophically appropriate to shift the baseline. However, we should be aware that this is what we are doing since after an ecosystem collapses, some species are lost, invasive species increase, larger species disappear or are reduced in number and there is more disease. This is a downward spiral in health in absolute terms, although some new stability should emerge. The reason we should be reluctant to shift our baseline to accommodate degradation and the downward spiral is that if many ecosystems collapse around the same time, then the global effect is compounded since the invading other species are also coming from a collapsed, or collapsing, ecosystem. Deciding on the baseline is a normative exercise. It sets a norm to which indicators and a final compass reading are responsible. The norm includes a concept of sustainability – to sustain a healthy ecosystem or a rate of degradation.

Costanza (1992) couples the baseline with sustainability in this way: "ecosystem health is closely linked to the idea of sustainability, which is seen to be a comprehensive, multi-scale, dynamic measure of system resilience, organization, and vigor ["vitality" for Rapport]." Here, sustainability is not meant in the sense of human/social weak sustainability but it [is] thought of in terms of an ecosystem. For Mageau et al. (1995) a healthy, sustainable, ecosystem "has the ability to maintain its structure and function over time in the face of [some] external stress." The important thing to note for the compass is to decide on indicators of resilience, organisation, vitality, structure, function and external stress.

Now comes a normative claim, worth discussing and debating:

Claim 15: (made by some ecological economists): The health of the economy depends on the health of society, and the health of society depends on the health of the ecosystem.

The normative stance of ecological economists, is that as a species, we can live well in the world if we adhere to certain norms that respect the "natural" (or baseline) flows of air, water, soil nutrient cycles and life-cycles. We then criticise institutions on the basis of the extent to which they align with, or deviate from, that norm – what it is to live 'normally' in the context of the natural systems that sustain us. We *should* make policies that bring us *towards* living within the natural flows, and prevent us from depleting our fund of low entropy – the non-renewable resources: oil, coal and gas. That is: indicators of resilience, organisation, vitality, structure, function and external stress are all used to measure the health of an ecosystem. An important key to recognising these is the second law of thermodynamics: the law of entropy. High biodiversity and vitality indicate low entropy, that is, a high level of order and organisation. Desserts, tundra and urban environments show low entropy, more chaos, less life and less organisation.

The norm sought by ecological economists is to align our lifestyles in such a way as to respect ecosystem health, where we can simplify this notion by thinking in terms of entropy. Sustainability consists in using up our fund of low entropy at as low a rate as possible, or at least one that stays within the bounds of what it is that nature can absorb and handle without suffering eco-system collapse. We should wean ourselves from using up our fund of low entropy: oil, coal, gas, uranium and plutonium.

The rate at which we wean ourselves and approach sustainability within the natural flows is culturally sensitive. There is a plurality of values. We value success in society, the ability to purchase material goods, the ability to afford luxurious goods, but we also value, family, friendship, cultural identity and our ability to live well in concordance with nature. We value nature for its own sake. It is a good in and of itself. These values should not be ignored in our economic thinking, where economics is about "the management of resources". Let us add that scarce resources depend on abundant resources so as humans we should manage our resources, and this includes leaving a lot of nature alone, so that it has the capacity to absorb our waste, to act as a buffer for disease (Quammen, 2012), to just intrinsically exist and be there for its own sake, so that we live with nature, appreciate it, learn from it, and not try to insulate ourselves from it.

To negotiate this plurality of values, we decide on a *culturally acceptable rate* of entropy production, pollution, disruption of flows and biodiversity loss (Mayumi, 2001, 45). That is, the normative stance of the ecological economist is a partly scientific and partly philosophical conception concerning our rate of deviance from how we can live 'normally' and sustainably on our planet. We would use this as the basis for a definition of what it is to live acceptably, with a view to increasing sustainability. The scientific idea is that insofar as we do not live sustainably, we shorten our time on Earth, or we compromise the quality of our time on earth because we shall see shorter life-spans, more human disease, psychological problems, political conflict over resources and so on.

The ideologically normative conception is more radical and is one step of generality up. We would like the human species to continue for a long time, and in some comfort with nature. We consciously endorse the above normative stance as a matter of *moral* principle. That is, we take an explicitly ideological stance, and encourage other humans to work towards living within the boundaries set by the conception of strong sustainability. In other words, instead of simply *observing and describing* the amount of deviance from the norm, we also think that we ought morally to try our very best to stay within the norm and encourage others to do likewise – as ideological, moral agents in our own right. So not only does the pluralism of values mean that we recognise people will have different values, we also recognise our own, and deliberately include them in the mix (table), and in our policy recommendations.

When we adapt the compass construction to align with the normative stance; strictly speaking, the ideological norm is separate. It does not affect the compass construction, only the wish compass and the analysis at the end, where we make policy *recommendations*.

7.2 Data Analysis for an Ecological Economics Institutional Compass

To align with the norm, we make a more elaborate compass construction, that starts with an addition to the analysis of data. We classify it not only in terms of the qualities but also in terms of whether it belongs to the ecology, society or the economy.

Step 3b: Classify data in terms of whether it is economic data, social data or ecological data.

We might find that we need more data. Often when making a generic compass we miss out ecological data or social data. The reason for the classification is that we are going to make tables and institutional compasses for each sphere separately: one representing the relationship of the institution with the economy, one for the relationship of the institution to the society and one representing the relationship of the institution to the natural environment. We now have nine sectors, three in each of three spheres. See Tables 7.1, 7.2 and 7.3.

Each table has its own values. Start with the economy table since it is the most familiar. Economic value, is value in *exchange*. The time-frame is short, since exchange value changes quickly. For the economic-sphere, you put on your neo-classical hat, you are now a businessman. The primary purpose of your business is to make a profit.

How do we make the quality classification concerning the econo-sphere? Harmony is indicated by fixed fees or prices, the steadiness of wages, low or no inflation, not much disparity between rich and poor within an institution, or with respect to others outside the institution, long-term employment (or confidence of being easily re-employed), market stability, stability in taxes. Excitement is indicated by money spent on leisure and luxury, expensive tours or luxury goods. Investment also belongs to excitement since it is risky and brings new opportunities, especially foreign investment, big financial projects, one-time investment in security or the military – anything that makes revenue jump or fluctuate. Discipline is indicated by poverty, bankruptcy, debt, loss of capital, big financial projects not making a return on investment. On the edge of discipline towards excitement we

Table 7.1 Table for the econo-sphere

TABLE FOR ECONOMIC COMPASS				
General Quality	Name of Indicator and Notes	Degree	length	Corrected length = log10(length) / #indicators in sector
Harmony	Stability in wages	70	.7	.7/3 = .23
Harmony	Profit shares increase around 2%	30	.9	.9/3 = .3
Harmony	Costs of supplies steady	110	.3	.3/3 = .1
Excitement	Major outside investment	140	.75	.75/4 = .18
Excitement	Money earning for charity drive	180	.3	.3/4 = .07
Excitement	Government sponsorship	200	.3	.3/4 = .07
Excitement	Partnership with other company	150	.5	.5/4 = 1.25
Discipline	Money ill spent on equipment	320	.75	.75/3 = .25
Discipline	Debt	310	.75	.75/3 = .25
Discipline	Firing employees	280	.45	.45/3 = .15

might find the monetary wealth gained from so-called "toxic debts". On the edge of discipline, but close to harmony are numbers of credit card debts that are regularly paid within the month – debts that are quickly paid back, so successfully managed debts.

Social value of an object, or institution is value in *use*. If an institution is used it is valued because it brings health, education, culture, comfort, familiarity, security and so on. The time-frame is longer than for the economic compass. For the socio-sphere think of health, education and security. We decide on base-lines, and these determine the length of arrows.

Table 7.2 Table for the socio-sphere

TABLE FOR SOCIAL COMPASS				
General Quality	**Name of Indicator and Notes**	**Degree**	**length**	**Corrected length = log10(length) / #indicators in sector**
Harmony	Families of employees healthy	100	.7	.7/3 = .23
Harmony	General good health of employees	30	.9	.9/3 = .3
Harmony	Management meetings short	90	.3	.3/3 = .1
Excitement	Quantity of people in festivities	140	.75	.75/3 = .25
Excitement	Launch of new public project	200	.3	.3/3 = .1
Excitement	Level of education of employees high	200	.3	.3/3 = .1
~~Excitement~~	~~Restructuring of computer provision~~	~~190~~	~~.1~~	~~.1/4 = .25~~
Discipline	Rules increasing	350	.75	.75/3 = .25
Discipline	Number of incidences of violence	300	.75	.75/3 = .25
Discipline	Disruption of work due to political strife in community	270	.45	.45/3 = .15

Harmony for health is then when infant mortality is low, childhood diseases are under control, for example, if enough children are vaccinated as to only "allow" a "normal" number of deaths or suffering from the disease. People live to a "normal" age, people who are ill or who have disabilities are looked after, healthy diet and preventive care. Discipline for health is ill health: disease, death, suffering and mental problems. Excitement for health concerns important medical interventions, new medical techniques, medical machines/technological compensators such as

Table 7.3 Table for the eco-sphere

TABLE FOR ECOLOGICAL COMPASS				
General Quality	**Name of Indicator and Notes**	**Degree**	**length**	**Corrected length = log10(length) / #indicators in sector**
Harmony	Quantity of natural land owned by company	10	.7	.7/3 = .23
Harmony	Agricultural goods used are all organic	50	.9	.9/3 = .3
Harmony	Quantity of organic farm land sponsored	100	.3	.3/3 = .1
Excitement	Quantity of industrial farmland sponsored	190	.75	.75/3 = .25
Excitement	Kept gardens in and around work area	150	.3	.3/3 = .1
Excitement	Green spaces within buildings	220	.3	.3/3 = .1
~~Excitement~~	~~Hydroponic gardening indoors~~	~~200~~	~~.1~~	~~.1/4 = .25~~
Discipline	Land covered by building	350	.75	.75/3 = .25
Discipline	Use of fund of low entropy for energy in buildings	270	.75	.75/3 = .25
Discipline	Quantity of waste produced by people working in buildings	260	.45	.45/3 = .15

wheel-chairs, or devices to teach deaf people to speak, eradication of a disease, technological health enhancements.

In education and culture, harmony is indicated by young children going to public school. Literacy and numeracy are high, family relations are good, there is good interaction between people of different cultures and religions. People are informed.

There is healthy debate, and people care for each other. Discipline is indicated when children or teenagers drop out of school, fail classes, there is distrust between cultures or a fear of other cultures, loss of a language or way of life, child labour or slavery. Excitement is indicated by international awards, art, museums, festivals and tourism.

Security is in harmony when there is low petty crime, people 'feel' safe at night, there are effective barriers and constructions to prevent accidents. Security is in the sector of discipline when there is violence and fear of violence, riots and wars. Security is in excitement when we have new safety standards or devices – as they become accepted and normalised, the arrow will shift into harmony. Security in excitement would also include self-defence classes and night-watch organisations. They are not in harmony because they are a reaction to fear.

Environmental value is intrinsic or existential value. The time-frame is long. For the ecological-sphere we have to decide on a baseline, as described in (Rapport & Maffi, 2010). The ideal baseline would be nature without humans, but this is unrealistic given the enormous human population on Earth. In a region which has been inhabited by humans for a long time, the baseline will be nature with humans as it was, say, before the population explosion and the green revolution to industrial agriculture. We look at the baseline from the point of view of nature, not of humans. Put on your domestic animal, family crops, algae, tree and beetle hat. That is, view the world from the point of view of a tree, squirrel, some plankton, an exotic fish... In particular, we are interested in the quality and naturalness of flows of heat, soil nutrients, air and water. We are also interested in biodiversity, eco-system health indicators (Jorgensen et al., 2010) and the use by humans of non-renewed resources and human waste. The people to ask about this are: biologists, ecologists, bird watchers, indigenous people, farmers, miners, hunters and so on. Areas that are in the baseline state are what are counted as harmonious, i.e., if there is a lot of such territory then this makes a longer arrow in that sector. The ecology is stable.

When we kill off species or eco-systems, cover soil with cement, or prevent growth of plants, insects, birds with synthetic pesticides, when we engage in mass deforestation, flooding to build a dam, when there is soil erosion, this is all part of discipline. Natural disasters also count except insofar as they are part of the baseline cycles.

When man encroaches and "improves" nature, especially in the direction of the agricultural green revolution or controls species and reproduction, this is excitement: GMO crops, large agricultural projects, organised tree plantations, irrigation, water treatment plants, fish farming... are all in the realm of excitement.

We have to be careful with the excitement quality in the ecosystem because it can easily tip an ecosystem into discipline. This is why maintaining or managing, say agricultural land, takes much more effort (entropy production) and is more delicate than "managing" a relatively wild forest area. Remember that the timeframe is long. Forest fires, floods, earthquakes, devastating contagious disease of plants and animals are also counted as discipline. But we should be careful. If there is a forest fire in keeping with the baseline cycles, then as it happens and shortly after, this indicator is in discipline, but the indicator might shift to harmony as nature recovers and inhabits the space again in a healthy way, showing resilience and vitality. So, we should note that indicators can shift from one general quality to another.

For the purposes of ecological economics, we make the following general recommendations for the indicators in all the tables. Consider that we live in a world subject to at least the first two laws of thermodynamics, so some indicators have got to reflect the entropy production of the institution; that the planet we live on is limited in space and resources, so when we use up the natural space, there is a debt to pay. The general idea is to follow Georgescu-Roegen (1971) and think in terms of the fund-flow model of the natural environment. We have a fund of low entropy that we can use up quickly or more slowly. This includes non-renewable (or too slowly renewed) resources: coal, oil, gas, uranium. To stay within the norm of human life on Earth, we want to use these up as slowly as possible – *aiming towards* the rate of replacement, although we know that it might be impossible to *achieve* the use of slowly replaced resources *at or below* the rate of replacement on pain of social unrest. There will be more said on this in a moment. Following Georgescu-Roegen again, we note that there is a flow of heat to the Earth from the sun and dissipation of heat from the Earth into space. Within this flow (over which we have influence through the emission of greenhouse gasses) we respect the rate at which natural resources such as: food, fibre, wood, replenish themselves naturally.

Another important sort of indicator comes from the thought that some of our practices have harmful and irreversible consequences on the natural environment. Here we use the metaphor of health of an organism and with some changes in the metaphor, apply it to whole eco-systems. Rapport (2012) has developed a number of these indicators. Most of them concern natural ecosystems that are stressed by human activity in the form of pollution.

So, the third, related, general idea is to think in terms of pollution, waste and clean-up. Once pollution has been released into the environment it starts to stress the natural eco-systems. There are limits beyond which the natural systems cannot cope and they become 'unhealthy' or 'collapse'. What replaces them is a *less healthy* natural eco-system (Rapport and Maffi, 2010). Some pollutants are dispersed quickly and others slowly, the effect of mixes between them is rarely known. The rates of dispersal should be respected and we should monitor the health of eco-systems to warn us of natural limits, in the case of accumulation or mixing of pollutants. Thus, the statistics falling under these three general ideas are what we use to find the relevant statistics for the eco-sphere.

To serve the ideological and moral ideas of ecological economics, of respecting the natural environment, we *should like* as many of our institutions as possible to be in the sector of harmony. That is, the wish spot is in harmony for the ecological economist. If we want to remain ideologically neutral, then we either consult the mandate of the institution to determine their ideology, and we ask members of the institution to choose their wish spot. Note that the same person might expect different qualities for different institutions.

7.3 The Mathematics for Constructing an Ecological Economics Institutional Compass

Regardless of the ideological orientation, we want to accommodate the descriptive part of ecological economics, the dependence relation represented by the sub-set relationship of the three spheres. We think that the environment has to be given priority over society, and the latter has priority over monetary economic considerations. This will now be represented by the relative *sizes of the compasses*, representing the three tables. For each table draw a sphere compass following steps 8–15. See Fig. 7.1.[2]

Step 14b: We place the compasses concentrically in the following proportions: the radius of the ecological compass is the longest. The radius of the economics compass is half the length of the ecological compass, and the length of the radius of the social compass is exactly half way between the two. See Fig. 7.2.[3]

The relative length of the radii of the three circles reflects how much more important we think, for example, ecology is with respect to society. To fend from confusion, remember that in the length of the indicator arrows on the tables is given as a proportion of the length of the radius of *that* circle. The corrected length is the length of each indicator arrow divided by the number of not-crossed out indicators in that sector. Thus, the calculations ensure that the ecological arrow has more influence in the final compass than the other two. As policy makers who share the worldview of ecological economists: look after the natural environment first, then look after society, and lastly look after the economy. We aggregate the three final arrows for the compasses by simple vector addition, as in step 8 (ignoring the sector demarcations).

Step 16: We draw our three 'final' sphere arrows, head to tail as in step 8 with the first one's tail starting at the centre of the circle.

Step 17: Erase the circumference of the social compass and the economics compass. Return to the general qualities. See Fig. 7.3.

Step 18: Add the three 'final' sphere arrows tail to head, and draw an arrow from the centre of the circle to the head of the last arrow. See Fig. 7.4.

Why do we do a simple vector addition here, rather than draw a triangle as in step 10? Because here we are aggregating three spheres, not tying three sectors. The method that we used to find the centre of the triangle in step 10 represents the average of the points in the triangle. We wanted to aggregate the three sectors, see which is pulling the most, and in what direction. Here, we aggregate final arrows of *spheres*, not *sector* arrows. So, we respect sphere arrows and leave them alone.

---

[2] We do not label the three qualities, but they are still there.

[3] We erase the lines indicating the three quality sectors, because that is not what is important in this part of the construction. They are still there but in the background.

Fig. 7.3 An ecological economics institutional compass, re-introducing the qualities

Fig. 7.4 Vector addition of arrows from the three spheres

Fig. 7.5 Final arrow for an ecological economics institutional compass

Step 19: Erase the sphere arrows. This is the final arrow for the institution, from the perspective of ecological economics. See Fig. 7.5.

This compass is constructed using the conceptual normative thinking behind ecological economics. If the environment is doing well, then we need not take care of it, and we can concentrate on society or the economy or both. Because the ecological compass arrows are more influential over the position and length of the final arrow, it is the statistics concerning the environment that we will heed most in our policy decisions – unless the ecology is doing well. In our particular example of Fig. 7.1 the socio-sphere is doing "well", since it points where many of us would like to have the wish spot. As policy makers we would then concentrate on promoting the socio-sphere harmony data and discouraging the eco-sphere and econo-sphere discipline data.

We are now in a position to make an analysis as per Sect. 5.6. We can then make policy recommendations. We use the recommendations to begin wider debate and include "non-experts" as in Sect. 5.6.1.

We turn to the delicate matters of ideology and sustainability.

7.4 Sustainability and the Ecological Economics Institutional Compass

It is politically in *vogue* to claim that an institution is "sustainable". Such a claim is almost empty when we consider the number of different definitions we might have for the word "sustainable". An industry might be deemed "unsustainable" just because it is not financially solvent; or we might be concerned with sustaining a certain standard of living; or we might be concerned with the stability of an ecological system. The word "sustainability" was used to refer to the natural environment, but has been appropriated by business and government because of the new, fashionable and strongly positive connotation. Since it is a vague term, it is subject to many interpretations. Since it is a positive term, its meaning is seldom made explicit by business or government, because most people agree. The problem is that they are agreeing to very different things if they have a different definition of "sustainability".

Ecological economists use the word in the older sense. This is to reflect the scientifically established reality of how it is that the environment is doing, and to acknowledge our dependence on that environment. For humans to live sustainably, we have to ensure that the eco-sphere is stable and not collapsing. It is only if the health of the eco-sphere is sustained, that we can think of sustaining society (within the bounds and context of the natural environment). This is recognised to be important for government, other public institutions, many non-profit organisations and many NGOs (non-governmental organisations); but, at least for the ecological economist, government ought to take very seriously the natural environment in which, and from which, the society lives. Furthermore, economic activity should not be "sustained" at the "cost" of society because there is the very real risk of social break-down. Thus, an ethical component is included in the notion of sustainability for the ecological economist. Similarly, a business institution which claims sustainability in the ecological economist's sense would take seriously both the social aspects internal to the institution and the external aspects: the society in which it is couched and the natural environment it affects. Thus, I put forward the claim that

Claim 16: For the ecological economist, an institution is sustainable if and only if the ecological-economics institutional compass's final arrow is in the harmony sector. Degree of sustainability is shown by the length of the arrow. The longer the arrow the more sustainable and the more resilient the institution.

'Sustainability' is here taken to set an ethical and normative standard – an ideology – reflecting what it is we want to sustain and what we are willing to sacrifice. Under ethical-normativity, we want the natural environment to remain relatively stable. In very basic terms we need to ensure that water, the air and the soil are natural and harmonious. It is only then that the bio-sphere can continue in a healthy manner. How do we know we are living sustainably?

We all know that increasing entropy damages the environment, and therefore, entropy production is one of the obvious choices for representing discipline with respect to the environment. Another environmental discipline indicator is pollution. Insofar as we are willing to sacrifice the environment to our social, material or economic ambitions, we think less and less in alignment with ecological economists. Let us be quite clear. There is the scientific aspect of ecological economics and the more normative, ethical and ideological aspect. It is this distinction that has been drawn out in the exercise of constructing our ecological-economic institutional compass.

References

Costanza, R. (1992). Towards an operational definition of ecosystem health. In R. Costanza (Ed.), *Ecosystem health: New goals for environmental management* (pp. 237–256). Island Press.

Friend, A. (2017). System of accounts for global entropy production (SAGE-P): The accounting in the topological domain space (TDS) of the econosphere, sociosphere an ecosphere. In S. Shmelev (Ed.), *Green economy reader* (pp. 99–137). Springer.

Georgescu-Roegen, N. (1971). *The entropy law and the economic process*. Harvard University Press.

Jorgensen, S. E., Fu-Liu, X., & Costanza, R. (2010). *Handbook of indicators for assessment of ecosystem health* (2nd ed.). Taylor and Francis.

Mageau, M. T., Costanza, R., & Ulanowicz, R. E. (1995). The development and initial testing of a quantitative assessment of ecosystem health. *Health, 1*, 201–213.

Mayumi, K. (2001). *The origins of ecological economics; The biomechanics of Georgescu-Roegen*. Routledge.

Quammen, D. (2012). *Spillover; Animal infections and the next human pandemic*. W.W. Norton and Company.

Rapport, D. J. (2012). Ecosystem health indicators. *The Berkshire Encyclopedia of Sustainability; Measurements, Indicators and Research Methods for Sustainability, 6*, 103–107.

Rapport, D. J. (2013). Ecosystem health. In *Achieving sustainability: Visions, principles and practices* (pp. 251–260). Cengage Learning.

Rapport, D. J., & Maffi, L. (2010). Eco-cultural health, global health and sustainability. *Ecological Research, Special Feature: Environmental Change, Pathogens and Human Linkages, 26*(6), 1039–1049.

Chapter 8
Further Manipulations and Extensions Using the Notion of Sphere

In Chap. 7, I explained the adaptation of the compass to ecological economics. Ecological economics has an ideological orientation, a normative element. We can reconsider the ideological orientation.

Remember the three spheres made from the three data tables? We could choose to change the relative sizes. For example, we could choose to emphasise society. In this case we would make the socio-sphere the largest. The other two spheres might be of the same size, or we might make one of them larger than the other. The different relative sizes and the very notion of sphere can be used to identify different ideological orientations.

For example, I submit that neoclassical economists can come in at least two different stripes – represented by sphere-size manipulations. A pure neoclassical economist only looks at the econo-sphere. The others are ignored, because *a priori* we are better off if the economy is better off and we enjoy the free market. Because the pure neoclassical economic position is *a prioristic*, there is no admissible counter-evidence. So, conceptually, the econo-sphere is the most important, and the socio-sphere arrow, if one bothered to construct one, would have a tendency to align with the econo-sphere sooner or later. Any deviance it temporary. For an argument showing why this is an erroneous view, see the appendix.

A less extreme neoclassical economist is one who thinks that society is better off with growth of the economy as a matter of fact, that is, *a posteriori*. This neoclassical economist also has an eye to society, and wants to vindicate the claim that society is better off with a healthy economy – a healthy economy is correlated with a healthy society and we should be able to observe the correlation. So, such a neoclassical economist might also consider the table for the socio-sphere, and make it smaller than the one for the econo-sphere. When the correlation of economic health to social health is not observed, it is then appropriate for government to intervene. This is a Keynesian conception of economics.

An environmental economist has a strong concern for the natural environment, and realises that we cannot neglect it altogether, but still believes that the prevailing remedy for ills in society or the environment is the economy, because it is thought

M. I. Friend, *The Institutional Compass: Method, Use and Scope*, Methodos Series 18, https://doi.org/10.1007/978-3-031-05453-2_8

that middle class or wealthy people pollute less and campaign more successfully against the destruction of the environment. Such an economist might make the econo-sphere the larger one and place the eco-sphere inside. Such an economist might be bold enough to express the value of nature in monetary terms. This the idea of re-inserting the externalities back into the economy. The trick is that nature becomes important in the compass construction because it, too, is part of the larger sphere. We notice nature because it is given a monetary value, and in compass terms, some of it belongs to the econo-sphere. This is a smart move, since the longer indicator arrows are the ones to which we pay special attention. Probably such an economist will not be blind to society, and so might also include the socio-sphere, probably in middle position between the econo-sphere and the eco-sphere – if there is any of the latter that has not been given a monetary value (i.e. remaining externalities). Thus, how we get to the final representation, which tables we include, and their relative sizes, depends on the ideological orientation of the compass constructor.

Now, of course, deciding on which sphere to emphasise does not have to be the decision of one person. The decision can be made democratically too. Not every society is ready to rebel against the conditioning they have received in neoclassical economic thinking. Different sub-groups will be more or less ready. This then becomes interesting, since we can now imagine different groups – ones with different ideological orientations with respect to the relative importance of the three spheres using the same data tables and coming up with different final arrows![1] Does this mean that there is no objective truth of the matter about the general quality displayed by an institution?

Rather than this being a cause for alarm and thinking that the exercise of constructing a compass is hopeless because completely subjective, we can use the different compasses to make our disagreements plain. Furthermore, one compass can be used as leverage for critique of an institution or critique of policy. We can also use the compass to predict the success of the institution, *according to different standards* (orientations). If we get the dependence relation wrong between the spheres, then the risk of failure is higher and the longevity of the institution is shorter. Of course, it might be very difficult to verify this, if there are no comparable institutions around.

---

[1] This will *not* happen only under the very unusual (but mathematically possible) situation where for all three spheres, the arrow is in the same place and has the same length relative to that sphere – or that they somehow cancel each other out perfectly with respect to the relative sizes. If this does happen, and we like where the arrow lies, then while there is an ideological disagreement, it is not important with respect to the functioning of the institution. On the condition that we do not like where the final arrow lies, then the ideological difference will come out with what we think we should do to put the arrow back in the right place – which table of data we favour.

8.1 Infrastructural Sphere

Here is another sphere to add to the mix. It might appeal to policy makers that have control over the infrastructure of a region. It is the infrastructural sphere. The information to construct a compass on the infrastructure of a region might already be in the tables for the other three spheres, but we might have a reason to tease out this information and treat it separately. The motivation for doing this might just be interest, for a report or academic project. It might be instrumental, that is, it might be something we can control or influence. In other words, we are politically and economically placed to address problems in infrastructure, and cannot do much directly about the other spheres. Our interest might also be couched in a wider ideological orientation. For example, we might think that infrastructure is, in some sense, the key to society functioning well, and this might be our priority and therefore, we might make a separate sphere representing the data concerning infrastructure. We extract the relevant data and make that sphere bigger.

There are two general types of infrastructure. They are material infrastructure and informational infrastructure. The material infrastructure includes transportation infrastructure: roads, railway lines, canals, transportation systems, delivery systems and fuel dispensation systems. But it also includes building infrastructure: factories, houses, schools; and resources infrastructure: mines, rivers, forests, stored oil and so on.

Informational infrastructure concerns information and communication. It supervenes on[2] a material infrastructure. It is agents who communicate. Agents include humans, but also animals, plants (Mancuso & Viola, 2018) and maybe spirits. The spirit of a river can communicate with human agents who are receptive to the communication. Humans communicate to each other through our senses. We use spoken language, writing, noises, art and body language. Communication can be successful or not. Acts of communication enjoy the three general qualities. Horror films belong to discipline, impressionist paintings belong to harmony, an exotic perfume belongs to excitement. They all contain information.

What would we measure in these acts of communication, once we have decided on the overall quality? Rate (frequency), quantity, duration and success. Rate is different from quantity. I can speak with someone every day, but only briefly. On the other hand, I might study the entire *oeuvre* of a novelist (quantity) during a period of my life (duration). Success is sometimes harder to measure; but not impossible. For example, it is the success in communication of the teacher that we measure by testing students.

[2] "Supervenience" is a relation. We say that "something supervenes on something else". When we say this, we mean that as the something-else changes so does the something. For example, communication by writing letters on paper supervenes on the postal system. If the postal systems break down, or is disrupted, this has an effect on the communication by written letter on paper. Telephonic communication supervenes on the material systems of telecommunication. If something goes wrong with the material system of telecommunication, this has an effect on communication by telephone.

Let us add normativity to the sphere, that is, our attitude towards the qualities. There could be some sorts of communication and information sharing that we wish to promote, and some that we wish to suppress. For example, in our institution, we might want to promote correct information about human health, but suppress mis-information. Normal, everyday health information we should like to see in the harmony sector. It should flow easily, regularly, quietly. There should be some such information, but not an overwhelming amount, explanations should be clear and succinct. If pictures accompany text, then these should not be too alarming.

Let us now move to excitement. Say, there is a real and sudden health hazard. Good information about this belongs to the excitement sector because of the suddenness. The quality of information should be good and clear, but also somewhat alarming, since, we should like people to notice and act in some prescribed manner to avoid the health hazard. We might also want a large quantity of information, available through many media. Mis-information, overly complicated, alarming (without solution) and about highly lethal health hazards belong to discipline. Moreover, we might want to supress mis-information about the health hazard. Wanting to supress mis-information is an ideological orientation.

A properly functioning information system would have the right sorts of information in the right places, and mis-information would not circulate very widely. The latter would be detected and replaced efficiently with better information or ignored altogether. For most institutions, we probably want the final arrow in harmony for our infrastructural sphere. If the arrow is in the wrong place, then we should address the problems, and promote the better practices.

If we want to subvert a government, then one effective way to do this is to control some of the information flow and spread mis-information. This adds confusion and frustration in the population. Similarly, we can disrupt the material infrastructure.

Let us then relate that sphere to the other spheres. Let us start with the easier econo-sphere. Some communication practices are costly. For example, printing books is expensive. The production of a film or television series is also expensive. Some communication practices are inexpensive. Blogs, imitating bird calls, speaking face to face are all inexpensive.

Data for the socio-sphere of the information infrastructure is quite interesting. We might be interested in quality and type of information being communicated, it's breadth and effect (reaching the right people, and not the wrong people), longevity and regularity of circulation. Depending on our ideological orientation, we might favour one type of information over another. So, for example, given my own ideological orientation, I might prefer, for example, a book about indigenous practices over a mass media campaign promoting a luxury consumer good.

Insofar as my democratic ideological tendencies prevail over my other ideological preferences, I might concede to wider public opinion about choices of quality and type of information. The several layers of enquiry and their interplay is what demonstrates the subtlety and artful aspect of compass construction, making it an inescapably philosophical project. It is also what ensures objectivity and robustness or weak objectivity by making the interconnections explicit and plain.

8.2 The Dance of the Spheres

What do, or can, these spheres represent? In the version of the compass designed to reflect the way of thinking of ecological economists, each sphere represents a table of data. The relative sizes represent our priorities. Söderbaum would call this an ideological orientation. Other ecological economists would resist this, and claim that the ecological economic compass reflects the scientific existential reality – that the economy *really does* depend on society and society *really does* depend on the environment. Such an ecological economist would probably accuse anyone who wants to change the relative sizes of the spheres of not seeing clearly, and being blinded by ideology, as opposed to being clear headed, scientific and recognising reality.

This shows us the dangers of using the word 'ideology'. If we have an ideology, it sounds as though we make a choice, since for every ideology there are alternatives. I do not want to solve the question now, as to whether the ecological economic compass reflects reality or an ideology; but I do want to point out that neoclassical economists who would have the economic sphere be the largest, and who would maintain that it is the economic sphere that holds society together, the *a prioristic* neo-classical economist, for example, *literally cannot appreciate* the ecological economist's conception of the dependence relation between the spheres.

For debates between the two camps, it will be important to recognise where the junctions of disagreement lie. We found out the junctions just now by re-considering the construction of the ecological economics compass. Through this re-consideration, ecological economists can have a sense of how other economists see the situation by constructing ideologically alternative compasses. We can then predict what the other group is going to think is the most pressing issue to attend to, and use this to negotiate trade-offs. We might also find that there are still important points of agreement.

Claim 17: The compasses can be used as a basis for mediation between differently oriented groups.

In other words, when we constructed the ecological economics compass, the spheres were used to emphasise the eco-sphere *over* the socio-sphere, and the latter *over* the econo-sphere. Moreover, this was done in the full recognition that this is a choice, and that the relative sizes of the spheres could be reversed or changed to reflect another ideology. So, where do we stand with compass construction?

The act of creating a sphere is an act of selection of certain data. We can do this with different purposes in mind. We can do so to reflect scientific and existential reality, we can do this to reflect an ideological perspective or we can do this to reflect what we think is the better sphere of influence *of the institution*. For example, members of a regional government might think that the environment just has to look after itself, but that society and material infrastructure are things that they can control best. It is only if the economy is *overwhelmingly* suffering or the ecology is *overwhelmingly* suffering that the regional government will intervene. Lastly, we might make a selection of certain types of data just out of scholarly interest. To use a term that has come into vogue in philosophy, we operationalise the exercise. That is, rather than looking with candid innocence and best scientific objectivity, we might be interested in what we think we can control and influence, and concentrate on these *as* an institution. This is a very deliberate meta-choice that we make and we should do so consciously. However, it is not recommended because we forget the wider context of the data. We lose the holism of the reading.

Claim 18: The more artificial and unrealistic meta-choices of worldviews are, the more limited the value of the compass reading.

The claim holds for the following reason. The more we are mistaken about reality, the greater the chance that things will go wrong. Our predictions are less likely to be realised. When we select a type of data and then amplify it to count more than what is supported by reality, we are in danger of deceiving ourselves into thinking that we are doing the very best we can to solve the problems around us with our institution when we could do better.

Here is the much *safer* approach that is equivalent. Construct a compass to reflect *reality* as best you can as an institution, without forgetting the democratic angle to prevent overlooking important information.

Know, what the responsibilities of the institution are and what it can feasibly influence and how. It is *that* information in the data table that you target with policy. So, now we are not so much concentrating on the degree relative to the wish spot, but on the content of the data – what we can control or best influence. After selection, we work out which ones need shortening and which ones need lengthening. You can select these data points from the tables and focus on them, but do *not* then go on to make a separate compass with them because that new compass omits the wider context. The awareness of the limitations of an institution are as important as knowing the strengths. If we obliterate the larger context, what I have been calling the existential and scientific reality, we fool ourselves. Moreover, the justifications for our policies are weaker because we do not include the wider context in the justification.

We also limit ourselves disingenuously. This is because if we become aware that something very good, or something very bad lies outside our power, as an institution, we can seek to support institutions that do have the good or the bad something within their power. Institutions can influence each other. In this manner the institution makes things better for itself indirectly by trying to influence other institutions to address the problem. Alternatively, the institution might seek to gain power over the problem area. After all, this is exactly what happens when laws are passed in parliament. We change the scope of the legal system to cope with a new problem.

Returning then to the spheres and their sizes, we know that by changing the relative sizes we change the relative emphasis of the spheres on the final compass arrow. It is a nice exercise to construct, say, an ecological economics compass and then re-normalise to make the spheres the same size. The data tables are the same. Only the normalised length changes. It turns out that if we have comprehensive tables, the difference is not always very stark. This is because we have already done a lot of work oriented towards ecological economics in our selection of data, that is, by including the relevant data from the ecological systems. If we make a generic compass, we might miss a lot of this data, and for this reason, generic compasses and ecological economics institutional compasses can look very different.

This play of the spheres gives us a visual way of representing the different conceptions of priorities or conceptions of what the world we live in is like metaphysically or existentially. It also gives us a way of understanding the differences in conceptions between people, be they ideological or scientific/ existential.

Claim 19: The play of the spheres is equivalent to a normalisation of the length in the data points.

The conception of sphere is a selection of a type of data. We then decide whether or not the selected data is *more important* than the data points belonging to other spheres. That relative importance is given a number calculation. This is a normalisation technique. When it is ideologically or normatively informed, then it is a *normative* normalisation, as opposed to a *mechanical* descriptive normalisation, one made for aesthetics, representation or communication purposes.

Reference

Mancuso, S., & Viola, A. (2018). *L'intelligence des Plantes. Traduit de l'italien par Renaud Temperini*. Albin Michel pour la production française.

Chapter 9
The Compass as a Representation

The compass represents a table of data, measuring each data point against the others in terms of its quality and strength. The representation is a sort of coded picture, and so, it can be used for communication. We interpret the arrow to tell us that our institution *overall* shows this general quality. We might be pleased, satisfied or alarmed by the final outcome. Because of the colours, the coded picture elicits emotions in its own right. Provided we select the colours well, we convey the message we want at an intuitive level. In the compasses we have a lighter area towards the centre, and the outer areas have a more intense colour. This is to emphasise the concept of the length of the arrow. A short arrow is balanced between the qualities, or is neutral between the qualities. Because of the strict geometry the compass also creates a sense of distance. We can look at it as a piece of information about the whole. We are then called upon to react to the position of the arrow, but also to reflect upon our own emotional reaction, especially when we are surprised by the position or length of the final arrow.

In this way, all representations are a type of distorting mirror. They reflect, but they also draw out some aspects of what they represent, and hide others. The data table is obliterated. We are not lost in the details, and not struck by particular details. This is an advantage since it also removes us from the latest data we were exposed to regarding the institution or some other concern that has recently captured our attention. The remove, affords us a *holistically objective perspective*. This has the advantage of preventing us from reacting to particulars. Instead, we are in a position to strategize and look ahead with a clear view of the whole. Similarly, with the democratic aspect of the compass construction, this affords us some distance from our particular perspective. Each actor in an institution, and each person affected by an institution sees different things. This is because we each have a different background of experience and knowledge.

We can also play with the representation. If, instead of three distinct colours, we bleed colours into each other we have something closer to Fig. 9.1.

We can also erase the lines between the thirds, and remove the names for the thirds. We then have something that looks like Fig. 9.2.

M. I. Friend, *The Institutional Compass: Method, Use and Scope*, Methodos Series 18, https://doi.org/10.1007/978-3-031-05453-2_9

Fig. 9.1 A more colour-sensitive compass

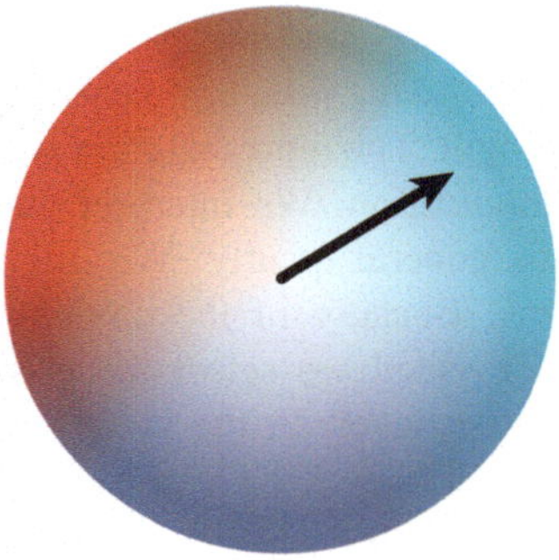

Fig. 9.2 An intuitive compass for people who are not colour-blind

Since we are using our intuitive reaction to colours, we can now think about how it is that the compass reading affects us: that the arrow sits in this colour and how it is that the neighbouring colours affect us. Colours have a psychological and a cultural dimension. Different cultures will associate slightly different colours with the three general qualities. To find out the culturally influenced reaction we have to do a little anthropology. This is important when constructing compasses in cultures other than our own if we want to communicate with the culture using the compass. We also want to be aware of general associations. Green, for Europeans tends to suggest ecological values. However, in the USA, green might still be associated with money, since all of the dollar notes are printed in a green colour. In Spain and Portugal, the bullfighters sometimes wear pink jackets, breeches or socks, whereas in Anglo-Saxon countries, pink is associated with girls and weakness.

The same applies to the words we use for the general qualities. When using the compass to communicate with people in a language other than English, the translation of: harmony, discipline and excitement should be carefully considered. It would be interesting, too, to consider a different trio of general qualities that come from other ancient traditions.[1]

[1] Salvador Peniche Camps made this suggestion to me. He had in mind some of the indigenous cultures in Mexico.

Having done our homework to culturally sensitively choose the colours and words for our compasses, the idea of bleeding the colours into each other adds the suggestion that the arrow can swing and change direction in analogue fashion, and in both directions, as opposed to jumping over the barrier that constitutes the line between the sectors. It is also more suggestive of the nuance of degree. This is equivalent to the exercise mentioned in Sect. 5.4.2 of considering a whole suite of adjectives, adding them to the three, and placing them at degrees around the circle.

Next consider that an arrow pointing upwards suggests progress, strength and virility, whereas pointing downward suggests something negative. Remember the meta-attitudes towards the qualities, and remember that we have an ideology. We can rotate the colour circle so that our preferred colour is at the top, where 'preferred' corresponds to the wish compass we constructed, and therefore, our meta-attitude towards the qualities. We locate the wish spot in the top third of the circle. See Sect. 9.1 and Chap. 11 for examples. Careful use of colours can replace words in the compass.

9.1 The Compass as a Labelling Device for Products

This is an easy introduction to the concept of institutional compass for people who are not experts in decision aides, and who rely on the market for food, material goods and services. To introduce the concept of an institutional compass, one can point out that we are given information about a product as a matter of course. There is a price, sometimes the country of origin, sometimes the ingredients, the brand etc.. . . We can then include a compass as a piece of information. Products are sold on the market with ideological orientations underlying them, and the preference in the orientation can be expressed in colour terms.

Consider toys. Some toys are meant to be calming and instructive, they belong to harmony. Others are all about power and destruction, they belong to discipline. Others are challenging, glamourous and exciting. They belong to excitement.

Having explored these ideas, we can then do the following exercise. We develop a circle with the colours arranged in a culturally suggestive way with our preferred quality-colour on top. We don't even need the arrow. We then develop a table of data for each product and construct a compass. The final reading with the preferred colour on top is used in the labelling of the product. It makes a very subtle suggestion to the purchaser. The colours replace words.

What is the point of the exercise? There are three points. One is to give a purely intuitive and suggestive indication to the purchaser of the general quality emphasised by the product (and how successful it is – indicated by the colour position). The other is to elicit enquiry. If the purchaser is curious about the logo, he, or she, can consult a sample flyer or web page to find out more. If he, or she, wants to enquire into the details underlying the compass, there is a file with the data table that the purchaser can consult. The curiosity can become a reason for participation. If the purchaser or producer disagrees with points on the data table, then his, or her, input can be taken into account on the data table, and the final compass reading ever so slightly shifted.

The third point of the exercise is to help the producer. Help comes in three ways. On a competitive or co-operative market, producers compete against each other or want to co-ordinate their efforts. One benefit comes if, for example, one producer notices that there are a lot of products that share the same compass reading, then maybe this is a hint to work on making one that occupies a less usual place – a niche market. Another benefit is to give the producer the opportunity to learn more about the alternative products, by also consulting the data sheets and improving his, or her, product. Of course, some producers might want to hide the data sheet for reasons of keeping secrets from competitors, but we display what we legally may, and indicate that some data points are missing. The point for the producers is to improve the product in the sense of making it stronger in the desired quality, or closer to a wish spot. But there is third possibility. The producer might point out that there is something important missing from the data sheet. We can add it in, and the compass reading shifts with the added information. This is a means of recognising the efforts made by producers, and acknowledging their creativity or innovative approach that is unique to them. For example, if the toys are made by an under-privileged minority, or they come from a family business, or some percentage of the earnings go to a charity, this can be included. The information is fed into the compass construction, and so the producer can communicate with a visual impression of the whole product.

The product label use of the compass is not important for institutional decision making, but it is an immediate way of communicating the compass concept to "lay" people – those who are not experts in decision making. It also shows us how basic and immediate the representation is.

Chapter 10
The Compass Used for Qualitative Accounting

Here is another creative use of the compass by an institution. We re-name the wish spot "responsibility spot". As an institution, it is not that we wish for the actual arrow to find itself in the wish spot, it is that we think we are successful as an institution when the arrow is in the responsibility spot. We fail in our responsibilities, as an institution when the actual compass arrow lies outside the responsibility spot. The further away, the less responsible we are.

Stronger still: as an institution we are held accountable for the direction and momentum of our institution. We can think of responsibility in terms of credit and debit. We are in credit when the institution is in the responsibility spot and we are in debit when the arrow lies outside. We can be more or less ambitious for our institution by making the responsibility spot smaller or larger. We can compare institutions by comparing the proximity they each have to their own declared responsibility spot, or to one that we choose ourselves. For example, we might hold an institution responsible to a higher standard (more restricted responsibility spot) than they declare.

For example, with the product label, as a customer, I might decide not to purchase products whose arrows lie outside an area of the compass that I associate with responsible production and distribution. If no products are available that fulfil a task – such as, say, a cleaning product, then I either do without, and forgo that function, or I make the responsibility spot wider for that type of product. This way of thinking is similar to the conception of "fair trade". The responsibility spot is then used as a certification.

Responsibility is an informal version of accountability. If we have a relatively robust, and therefore, objective compass, then there is nothing preventing us from making the responsibility spot into an accounting device. We hold the institution accountable to the responsibility spot.

How would this work in practice? Take, for example a small business. The business chooses, and maybe advertises publicly its responsibility spot. Decisions are made in order to ensure that the compass arrow lies within the responsibility spot. When it lies outside, this is time for policy to change, and a final arrow outside the

M. I. Friend, *The Institutional Compass: Method, Use and Scope*, Methodos Series 18, https://doi.org/10.1007/978-3-031-05453-2_10

responsibility spot marks failure of the business. The success or failure is holistically conceived, not monetarily. But it can be used to justify loans, for example. It is a qualitative and quantitative accounting, not a purely monetary accounting. It is quantitative because we measure how far outside the responsibility/ accountability spot the arrow lies, or how close to the centre.

Imagine this at government level. Government informs the governed or decides with the governed, where they wish to find themselves qualitatively. A wish spot is determined. Government is successful when the actual arrow falls within the wish/ responsibility spot. It is failing otherwise. Different government policies will influence where the arrow points.

Failure can be overcome in four ways. Gerrymander the indicator arrows. This is not recommended. The second way is to make different decisions, that is, change policy. A third way is to change the identity of the institution, that is, its boundary conditions to encompass institutions whose compasses added to that of the original institution will result in pulling the arrow back into the responsibility spot. Of course, mergers take negotiation and agreement not only in the boundary conditions of the institution, but also in the location and extent of the responsibility spot for the new institution. At government level, this is realised through colonisation, occupation, or more mildly, agreements for trade or support.

The fourth way to overcome failure is to change the size or location of the responsibility spot. When done honestly, this amounts to re-thinking the ideological orientation of the institution. It is a highly normative and philosophical reflection. For, example, we might acknowledge that the situation of our institution is very difficult, and lies in discipline, but relatively speaking it is much better than it could be, so we rest content with the length of the arrow in discipline not being too long. This is important to understand, especially when working on government decisions and using an ecological economics compass – or including ecological, social and economic information in our compass construction. Unless we are very cynical about our base-line (choose it to be in keeping with the gradual destruction of the eco-system), most regional compasses will find that the actual arrow is in discipline. This is because the environment is suffering irreparably. And this is a global problem. If this is what we are finding, then to be realistic, and to think in terms of democratic feasibility, we might hold ourselves accountable to shortening the arrow, and so not be too ambitious. When working with eco-system collapse around us, sobriety is more important than hyperbole and false hopes.

The attraction of thinking of government using this accounting method instead of, or in parallel with, a monetary one, is that it explicitly acknowledges a region's qualitative sense of identity. In contrast, this is not well captured by GDP. Yet, this has become an iconic number for comparing nations and rating them. A nation is not a for-profit business (except under a very narrow neoclassical economics ideology). Instead, national, or regional, identity is qualitative and power-positional. For example, Canadians think of Canada as a nation that is good at compromise. It is a negotiating nation, where members negotiate with each other and Canada positions itself internationally to play a mediating role between other nations. The conception might be accurate or very far from reality. Construct a compass to find out. The responsibility spot would be somewhere in harmony, since compromise is usually to that end. It involves some sacrifice: discipline, but in an equal and negotiated way: back to harmony. So, the responsibility spot for Canada lies in harmony, and towards discipline. If Canadians identify with this image of Canada, then they can hold government accountable to the responsibility spot in the institutional compass for Canada. If this is the favoured image that Canadians have of Canada, and the final arrow for the compass for Canada lies within the accountability spot, then the government is doing what it should. If government is failing according to the compass, then a competing party who wants to gain power in the next election could promise to outdo the present government by promising policy decisions that address indicator arrows in the table in the appropriate way – favouring the ones that point on the for side of the responsibility spot, and discouraging those that pull the final arrow in the opposite direction to rotate the final arrow.

Say the government is failing with respect to the accountability spot. There might be good reason for this, outside the control of government. That is, it is not a matter of policy made by government, but of the world context Canada finds itself in. In this case government policy should aim indirectly at changing the arrow by influencing the context. Pandemics are an example. How government reacts is important. Pandemics together with government and public reaction are a social and economic stressor. Say, the effects are such that the arrow rotates out of the accountability spot. The cause of the pandemic is independent of government policy, but government reaction to it is not. Government can react internally by legislating in such a way as to: decrease the spread of disease, to keep the economy healthy, to ensure social and psychological ease or to use the occasion to decrease CO_2 emissions and so on. The government can also act externally to decrease the global spread of disease, by restricting travel across its borders or by helping other nations to vaccinate their populations and stem the spread of the pandemic.

Say, this time that the reason for compass-accountability failure has to do with past policy. The policy needs then to be reversed or changed in some way, or some compass-direction-compensating policy needs to be adopted, and sufficiently to pull the arrow back to the accountability spot. The compass holds us accountable. When we use compasses, there is less room for dishonesty or gerrymandering.

Compare GDP as a means of comparing nations, to the compass as a means of comparing nations. We look at GDP per capita, and look at rate of growth of GDP. The rate is less important in "developed" economies. We tell the difference between the two with the GDP per capita.

The compass is a more subtle way to make comparisons. There are two ways for a nation to boast using a compass. One is to show that the nation is doing well by its internal qualitative conception of identity. It's choice of where to put the responsibility spot corresponds to the direction of the final arrow for that country. The second is in terms of an externally decided upon accountability spot; where we might decide for ourselves that we would not want to live in such a region, even if it is doing well according to its internally decided criteria. This decision is made simply because we do not share the values of that region.

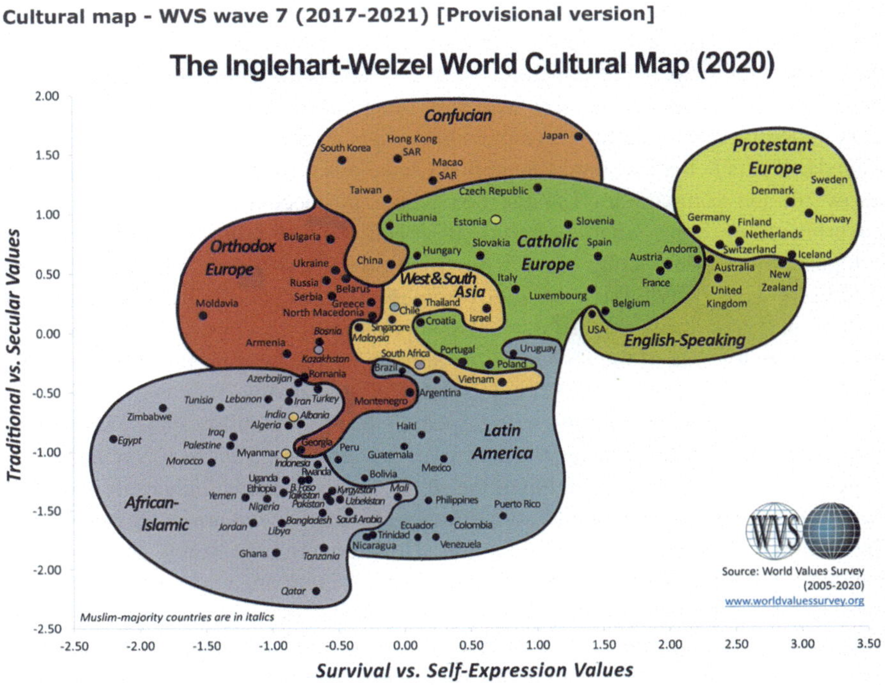

Fig. 10.1 The grouping of countries according to the value structure in Schwartz' theory. (The Inglehart-Welzel World Cultural Map – World Values Survey 7 (2020) [Provisional version]. Source: http://www.worldvaluessurvey.org/, Shmeleva (2017))

For example, nations can be compared on the basis of their sense of security, adherence to tradition, hedonism and so on (Shmeleva, 338). See Fig. 10.1. The colour groupings represent culturally similar values. This is what is done by Inglehart (2015) when he uses the Schwartz theory of values to compare nations. (Shmeleva 2017, 344). But here, I am proposing to use the compass not as a comparison of actual character of the members of a nation, but also compare the success of that nation in *preserving* certain values that figure in their sense of identity. Would this not be a more interesting and honest means of comparison, rather than GDP? It would be more sensitive to differences in values and in national character, promoting and recognising a plurality of values. Of course, a nation that wants to boast of its ecological consciousness, had better be using an ecological economics compass, similarly for anyone interested in comparing countries or regions with respect to strong sustainability. We might well find that many of the poorer nations come out on top with this basis of comparison, and for that reason alone they should be appreciated, supported and turned to for advice.

In summary, the compass conception is very flexible in its adaptations. It is not static or completed. It is a way of looking at the world, and of comparing institutions. The exercise of constructing a compass elicits philosophical enquiry in a structured way. This is important when making decisions in a complex context, and when there are appreciable tensions.

References

Inglehart, R. (2015). *World values survey*. http://www.worldvaluessurvey.org/wvs.jsp
Shmeleva, I. (2017). Human values and sustainable development. In S.E. Shmelev (Ed.), *Green economy reader; Lectures in ecological economics and sustainability* (pp. 333–366). Springer.

Part IV
Actual Case-Studies and Conclusion

We shall see three case studies. The first is by Ana Mulió Álvarez. She was a student of mine at George Washington University, and did this project as part of a graduate course I taught on philosophy of the environment and policy. She subsequently acquired a master's degree from the London School of Economics in the programme on environment and policy. She re-worked her class project as a case study for this book. Because it was done as a class project, she did not have the opportunity or resources to make the project consultative or democratic. It was an armchair project. It is the preliminary stage. The next stage would have been to go with the results to the World Health Organisation to see their reactions to the final recommendations and re-visit the data and the data analysis.

The second case study is for using the compass as a product label as per Chap. 12. This was also done with the help of an ex-student: Quinn Samouilidis. He did the data analysis for all of the products sold in the shop. The chapter is a report of what transpired.

The third case study was done in conjunction with Ahmed Yaman Abdin, a student who was visiting from Saarland University. He did the majority of the data collection. We did the data analysis and compass construction together. Again, because of limited resources or time and personnel, we have not yet done the further step of including participants.

The purpose of including these partial case studies it to show the compass construction in action. We read of the conceptual struggles of the authors, we witness different colours of the compasses and different styles of writing. The colours are not fixed in advance, and we should not develop a fetish for them. I left the footnotes and references at the bottom of the page for these chapters in order not to mix them with the bibliography of the rest of the book. These references serve a very different purpose. They are the sources of data. The compass takes on a life of its own in the shared hands of others.

We end this part with some concluding philosophical remarks that return us to the beginning.

Chapter 11
Case Study I: The World Health Organisation, by Ana Mulió Álvarez

11.1 Philosophical Considerations

The world currently faces the greatest challenge ever experienced by humankind. Climate change and environmental degradation threaten nearly every ecological cycle and living organism. Humans have disrupted the bio-sphere: from the composition of the atmosphere to the nutrient cycles of the soil.[1] As recently stated by the UN "75% of land environment and some 66% of the marine environment have been significantly altered by human actions."[2] We are already experiencing changes in precipitation patterns, rising sea levels, and stronger and more destructive storms due to climate change.[3] In a recent study, UK researchers found microplastics in every marine organism surveyed, in fact, by 2050 plastic will outweigh fish in the ocean.[4,5] Such realizations inevitably lead us to wonder about how we got to this point and what we are going to do about it. More specifically, what is our role and purpose in our relationship with the environment? These concerns are deeply philosophical and real. The institutional compass provides a practical tool and a holistic framework of analysis for these complicated philosophical and political inquiries.

By analyzing an institution through an ecological economics ideological orientation, the compass helps us to understand the contribution of an institution to the

---

The footnotes of this chapter are references for sources of data.

---

[1] https://www.sciencedaily.com/releases/2009/06/090604144322.htm

[2] https://www.npr.org/2019/05/06/720654249/1-million-animal-and-plant-species-face-extinction-risk-u-n-report-says

[3] https://climate.nasa.gov/effects/

[4] https://www.theguardian.com/environment/2019/jan/31/microplastics-found-every-marine-mammal-uk-study

[5] https://www.washingtonpost.com/news/morning-mix/wp/2016/01/20/by-2050-there-will-be-more-plastic-than-fish-in-the-worlds-oceans-study-says/?noredirect=on&utm_term=.2b05bca5f32e

M. I. Friend, *The Institutional Compass: Method, Use and Scope*, Methodos Series 18, https://doi.org/10.1007/978-3-031-05453-2_11

environmental puzzle we are trying to solve. In this way, an ecological economics institutional compass proposes a change of paradigm for institutions: the economy should not shape society and the environment, but the other way around. We use it to challenge institutions to question their priorities to ensure the survival of the human species: what is the institution's relationship towards the environment and society? What does our future look like if we continue to ignore the physical reality of our dependency on our planet and its ecological goods and services? Unfortunately, the answers to these questions are becoming clearer with every season.

11.2 The Institution: World Health Organization

I have chosen the World Health Organization (henceforth: WHO) as the institution to analyze for many reasons. First, it is a well-established institution with a lot of reliable information that can provide a robust analysis. Second, it is an extremely relevant institution as the leading international organization for public health. Particularly now in recent times with the development of the COVID-19 world pandemic, public health leadership and consensus is more important than ever. Thirdly, I chose the WHO because of its focus on health. I believe health to be the key indicator of well-being that can be observable in all three spheres of the ecological-economic compass. I also believe that the objective of "good health," while still somewhat subjective, is a widely shared cultural goal making this analysis relevant and useful. I hope that by reframing the WHO under an ecological economics analysis, afforded by the institutional compass, I shall provide insight into some of the ways we could really improve public health around the world.

To begin the analysis and get a sense of how the organization works and its goals, it is informative to look at its mission statement: "our goal is to build a better, healthier future for people all over the world." The WHO's constitutional principles are as follows:

- Health is a state of complete physical, mental and social well-being and not merely the absence of disease or infirmity.
- The enjoyment of the highest attainable standard of health is one of the fundamental rights of every human being without distinction of race, religion, and political belief, economic or social condition.
- The health of all peoples is fundamental to the attainment of peace and security and is dependent on the fullest cooperation of individuals and States.
- The achievement of any State in the promotion and protection of health is of value to all.
- Unequal development in different countries in the promotion of health and control of diseases, especially communicable diseases, is a common danger.
- The healthy development of the child is of basic importance; the ability to live harmoniously in a changing total environment is essential to such development.

- The extension to all peoples of the benefits of medical, psychological, and related knowledge is essential to the fullest attainment of health.
- Informed opinion and active co-operation on the part of the public are of the utmost importance in the improvement of the health of the people.
- Governments have a responsibility for the health of their peoples which can be fulfilled only by the provision of adequate health and social measures.

These principles provide a deeper look into the priorities of the institution and give us a sense of what the analysis may find. The initial mission statement is vague and limited to "improving health for all people" which only considers the socio-sphere, meaning it only considers the health of human beings, not that of other beings, ecosystems, etc. The constituting principles, do provide a definition of health "A state of complete physical, mental and social well-being". The principles also emphasize that health is a fundamental right to every person regardless of race, religion, etc. This will be a key point of analysis. Does the WHO formulate policies that bring health to everyone equally, or does it prioritize the wellbeing of Western nations? While the main focus remains in the socio-sphere, there are some hints of the consideration of the econo-sphere as "unequal development" is mentioned as a danger to health, implying development must occur everywhere, similarly, for the success of public health. However, as we know, it is often Western-style economic development that is to blame for world health issues. In the constitution, there is only one reference to the "environment" but it is not clear if it is a reference to the natural environment or to the social environment: "Healthy development of the child is of basic importance; the ability to live harmoniously in a changing total environment is essential to such development." Thus, we already notice that the emphasis is on the socio-sphere, and there is a woeful neglect of the eco-sphere and its effect on the health of humans, or of the effects of the econo-sphere on the eco-sphere. The shortsightedness of the WHO in neglecting these important relationships will be revealed by the ecological economics institutional compass and the analysis.

11.3 Methods

(i) This case study will create an institutional compass of the WHO under the ideological framework of ecological economics. It will entail the construction of three compasses, one per sphere (eco-sphere, socio-sphere, econo-sphere). Following Friend's methodology, each sphere will be divided into the three qualities (discipline, excitement, harmony). The indicator table will be organized by both spheres and qualities. There will be roughly 10 selected indicators per quality and per sphere, with a total of roughly 90 indicators which should provide certain robustness to the analysis.

(ii) The process of establishing arrow length will be subjective because there is no comparable institution and because of limited time and resources. The ideological principles will be those of ecological economics. The analysis is both a social scientific exercise and a deeply philosophical evaluation of the institution. A thorough explanation of how each length was determined will be detailed in the next section. Generally, lengths will be determined in comparison to other indicators, the strength of the quality, and the impact of the indicator in achieving the mission of the institution. Establishing arrow degrees will also be the result of a deep philosophical and analytical process explained in further detail in the next section.

11.4 Critique of Data

All indicators were selected because they contributed meaningfully to the reflexive exercise of the compass. Data was selected that was as up-to-date as possible. Because of the holistic nature of the situation, the data collection and analysis processes require the compass designer to think from different perspectives and with different priorities in mind which is one of the benefits of the tool. I wanted the indicators to capture the holistic nature of the compass as well as the complexity of the issue of public health. Because health is such a widely encompassing topic, all indicators are at some level interconnected and this connection is something I kept in mind when analyzing the data and deciding on the sphere, quality, length, and degree of the indicators. Some indicators I found by directly looking for information about a specific phenomenon I wanted to include, such as the contribution of healthcare to air pollution, others I discovered along the way and decided to include. I selected both very concrete indicators such as deaths by a particular disease, and very broad indicators such as life expectancy, to add variety and make the research as robust as possible.

Overall, most of the information available was related to the socio-sphere (human health indicators), since there was little updated information connecting the econo-sphere with the WHO and its policies and also very little information on WHO policies related to the eco-sphere (ecosystem health). While sections of the WHO website mention the importance of tackling environmental issues such as climate change and biodiversity loss for public health, specific data on WHO policies and their impact assessment was scarce. For example, the WHO indicator "Deaths Attributable to the Environment" has not been updated since 2012.[6] Moreover, the WHO has recently changed its website and made most of its content unavailable or available only through a convoluted database. This made the data collection difficult as many links containing critical information no longer existed.

[6]WHO. (2015, June 3) "Biodiversity and Health." *World Health Organization: Newsroom Fact Sheets, Biodiversity and Health.* World Health Organization.
Retrieved from https://www.who.int/news-room/fact-sheets/detail/biodiversity-and-health

In regards to the particular content of the indicators, I wanted to find indicators that showed the connections between public health programmes and their actual impact on health. For example, when working within the econo-sphere I looked at how a booming economy contributed, or not, to human health. What I confirmed is a phenomenon well known to public health experts. While a growing economy helps improve health in areas such as water and sanitation, in many cases the accumulation of wealth leads to high obesity rates, cancer, and other rich-country maladies. Therefore, in constructing the compass I found not only indicators for the priorities of the WHO, but also contradictions in those priorities. These can be explained by the contributions of the eco-sphere and the econo-sphere to the socio-sphere. Discussing these contradictions is not a mere critique of the current global public health regime but also highlights that there is hope. If the WHO changes policies to prioritize the health of the natural environment, then the health of humans is likely to improve. The health of humans depends on the health of the natural environment and on the health of eco-systems. See Sect. 7.1.

11.5 Indicator Analysis

11.5.1 Econo-Sphere

11.5.1.1 Harmony

- Indicator "WHO Budget in 2020–2021 was 4.840.4 million US Dollars, an 11% increase compared to 2018–2019."[7] I selected this indicator because under the current neoclassical economic system any increased spending that adds to the Gross Domestic Product means the economy is growing and everyone is better off. This is why the indicator is in the harmony quality. In this case, however, while the budget increased considerably, so did the financial needs of the organization due to the ongoing COVID-19 pandemic. Therefore, while it was good that the budget increased to serve these needs, it did not directly correlate with better public health, rather the contrary. The increase fell short of the needs.
  - Length: I gave this indicator a length of 0.7 because the level of growth and the importance of such increase are significant under the current COVID-19 crisis. The increase in the budget provided considerable resources to tackle the increasing needs of the global public health regime.

[7] Global Health Observatory. (2016, March 9). "Deaths Attributable to the Environment (%)." *World Health Organization: Global Health Observatory Indicators*, World Health Organization. Retrieved from www.who.int/data/gho/data/indicators/indicator-details/GHO/deaths-attributable-to-the-environment-(-).

- Degree: I gave this indicator a degree of 10 because I believe the indicator is closer to excitement than to discipline. The increase in spending is quite exciting, unexpected, and in terms of total numbers, rather spectacular.

- Indicator "Rates of vaccination against pneumococcal, Haemophilus influenza type b, pneumonia, meningitis, rotavirus, pertussis, measles, and malaria over the next ten years will save $145 billion in productivity losses."[8] I selected this indicator because vaccinations are considered one of the greatest advances in medicine and they have an often overlooked harmonious effect on the economy. I believe this indicator is particularly relevant in the wake of the COVID-19 vaccination campaign as it provides some insight into how useful such vaccinations can be to bring balance to the economy.
  - Length: I gave this indicator a length of 0.5 because although the savings are significant, they do not appear that large if we consider world GDP.
  - Degree: I gave this indicator a degree of 10 because of the exciting potential of the indicator. Vaccinations are new and exciting discoveries that require governments and organizations to be constantly active.

- Indicator "Investments in expanding Universal Health Coverage over the next five years will result in 24.4 million lives saved. Each dollar invested will result in a return of US$ 1.40."[9] I selected this indicator because it shows the positive and harmonious effect of investing in health for everyone. Improving public health has a positive multiplier effect in all spheres: it saves people, promotes a healthy environment, and it leads to economic growth.
  - Length: I gave this indicator a length of 0.8 because I believe a return in investment of 1.4 is quite positive.
  - Degree: I gave this indicator a degree of 30 because the indicator is exciting but I wanted to keep the arrow closer to the mid-point of harmony.

- Indicator "Donations to WHO to fight COVID 608,516,234 US Dollars."[10] It is a similar indicator as the first one, but more specific to COVID. The amount of economic effort put into fighting the COVID-19 pandemic sheds light on the incredible capacity of world-leading donors to come together with a common purpose.

---

[8] Stack, M. L., Ozawa, S., Bishai, D. M., Mirelman, A., Tam, Y., Niessen, L., Levine, O. S. (2011, June 30). "Estimated economic benefits during the 'decade of vaccines' include treatment savings, gains in labor productivity." Health Affairs. Retrieved from https://www.ncbi.nlm.nih.gov/pubmed/21653952

[9] Stack, M. L., Ozawa, S., Bishai, D. M., Mirelman, A., Tam, Y., Niessen, L., Levine, O. S. (2011, June 30). "Estimated economic benefits during the 'decade of vaccines' include treatment savings, gains in labor productivity." Health Affairs. Retrieved from https://www.ncbi.nlm.nih.gov/pubmed/21653952

[10] WHO. (2018). "A healthier humanity: the WHO investment case." World Health Organization. *World Health Organization.* Retrieved from https://apps.who.int/iris/bitstream/handle/10665/274710/WHO-DGO-CRM-18.2-eng.pdf

- Length: I gave this indicator a length of 0.8 because the amount is quite significant. However, the arrow is not longer than the first indicator because the specific allocation of the funds is an assumption.
- Degree: I gave this indicator a degree of 20 because it is almost as exciting as it is harmonious.

• Indicator "WHO establishes Council on the Economics of Health for All. The Council, comprising top economists and health experts, will focus on investments in health, and achieving sustainable, inclusive, and innovation-led economic growth."[11] It surprised me to find that this council was formed this year in 2021 and that such an organization did not exist before. I included this indicator because I believe it indicates that the WHO's concept of health is becoming more holistic and inclusive, and thus more harmonious.

  - Length: I gave this indicator a length of 0.3 because while it is a positive step likely to bring harmony, its effectiveness is yet to be evaluated.
  - Degree: I gave this indicator a degree of 10 because it is almost as exciting as it is harmonious, and because it is a new idea.

• Indicator "Investments in reducing patient harm can lead to significant financial savings, and more importantly better patient outcomes. An example of prevention is engaging patients, if done well, it can reduce the burden of harm by up to 15%."[12] I struggled to categorize this indicator but I decided to qualify it as harmony because I found it extremely hopeful and a harmonious approach to improve health.

  - Length: I gave this indicator a length of 0.5 because it is quite positive that the benefits of reducing patient harm are being evaluated and that the WHO considers it a critical focus of improvement. However, how much of these policies are being applied is yet to be reported on which is why the length is limited.
  - Degree: I gave this indicator a degree of 30 because I believe these policies for patient harm reduction will bring harmony, but the excitement is unclear.

[11] WHO. (2021, August 31). "COVID-19 Response Fund." World Health Organization Diseases: COVID-19. *World Health Organization*. Retrieved from https://www.who.int/emergencies/diseases/novel-coronavirus-2019/donors-and-partners/funding

[12] WHO. (2020, November 13). "WHO Establishes council on the economics of health for all." World Health Organization News. *World Health Organization*. Retrieved from https://www.who.int/news/item/13-11-2020-who-establishes-council-on-the-economics-of-health-for-all

11.5.1.2 Excitement

- Indicator "US$ 25 billion to procure and deliver a safe and effective COVID-19 vaccine to the world's poorest countries, this could yield a benefit-to-cost ratio of 4.8 to 1. In other words, for every US$ 1 spent, wealthier countries would get back about US$ 4.80 in terms of the avoided economic costs."[13] I selected this indicator because it provides insight into the incredible potential of COVID-19 vaccine distribution in areas that currently lack access. This potential is exciting tending towards harmony.
  - Length: I gave this indicator a length of 0.8 because the potential is quite significant and hence exciting.
  - Degree: I gave this indicator a degree of 110 because it is as exciting as it is harmonious.
- Indicator "Noncommunicable diseases (NDCs) kill 41 million people each year, equivalent to 71% of all deaths globally."[14] I selected this indicator because it highlights what I believe to be a huge contradiction in public health. The fact that over half of deaths are from NCDs, most of them preventable, is not only alarming but also exciting as it shows great potential for the improvement of public health. At the same time, it highlights some of the failures of the current public health policies that have not successfully tackled NCDs.
  - Length: I gave a length of 0.8 to this indicator because the statistic is quite alarming but also exciting because it shows a great margin for change.
  - Degree: I gave a degree of 10 to this indicator because I believe it is almost as close to discipline as it is to excitement, given the alarming nature of the data.
- Indicator "People who eat the most subsidized foods have a 37% higher risk of obesity."[15] I selected this indicator for similar reasons to the previous indicator. The spectacular amount of activity, money, and resources that go into food subsidies that later make people ill is an alarming contradiction and a waste of resources.
  - Length: I gave this indicator a length of 0.7 because of the huge contradiction it entails. The government is directly funding foods that later create obesity that they have to spend money on treating.

---

[13] WHO. (2019, September 13). "Patient Safety Fact Sheet." World Health Organization Newsroom. *World Health Organization*. Retrieved from https://www.who.int/news-room/fact-sheets/detail/patient-safety

[14] The Vaccine Alliance. (2020, November 26). "Equal, rapid access to COVID-19 vaccines won't just save lives; it will save money." Gavi. *The Vaccine Alliance*. https://www.gavi.org/vaccineswork/equal-rapid-access-covid-19-vaccines-wont-just-save-lives-it-will-save-money

[15] WHO. (2021, April 13). "Non-communicable diseases Fact Sheet." World Health Organization Newsroom. *World Health Organization*. Retrieved from https://www.who.int/news-room/fact-sheets/detail/noncommunicable-diseases

  - Degree: I gave this indicator a degree of 10 because I believe it is almost as disciplinary as it is exciting.

- Indicator "15% of hospital expenses can be attributed to treating patient safety failures in OECD countries."[16] I selected this indicator because I also found it provides extremely alarming information. The fact that the richest countries on earth still suffer from so many failures in patient safety is very confusing, concerning, and wasteful.

  - Length: I gave this indicator a length of 0.5 because it is quite a significant percentage but probably not as high as in non-OECD countries.
  - Degree: I gave this indicator a degree of 30 because it is close to discipline, but remains significantly under excitement.

11.5.1.3 Discipline

- Indicator "Global health workforce shortage is of 7.2 million health workers."[17] I selected this indicator because I wanted to bring another aspect into consideration into the eco-sphere, which is employment. I believe this indicator belongs in the discipline quality due to the loss of opportunity correlated to economic suffering and its impeding of the WHO goals overall.

  - Length: I gave this indicator a length of 0.7 because it is a significant shortage but distribution is unclear, therefore, I do not want to overestimate its length.
  - Degree: I gave this indicator a degree of 100 degrees because the shortage is detrimental to public health and an exciting opportunity for economic growth and health improvement.

- Indicator "Medical costs increased 8.2% globally for employers in 2017."[18] I selected this indicator because many economies depend in large part on how their employers, particularly small and medium-sized companies, perform. Increasing medical costs at such a high rate create a burden on such employers.

  - Length: I gave this indicator a length of 0.7 because I thought this was quite a significant increase for just one year, and it could become an unbearable burden to many employers, however, distribution remains unclear.

---

[16] Siegel, K. R. (2016, August 01). "Consumption of Subsidized Foods and Cardio metabolic Risk in US Adults." JAMA Internal Medicine. *JAMA Network*. Retrieved from https://jamanetwork.com/journals/jamainternalmedicine/fullarticle/2530901

[17] WHO. (2019, September 17). "World Patient Safety Day 2019." World Health Organization Campaigns. *World Health Organization*. Retrieved from https://www.who.int/campaigns/world-patient-safety-day/2019

[18] WHO. (2014, May 20). "Global health workforce shortage to reach 12.9 million in coming decades." World Health Organization News. *World Health Organization*. Retrieved from http://www.who.int/mediacentre/news/releases/2013/health-workforce-shortage/en/

- Degree: I gave this indicator a degree of 100 because such an increase in costs seems far from balanced and harmonious, but rather a dramatic change likely to create unemployment and business failure, hence closer to the quality of excitement.

- Indicator "Cardiovascular disease costs $126.4 billion in lost productivity annually in the US."[19] I selected this indicator because I believe it shows the lack of action to address the number one cause of death in developed countries which is easily preventable.
  - Length: I gave this indicator a length of 0.8 because of the high losses which could be saved by preventing cardiovascular disease.
  - Degree: I gave this indicator a length of 100 degrees because of the unbalance and confusion that these losses create making the indicator close to excitement.
- Indicator "COVID-19 cost women globally over $800 billion in lost income in one year"[20]: I selected this indicator because I believe its an insightful example of how pandemics, whether diabetes, drug abuse, or COVID affects the economy negatively. However, it is much easier to realize the true impact of such pandemics when they are sudden and with high mortality rates than when it's a slow process over decades that becomes normalized.
  - Length: I gave this indicator a length of 0.9 because I believe it is particularly pervasive and will set income inequality back decades.
  - Degree: I gave this indicator a degree of 60 because I believe it represents discipline completely.
- Indicator "Climate change the direct damage costs to health (i.e., excluding costs in health-determining sectors such as agriculture and water and sanitation), is estimated to be between USD 2–4 billion/year by 2030."[21] This is perhaps one of the most important indicators I have selected because it connects all spheres under consideration. Public health policies often overlook the direct costs of environmental degradation, therefore, I found it important to include this indicator. Note that the estimate of damage costs does not include many critical sectors such as agriculture (famine), water, and sanitation (cholera and other diarrheal diseases).

[19] Aon plc. (2018). "2018 Global Medical Trends Report." *Health Resources Aon*. Retrieved from http://healthresources.aon.com/global-benefits/2018-global-medical-trends-report?_ga=2.50988718.604973933.1525063962-489636635.1525063962

[20] National Center for Chronic Disease Prevention and Health Promotion. (2017, June 28). "Chronic Disease Prevention and Health Promotion." *Centers for Disease Control and Prevention*. Retrieved from https://www.cdc.gov/chronicdisease/overview/index.htm

[21] OXFAM International. (2021, April 29). "COVID-19 cost women globally over $800 billion in lost income in one year." OXFAM Press Releases. OXFAM International. Retrieved from https://www.oxfam.org/en/press-releases/covid-19-cost-women-globally-over-800-billion-lost-income-one-year#:~:text=The%20COVID%2D19%20crisis%20cost,3.9%20percent%20loss%20for%20men.

- Length: I gave this indicator a length of 0.9 because I believe it is significantly destructive.
- Degree: I gave this indicator a degree of 60 because I believe it represents discipline completely.

- Indicator "Governments provide an average of 51% of a country's health spending, while more than 35% of health spending per country comes from out-of-pocket expenses. One consequence of this is 100 million people are pushed into extreme poverty each year."[22] I selected this indicator because it shows the hardship many people face. They have an unbearable burden of healthcare costs which in turn has negative effects on the economy as well.
  - Length: I gave this indicator a length of 0.6 because while it is quite significant, the government still carries over 50% of the burden.
  - Degree: I gave this indicator a degree of 30 because I believe it is well into discipline but on its way to harmony due to the COVID-19 pandemic which has led decision-makers to realize the importance of universal healthcare.
- Indicator "In 2019, the proportion of funding provided by external aid dropped to less than 1% of global health expenditure. Almost half of these external funds are devoted to three diseases – HIV/AIDS, Tuberculosis (TB), and malaria."[23] This indicator surprised me because I had the false impression that external aid for healthcare was quite significant, yet it dropped under 1% in 2019 which I find quite destructive. While these numbers probably changed during the COVID-19 health crisis, the question remains as to the future level of expenditure in public healthcare and external aid in the post-COVID world.
  - Length: I gave this indicator a length of 0.7 because this is an alarming trend, but perhaps not the trend anymore. The length is likely to change soon and significantly.
  - Degree: I gave this indicator a degree of 60 because I believe it very well represents the discipline quality.

[22] WHO. (2018, February 1). "Climate Change and Health Fact Sheet." World Health Organization Newsroom. *World Health Organization.* Retrieved from https://www.who.int/news-room/fact-sheets/detail/climate-change-and-health

[23] WHO. (2018, February 1). "Climate Change and Health Fact Sheet." World Health Organization Newsroom. *World Health Organization.* Retrieved from https://www.who.int/news-room/fact-sheets/detail/climate-change-and-health

11.5.2 Socio-Sphere

11.5.2.1 Harmony

- Indicator "Globally, life expectancy has increased by more than 6 years between 2000 and 2019 – from 66.8 years in 2000 to 73.4 years in 2019."[24] I selected this indicator because life expectancy is one of the best indicators of health, although not it is not perfect and it might be misleading. As with any global data, it hides the existing inequalities between countries. Moreover, life expectancy accounts for expectancy at birth which may change in the face of unforeseen events.
  - Length: I gave this indicator a length of 0.8 because life expectancy has increased quite significantly in a short period however, it is not a 10 because it could have increased more if we acted more firmly against ongoing preventable health issues such as obesity and air pollution.
  - Degree: I gave this indicator a degree of 30 degrees because this increase in life span is harmonious and leading to excitement for humanity. It is not closer because of the potential challenging results of this population increase for the quality of life of many people, especially in developing regions which struggle to provide services to the growing population.
- Indicator "New HIV infections have been reduced by 47% since the peak in 1998."[25] I selected this indicator because HIV has been one of the most pressing issues in public health for the last few decades, and it has proven especially difficult to address because of the social stigma associated with the condition.
  - Length: I gave this indicator a length of 0.5 because although it is positive and harmonious that HIV infections are decreasing, it appears to be a quite small decrease for such a long period, especially since it is a main focus of WHO policies and programmes.
  - Degree: I gave this indicator a degree of 30 because the fight against HIV has brought a lot of constructive and positive breakthroughs to the affected communities, but it has also required a lot of action and organizing.
- Indicator "One of the largest declines in the number of deaths is from diarrheal diseases, with global deaths falling from 2.6 million in 2000 to 1.5 million in

[24] WHO. (2018, February 1). "Climate Change and Health Fact Sheet." World Health Organization Newsroom. *World Health Organization.* Retrieved from https://www.who.int/news-room/fact-sheets/detail/climate-change-and-health

[25] WHO. (2006–2019). "GHE: Life expectancy and healthy life expectancy." Global Health Observatory. *World Health Organization.* Retrieved from https://www.who.int/data/gho/data/themes/mortality-and-global-health-estimates/ghe-life-expectancy-and-healthy-life-expectancy

2019."[26,27] I selected this indicator because diarrheal diseases are one of the main causes of death in the world while also being one of the most preventable ones as it is related to water quality. It shows our potential to improve public health.

- Length: I gave this indicator a length of 0.7 because this is an impressive decrease but not a very impressive decrease for a 10 year time period, especially if we consider how preventable these diseases are. The fact is that diarrheal diseases are still the leading cause of death in children. It is preventable by simply providing clean water.[28]
- Degree: I gave this indicator a degree of 60 degrees because it indicates growing harmony with our surroundings.

• Indicator "In the period 2010–2019, total malaria cases in the 21 E-2020 countries was reduced by 79%."[29] I selected this indicator because Malaria is also one of the biggest focuses and challenges of the WHO. The E-2020 countries are 21 countries, including South Africa, Mexico, and China, selected for Malaria elimination programmes by the WHO with quite encouraging results

- Length: I gave this indicator a length of 0.8 because of the quite significant progress.
- Degree: I gave this indicator a degree of 30 because of the exciting potential of this programme when applied worldwide.

• Indicator "COVAX offers Doses for at least 20% of countries' populations."[30] COVAX is a WHO pro-vaccination initiative aiming for equal vaccine distribution. I selected this indicator because it aims to reach harmony between countries.

- Length: I gave this indicator a length of 0.5 because while 20% is significant, it falls short of what we need to overcome the COVID-19 pandemic.
- Degree: I gave this indicator a degree of 100 because while it remains in harmony, with current vaccination inequalities and protective patent policies it seems like COVAX's efforts might not be enough.

---

[26] UN AIDS. (1990–2021) "Global HIV & AIDS statistics Fact sheet." United Nations AIDS Press Center. *United Nations*. Retrieved From https://www.unaids.org/en/resources/fact-sheet

[27] WHO. (2020, December 9). "The top 10 causes of death." World Health Organization Newsroom. *World Health Organization*. Retrieved from https://www.who.int/news-room/fact-sheets/detail/the-top-10-causes-of-death

[28] UNICEF. (2021, April). "Diarrhoea remains a leading killer of young children, despite the availability of a simple treatment solution." United Nations Children's Fund: Diarrheal Disease. *UNICEF*. Retrieved from https://data.unicef.org/topic/child-health/diarrhoeal-disease/

[29] PAHO. (2021, April 21). "World Malaria Day: WHO launches effort to stamp out malaria in 25 more countries by 2025." Pan American Health Organization News. *World Health Organization*. Retrieved from https://www.paho.org/en/news/21-4-2021-world-malaria-day-who-launches-effort-stamp-out-malaria-25-more-countries-2025

[30] COVAX. (2021) "Working for global equitable access to COVID-19 vaccines." World Health Organization: COVAX. *CEPI, Gavi and WHO*. Retrieved from https://www.who.int/initiatives/act-accelerator/covax

- Indicator "G7 announces pledges of 870 million COVID-19 vaccine doses, of which at least half to be delivered by the end of 2021."[31] This indicator incites similar reactions to the previous one as they are both pledges yet to be fulfilled. However, they show a pattern of developed countries and international organizations setting unsubstantiated goals.
  - Length: I gave this indicator a length of 0.5 because while 870 million is significant, it also falls short of what we need to overcome the COVID-19 pandemic.
  - Degree: I gave this indicator a degree of 100 because while it remains in harmony, with current vaccination inequalities and protective patent policies it seems like the G7 efforts will not be enough.

11.5.2.2 Excitement

- Indicator "Number of plastic surgery procedures increased 6.7% from 2018 to 2019."[32] I selected this indicator because it shows the magnitude of the relatively new phenomenon which is plastic surgery. A small percentage of plastic surgery is for correcting really disfiguring features. However, the great majority is merely to "enhance" beauty. While at least half of the world's population does not have access to basic healthcare, others have surgery by choice. It is quite a contrast that shows the contradictions of the industrialized world.
  - Length: I gave this indicator a length of 0.7 because of the novelty and extravagance of the indicator.
  - Degree: I gave this indicator a degree of 60 degrees because I do not want to characterize plastic surgery as constructive or destructive, but rather an interesting pattern to observe that might provide us with information about society.
- Indicator "One-quarter of all deaths from heart disease and stroke are preventable."[33] I found this indicator while searching for the most common causes of death and WHO programmes to decrease them. I was shocked to find that there are little, to no, international programmes to prevent these conditions.
  - Length: I gave this indicator a length of 0.8 because of its severity.
  - Degree: I gave this indicator a degree of 10 degrees because I believe it is almost as destructive as it is contradictory.

---

[31] WHO. (2021, June 13) "G7 announces pledges of 870 million COVID-19 vaccine doses, of which at least half to be delivered by the end of 2021." World Health Organization News. *World Health Organization.* Retrieved from https://www.who.int/news/item/13-06-2021-g7-announces-pledges-of-870-million-covid-19-vaccine-doses-of-which-at-least-half-to-be-delivered-by-the-end-of-2021

[32] ISAPS. (2019). "ISAPS Global Statistics." *International Society of Aesthetic Plastic Surgery.* Retrieved from https://www.isaps.org/medical-professionals/isaps-global-statistics/

[33] LeWine, H., MD. (2013, September 04). "200,000 heart disease, stroke deaths a year are preventable." Harvard Health. *Harvard University.* Retrieved from https://www.health.harvard.edu/blog/200000-heart-disease-stroke-deaths-a-year-are-preventable-201309046648

- Indicator "Reduction of Polio infections: Since 1998 there has been a 99.9% reduction in annual cases of polio."[34] This indicator is quite opposite of the last indicator. Polio has now been nearly eradicated, unlike heart disease, as a result of global efforts by the WHO, Rotary International, UNICEF, etc. These coordinated campaigns have been extremely successful and have required incredible amounts of work. The efforts have been rewarded by spectacular results.
  - Length: I gave this indicator a length of 0.9 because of how spectacular the drop has been.
  - Degree: I gave this indicator a degree of 110 because while it is very exciting, it has also brought a lot of wellness and balance.
- Indicator "One in 100 deaths is by suicide."[35] I included this indicator because I wanted to look at health holistically, including mental health which is often ignored. What I found stunned me. Suicide is most common in younger adults with victims being overwhelmingly male.
  - Length: I gave this indicator a length of 0.7 because of the severity of the statistic.
  - Degree: I gave this indicator a degree of 10 because it is as destructive as it is shocking.
- Indicator "While healthy life expectancy (HALE) has also increased by 8% from 58.3 in 2000 to 63.7, in 2019, this was due to declining mortality rather than reduced years lived with disability. In other words, the increase in HALE (5.4 years) has not kept pace with the increase in life expectancy (6.6 years)."[36] I included this indicator because it provided depth to the previous indicator in life expectancy and added robustness to the research. Life expectancy has increased quite a bit, but the years lived with disabilities have not decreased at the same rate, which means public health policies have been mostly focused on reducing mortality rather than increasing wellness.
  - Length: I gave this indicator a length of 0.5 because the indicator shows a somewhat significant contradiction in public health policy.
  - Degree: I gave this indicator a degree of 20 because it shows a lack of policies promoting quality of life – maybe because this is difficult to measure or to take into account.

---

[34] WHO (2017). "Global Polio Eradication Initiative: Semi-annual Status Report January – June 2017." WHO's Progress against the polio Eradication & Endgame Strategic Plan. *World Health Organization.* Retrieved from http://polioeradication.org/wp-content/uploads/2017/12/WHO-Polio-Donor-Report-january-june-2017-web-30112017.pdf

[35] WHO. (2021, June 17). "One in 100 deaths is by suicide." World Health Organization News. *World Health Organization.* Retrieved from https://www.who.int/news/item/17-06-2021-one-in-100-deaths-is-by-suicide

[36] WHO. (1990–2019). "GHE: Life expectancy and healthy life expectancy." Global Health Observatory. *World Health Organization.* Retrieved from https://www.who.int/data/gho/data/themes/mortality-and-global-health-estimates/ghe-life-expectancy-and-healthy-life-expectancy

- Indicator "1.9 billion Adults are overweight or obese, while 462 million are underweight.[37] This indicator again brings up the contradictions of public health. While some populations are overweight others are underweight, highlighting how many of these health issues are not a matter of lack of resources, but rather a distribution of both.
  - Length: I gave this indicator a length of 0.7 because of the significant disparity.
  - Degree: I gave this indicator a length of 60 because I will later qualify other similar indicators as destructive and I would like to highlight the contradictory nature of this data.

11.5.2.3 Discipline

- Indicator "Number of people without access to essential health services: At least half of the world's population cannot obtain essential health services."[38] I selected this indicator because I thought it captures the gravity of the healthcare challenge: it is 2021 and at least half of the world's population cannot obtain healthcare services. I believe this is a robust indicator of major importance to the compass.
  - Length: I gave this indicator a length of 9 because it is politically suppressive and destructive. One may argue that it is a long length considering that the other half does have access to essential healthcare, but I think that still, the gravity is too high for a shorter length.
  - Degree: I gave this indicator a degree of 100 degrees because of how spectacular the data is while being extremely unbalanced at the same time, therefore the degree leans towards excitement much more than to harmony.
- Indicator "Assuming continued economic growth and health progress, [it was] concluded that climate change is expected to cause approximately 250,000 additional deaths per year between 2030 and 2050; 38,000 due to heat exposure in elderly people, 48,000 due to diarrhoea, 60,000 due to malaria, and 95,000 due to childhood undernutrition."[39] This indicator complements the Climate Change indicator in the econo-sphere and provides specific data on deaths. However, recent data shows already 150,000 people die each year directly from climate change so the datum might be underestimated.[40] Moreover, climate change is

---

[37] WHO. (2021, June 9) "Malnutrition Factsheet." World Health Organization News. *World Health Organization.* Retrieved from https://www.who.int/news-room/fact-sheets/detail/malnutrition

[38] WHO. (2018, March 23). "Tracking universal health coverage: 2017." Global Monitoring Report. *World Health Organization.* Retrieved from http://www.who.int/healthinfo/universal_health_coverage/report/2017/en/

[39] SOGA. (2017). "A Special Report on Global Exposure to Air Pollution and its Disease Burden." *State of Global Air & Health Effects Institute.* Retrieved from https://www.stateofglobalair.org/sites/default/files/SOGA2017_report.pdf

[40] WHO. (2021). "Deaths from Climate Change. "Health and Environment Linkages Initiative. *World Health Organization.* Retrieved From https://www.who.int/heli/risks/climate/climatechange/en/

more of a threat multiplier than a cause of death itself, so the deaths caused by floods, typhoons, etc. might not be considered to be directly linked to climate change but are precipitated by such.

- Length: I gave this indicator a length of 0.8 because of the destructive characteristics of the indicator.
- Degree: I gave this indicator a length of 60 because it is purely disciplinary.

- Indicator "Over 90% of the world's population lived in areas with unhealthy air in 2015."[41] I selected this indicator because it demonstrates the magnitude of the impact humans have in the environment which in turn affects society overall. Air pollution is a common externality of industrial processes and transportation, but it contributes greatly to strokes, cardiovascular disease, respiratory diseases, etc. Something to take into consideration, however, is that most people nowadays live in urban areas which tend to have the worst air quality, rather than the air being polluted equally across the globe.
  - Length: I gave this indicator a length of 0.9 because it is extremely destructive to human health.
  - Degree: I gave this indicator a degree of 60 degrees because it is purely disciplinary.
- Indicator "Worldwide obesity has nearly tripled since 1975."[42] I selected this indicator because obesity is a relatively new issue (at least at this scale) which contributes greatly to the new health challenges of developed nations such as diabetes. It is a global trend that has been observed over a few years which adds to the robustness of the indicator.
  - Length: I gave this indicator a length of 0.9 because the consequences of obesity at this scale are devastating, especially if we consider that most cases are preventable.
  - Degree: I gave this indicator a degree of 100 degrees due to the novelty of the epidemic of obesity.
- Indicator "Diabetes has entered the top 10 causes of death, following a significant percentage increase of 70% since 2000. Diabetes is also responsible for the largest rise in male deaths among the top 10, with an 80% increase since 2000."[43] Similar to the last indicator, the rise of diabetes is linked to western-style development

[41] WHO. (2021, June 21). "Chronic Obstructive Pulmonary Disease Factsheet." World Health Organization Newsroom. *World Health Organization*. Retrieved from https://www.who.int/news-room/fact-sheets/detail/chronic-obstructive-pulmonary-disease-(copd)

[42] WHO. (2018, February 09). "Obesity and overweight." World Health Organization News. *World Health Organization*. Retrieved from http://www.who.int/mediacentre/factsheets/fs311/en/

[43] WHO. (2020, December 9). "The top 10 causes of death." World Health Organization Newsroom. *World Health Organization*. Retrieved from https://www.who.int/news-room/fact-sheets/detail/the-top-10-causes-of-death

and is highly preventable. Diabetes not only can cause death but it can greatly affect quality of life if not properly handled.

- Length: I gave this indicator a length of 0.8 because of the high rate of deaths.
- Degree: I gave this indicator a degree of 100 due to the novelty of the epidemic of diabetes.

• Indicator "The world's biggest killer is ischemic heart disease, responsible for 16% of the world's total deaths. Since 2000, the largest increase in deaths has been due to this disease, rising by more than 2 million to 8.9 million deaths in 2019."[44] Earlier we saw that one-third of deaths by heart disease and stroke are preventable. Now we look more narrowly at ischemic heart disease is the cause of 16% of the world's deaths.

  - Length: I gave this indicator a length of 0.8 because of the magnitude of the death toll.
  - Degree: I gave this indicator a degree of 60 because I believe it is purely destructive and shows the lack of focus on preventative medicine.

• Indicator "Worldwide, 3 million deaths every year result from harmful use of alcohol, this represents 5.3 % of all deaths."[45] I included this indicator because I wanted to add more aspects to the idea of health. Drug abuse, including alcohol, is a real epidemic in many countries including the US and Russia, yet I was surprised to find that alcohol use alone is responsible for 5.3% of all deaths. I believe these deaths are the result of unaddressed mental health issues hence the reason I qualified it as discipline.

  - Length: I gave this indicator a length of 0.9 because the death toll is incredibly high.
  - Degree: I gave this indicator a degree of 60 because of the destructive nature of the indicator.

11.5.3 Eco-Sphere

11.5.3.1 Harmony

• Indicator "Record-breaking 2020 Antarctic ozone hole finally closed at the end of December."[46] I selected this indicator because the loss of the Ozone layer is an

---

[44] WHO. (2020, December 9). "The top 10 causes of death." World Health Organization Newsroom. *World Health Organization*. Retrieved from https://www.who.int/news-room/fact-sheets/detail/the-top-10-causes-of-death

[45] WHO. (2021, September 21). "Alcohol." World Health Organization Newsroom. *World Health Organization*. Retrieved from https://www.who.int/news-room/fact-sheets/detail/alcohol

[46] WMO. (2021, January 6). "Record-breaking 2020 ozone hole closes." World Meteorological Organization News. *World Meteorological Organization*. Retrieved from https://public.wmo.int/en/media/news/record-breaking-2020-ozone-hole-closes

environmental issue caused by human activity that affects not only ecosystem health worldwide but also human health directly. However, it has also been one of the issues most effectively addressed by the international community and it is often used as an example of international cooperation for environmental action from which to draw inspiration for other issues such as climate change. I thought it would be important to represent such efforts in the compass.

- Length: I gave this indicator a length of 0.9 because this indicator was very positive and constructive.
- Degree: I gave this indicator a degree of 60 degrees because finally harmony has been restored to the Ozone Layer.

• Indicator "China wildlife crime prosecutions [went] up sharply after COVID-19 outbreak. China prosecuted more than 15,000 people for wildlife-related crimes in the first nine months of the year, up 66% from 2019.[47] I selected this indicator because it shows a shift in Chinese policy to live in harmony with its wildlife in order to avoid zoonotic diseases such as COVID-19. It is a quite exciting change that brings hope to NGOs fighting for wildlife and biodiversity conservation around the globe.

  - Length: I gave this indicator a length of 0.7 because of the fast and encouraging change.
  - Degree: I gave this indicator a degree of 10 because while this indicator brings harmony to the ecosphere, it is also incredibly exciting and it entails a lot of renewed action against wildlife trafficking.

• Indicator "Marine ecosystem resilience has been observed by 80% of the surveyed experts on all ecosystems."[48] I selected this indicator because I believe it adds to the discussion around the complexity of health. Human health is intrinsically linked to biodiversity and marine ecosystems. This indicator demonstrates the resilience of species within ecosystems and their ability to find harmony, the fact that 80% of the experts saw resilience on all ecosystems of the most major marine biodiversity hotspots studied means that they saw these ecosystems under stress due to human activities. The level of such resilience varies among and within ecosystems, moreover, elements of the ecosystem may be becoming more resilient while others might be disappearing completely.

  - Length: I gave this indicator a length of 0.5 because while it is positive that ecosystems are showing some level of resilience to environmental pressure, the complexity of the indicator shows limited harmony.

[47] Stanway, D. (2020, November 9). "China wildlife crime prosecutions up sharply after COVID-19 outbreak." Reuters Environment. *Reuters*. Retrieved from https://www.reuters.com/article/us-china-environment-wildlife-idUSKBN27P35B

[48] O'Leary, J. K., Micheli, F., Airoldi, L., Boch, C., De Leo, G., Elahi, R., Wong, J. (2017, February 1). "Resilience of Marine Ecosystems to Climatic Disturbances." Oxford Academic: BioScience. *Oxford University*. Retrieved from https://academic.oup.com/bioscience/article/67/3/208/2900174

- Degree: I gave this indicator a degree of 100 degrees because while I believe the indicator is positive in that ecosystems are adapting, the fact that they are under pressure to adapt is quite disciplinary.

- Indicator "4 billion people rely primarily on natural medicines."[49] I selected this indicator because it shows our dependency health-wise on nature and how on some level we are still in harmony with it.
  - Length: I gave this indicator a length of 0.8 because the statistic encompasses over half of the world's population which is quite significant.
  - Degree: I gave this indicator a degree of 60 because the indicator is a great example of living in harmony with nature.

11.5.3.2 Excitement

- Indicator "The Food and Agriculture Organization of the United Nations reports that 800 million people worldwide grow vegetables or fruits or raise animals in cities, producing an astonishing 15 to 20 percent of the world's food."[50] This indicator was quite shocking and confusing to find. I could not help but wonder how all this agricultural activity is taking place in cities and whether it is happening chaotically in slums or harmoniously in city gardens which is why I classified it under excitement.
  - Length: I gave this indicator a length of 0.7 because the statistic quite significant.
  - Degree: I gave this indicator a degree of 110 because it also has a strong harmony aspect a well in terms of maintaining our relationship with nature.

- Indicator "Thirty percent of the drugs sold worldwide contain compounds derived from plant material."[51] This indicator complements the previous indicator about medicine. It also shows our intrinsic relationship with the environment and the level of extraction we derive from it.
  - Length: I gave this indicator a length of 0.5 because the percentage is significant but could be greater.
  - Degree: I gave this indicator a degree of 110 because it also has a strong harmony aspect a well in terms of maintaining our relationship with nature.

---

[49] UN. (2019, May 6). "UN Report: Nature's Dangerous Decline 'Unprecedented'; Species Extinction Rates 'Accelerating'" United Nations Blog. *United Nations.* Retrieved from https://www.un.org/sustainabledevelopment/blog/2019/05/nature-decline-unprecedented-report/

[50] Royte, E. (2015, May 5) "Urban farms now produce 1/5 of the world's food." GreenBiz and Food & Environment Reporting Network. *GreenBiz*. Retrieved from. https://www.greenbiz.com/article/urban-farms-now-produce-15-worlds-food

[51] FAO. (2020) "Trade in Medicinal Plants." Economic and Social Department Food and Agriculture Organization of the United Nations. United Nations. Retrieved from http://www.fao.org/3/af285e/af285e00.pdf

- Indicator "Plants have globally increased their water use efficiency at the leaf level in proportion to the rise in atmospheric CO_2."[52] I selected this indicator because it demonstrates the unpredictable response of ecosystems to human impacts. The phenomenon is new and it has yet to be understood, therefore, one could argue that this indicator lacks robustness. However, I believe it is important to represent the high level of uncertainty that ecosystem health entails.
  - Length: I gave this indicator a length of 0.6 because this is a relatively new phenomenon but it is poorly understood, therefore, I did not feel it was strong enough for a longer length.
  - Degree: I gave this indicator a length of 20 degrees because it is so uncertain that it is hard to predict if the effects will be harmonious or disciplinary. Water efficiency sounds like could bring benefits to ecosystems dealing with increasing drought due to climate change, but typically a change, as subtle as might be, can create enormous unforeseen consequences.
- Indicator "On average, the researchers found 20 microplastic particles per 10g of stool."[53] Discoveries around the prevalence of microplastics new and alarming. We do not understand yet the consequences of these microplastics and research is ongoing which is why I classified this indicator under excitement.
  - Length: I gave this indicator a length of 0.8 because the statistic is quite significant.
  - Degree: I gave this indicator a degree of 10 because it demonstrates the level of impact we are having on the environment rather than living in harmony with it.

11.5.3.3 Discipline

- Indicator "In the US in 2013, the health care sector was also responsible for acid rain (12%), greenhouse gas emissions (10%), smog formation (10%) criteria air pollutants (9%), stratospheric ozone depletion (1%), and carcinogenic and non-carcinogenic air toxics (1–2%)."[54] I specifically searched for this indicator because I had analyzed the role of air pollution in other indicators, so I wanted to include the role of healthcare itself in air pollution which is quite staggering. A weakness of this indicator is that although it is quite specific, it is limited to the US.

---

[52] Keeling, R. F., Graven, H. D., Welp, L. R., Resplandy, L., Bi, J., Piper, S. C., Meijer, H. A. (2017, September 26). "Atmospheric evidence for a global secular increase in carbon isotopic discrimination of land photosynthesis." *Proceedings of the National Academy of Sciences of the United States of America.* Retrieved from http://www.pnas.org/content/114/39/10361

[53] Paskins, L. (2018, October 2022). "Microplastics discovered in human stools across the globe in 'first study of its kind'" *EurekAlert.* Retrieved from https://www.eurekalert.org/pub_releases/2018-10/sh-mdi101518.php

[54] Eckelman, M. J., & Sherman, J. (2016, June 9). "Environmental Impacts of the U.S. Health Care System and Effects on Public Health." *PLOS ONE.* Retrieved from http://journals.plos.org/plosone/article?id=10.1371/journal.pone.0157014

- Length: I gave this indicator a length of .5 because it is quite an important contribution to air pollution but it is not close to being the main or a large contributor.
- Degree: I gave this indicator a degree of 100 degrees because of the novelty of these contributions.

- Indicator "Severe pathogen pollution is estimated to affect around a quarter of Latin American river stretches, around 10 to 25% of African river stretches and about a third to one-half of Asian river stretches."[55,56] I selected this indicator because it deals specifically with faecal pathogen pollution, which could be prevented with proper sanitation and sewage management, yet it is not. It is a concrete example that provides depth to previous indicators about diarrheal diseases.
  - Length: I gave this indicator a length of .8 because of the tremendous harm that derives from water pollution, and the prevalence of such pollution in streams in these three regions.
  - Degree: I gave this indicator a degree of 60 degrees because of the lack of tendency either towards excitement or harmony.
  - Indicator "Particulate Matter concentrations increased by 11.2% from 1990 to 2015 worldwide."l Particulate matter is a type of air pollution made of organic material small enough to travel through the main respiratory tracks to then get stuck on the lung tissue and even sometimes penetrate the bloodstream causing all sorts of respiratory and other health issues. This indicator also adds depth to other indicators about air quality and demonstrates how it is a worsening issue.
  - Length: I gave this indicator a length of 0.7 because of the significant worsening of just one type of air pollutant.
  - Degree: I gave this indicator a degree of 60 because the indicator shows a lack of policies and actions to address increasing air pollution.

- Indicator: Soil degradation has reduced the productivity of 23% of the global land surface.[57] Productive and healthy soil is fundamental for human health. I selected this indicator because the loss of productive soil is destructive and indirectly impacts human health because it reduces the nutrition in food. The amount of vitamin C in a typical apple in the 1950s was 80% higher than it is today.

[55] UNEP. (2016). "A Snapshot of the World's Water Quality: Towards a global assessment." *United Nations Environmental Programme*. Retrieved from https://uneplive.unep.org/media/docs/assessments/unep_wwqa_report_web.pdf

[56] SOGA. (2017). "A Special Report on Global Exposure to Air Pollution and its Disease Burden." *State of Global Air & Health Effects Institute*. Retrieved from https://www.stateofglobalair.org/sites/default/files/SOGA2017_report.pdf

[57] UN. (2019, May 6). "UN Report: Nature's Dangerous Decline 'Unprecedented'; Species Extinction Rates 'Accelerating'" United Nations Blog. *United Nations*. Retrieved from https://www.un.org/sustainabledevelopment/blog/2019/05/nature-decline-unprecedented-report/

  - Length: I gave this indicator a length of 0.7 because of the severity of the destruction.
  - Degree: I gave this indicator a degree of 60 because it is purely disciplinary.

- Indicator "75%: terrestrial environment "severely altered" to date by human actions (marine environments 66%)"[58] This indicator complements the previous indicator on land productivity degradation. Not only has 23% of land lost its productivity but 75% of terrestrial ecosystems have been severely altered, which demonstrates the level of environmental disruption due to human activity.

  - Length: I gave this indicator a length of 0.8 because of the severity of the indicator.
  - Degree: I gave this indicator a degree of 60 because it is purely disciplinary.

- Indicator "85% of wetlands present in 1700 had been lost by 2000 – loss of wetlands is currently three times faster, in percentage terms than forest loss."[59] Wetlands are critical areas of biodiversity, water purification, and storm mitigation. They are very vulnerable to human activity and very important for ecosystem and human health. Their destruction is a direct threat to human life which is why I decided to include this indicator.

  - Length: I gave this indicator a length of 0.9 because most wetlands have been lost.
  - Degree: I gave this indicator a degree of 60 because it is purely disciplinary.

- Indicator "Ocean acidification increased by 30% since Industrial Revolution."[60] Ocean acidification is due to increasing CO_2 concentrations in the ocean. It is a direct threat to food security and, therefore, to the health of millions of people around the world. Ocean acidification is often overlooked as a side effect of climate change which is why I selected this indicator.

  - Length: I gave the indicator a length of 0.8 because of the gravity of the increase.
  - Degree: I gave this indicator a degree of 60 because it is purely disciplinary.

---

[58] UN. (2019, May 6). "UN Report: Nature's Dangerous Decline 'Unprecedented'; Species Extinction Rates 'Accelerating'" United Nations Blog. *United Nations.* Retrieved from https://www.un.org/sustainabledevelopment/blog/2019/05/nature-decline-unprecedented-report/

[59] UN. (2019, May 6). "UN Report: Nature's Dangerous Decline 'Unprecedented'; Species Extinction Rates 'Accelerating'" United Nations Blog. *United Nations.* Retrieved from https://www.un.org/sustainabledevelopment/blog/2019/05/nature-decline-unprecedented-report/

[60] NOAA. (2021) "A primer on Ph." Pacific Marine Environmental Laboratory: Carbon Program. *National Oceanic and Atmospheric Administration.* Retrieved from https://pmel.noaa.gov/co2/story/A+primer+on+pH

11.6 Indicator Table 11.1

Table 11.1 WHO Table

Sphere	Quality	Indicator	Degree	Length
Econo-sphere	Harmony	WHO Budget in 2020–2021, 4,840.4 million US Dollars, 11% increase compared to 2018–2019.	10	0.7
Econos-phere	Harmony	Savings in productivity losses from vaccination rates: Rates of vaccination against pneumococcal, Haemophilus influenza type b pneumonia and meningitis, rotavirus, pertussis, measles, and malaria over the next 10 years will save $145 billion in productivity losses.	10	0.5
Econo-sphere	Harmony	Investments in expanding Universal Health Coverage over the next 5 years will result in 24.4 million lives saved. Each dollar invested will result in a return of US$ 1.40.	30	0.8
Econo-sphere	Harmony	Donations to WHO to fight COVID 608,516,234 US Dollars.	20	0.8
Econo-sphere	Harmony	WHO establishes Council on the Economics of Health for All The Council, comprising top economists and health experts, will focus on investments in health, and achieving sustainable, inclusive and innovation-led economic growth.	10	0.3
Econo-sphere	Harmony	Investments in reducing patient harm can lead to significant financial savings, and more importantly better patient outcomes (2). An example of prevention is engaging patients, if done well, it can reduce the burden of harm by up to 15%.	30	0.5
Econo-sphere	Excitement	US$ 25 billion to procure and deliver a safe and effective COVID-19 vaccine to the world's poorest countries, this could yield a benefit-to-cost ratio of 4.8 to 1. In other words, for every US$ 1 spent, wealthier countries would get back about US$ 4.80 in terms of the avoided economic costs.	110	0.8
Econo-sphere	Excitement	Noncommunicable diseases (ncds) kill 41 million people each year, equivalent to 71% of all deaths globally.	10	0.8
Econo-sphere	Excitement	Relation between subsidized foods and obesity: People who eat the most subsidized foods have a 37% higher risk of obesity.	10	0.7
Econo-sphere	Excitement	**15%** of hospital expenses can be attributed to treating patient safety failures in OECD countries.	30	0.5
Econo-sphere	Discipline	Global health workforce shortage: Global health workforce shortage is of 7.2 million health workers.	100	0.7

(continued)

Table 11.1 (continued)

Sphere	Quality	Indicator	Degree	Length
Econo-sphere	Discipline	Increase of medical costs: Medical costs increased 8.2% globally for employers in 2017.	100	0.7
Econo-sphere	Discipline	Cost of productivity losses of cardiovascular disease: Cardiovascular disease costs $126.4 billion in lost productivity annually in the US.	100	0.8
Econo-sphere	Discipline	COVID-19 cost women globally over $800 billion in lost income in 1 year.	60	0.9
Econo-sphere	Discipline	Climate change the direct damage costs to health (i.e. Excluding costs in health-determining sectors such as agriculture and water and sanitation), is estimated to be between used 2–4 billion/year by 2030.	60	0.9
Econo-sphere	Discipline	Governments provide an average of 51% of a country's health spending, while more than 35% of health spending per country comes from out-of-pocket expenses. One consequence of this is 100 million people pushed into extreme poverty each year.	30	0.6
Econo-sphere	Discipline	The proportion of funding provided by external aid has dropped to less than 1% of global health expenditure. Almost half of these external funds are devoted to three diseases – HIV/AIDS, Tuberculosis (TB) and malaria.	60	0.7
Socio-sphere	Harmony	Globally, life expectancy has increased by more than 6 years between 2000 and 2019 – from 66.8 years in 2000 to 73.4 years in 2019.	30	0.8
Socio-sphere	Harmony	New HIV infections have been reduced by 47% since the peak in 1998.	30	0.5
Socio-sphere	Harmony	One of the largest declines in the number of deaths is from diarrheal diseases, with global deaths falling from 2.6 million in 2000 to 1.5 million in 2019.	60	0.7
Socio-sphere	Harmony	In the period 2010–2019, total malaria cases in the 21 E-2020 countries reduced by 79%.	30	0.8
Socio-sphere	Harmony	COVAX offers Doses for at least 20% of countries' populations.	100	0.5
Socio-sphere	Harmony	G7 announces pledges of 870 million COVID-19 vaccine doses, of which at least half to be delivered by the end of 2021.	100	0.5
Socio-sphere	Excitement	Number of plastic surgery procedures increased 6.7% from 2018 to 2019.	60	0.7
Socio-sphere	Excitement	Preventability of deaths by stroke and heart disease: One-quarter of all deaths from heart disease and stroke are preventable.	10	0.8
Socio-sphere	Excitement	Reduction of Polio infections: Since 1998 there has been a 99.9% reduction in annual cases of polio.	110	0.9
Socio-sphere	Excitement	One in 100 deaths is by suicide.	10	0.7

(continued)

Table 11.1 (continued)

Sphere	Quality	Indicator	Degree	Length
Socio-sphere	Excitement	While healthy life expectancy (HALE) has also increased by 8% from 58.3 in 2000 to 63.7, in 2019, this was due to declining mortality rather than reduced years lived with disability. In other words, the increase in HALE (5.4 years) has not kept pace with the increase in life expectancy (6.6 years).	20	0.5
Socio-sphere	Excitement	1.9 billion Adults are overweight or obese, while 462 million are underweight.	60	0.7
Socio-sphere	Discipline	Number of people without access to essential health services: At least half of the world's population cannot obtain essential health services.	100	0.9
Socio-sphere	Discipline	Assuming continued economic growth and health progress, concluded that climate change is expected to cause approximately 250,000 additional deaths per year between 2030 and 2050; 38,000 due to heat exposure in elderly people 48,000 due to diarrhea, 60,000 due to malaria, and 95,000 due to childhood undernutrition.	60	0.8
Socio-sphere	Discipline	Percentage of people living in areas with unhealthy air: Over 90% of the world's population lived in areas with unhealthy air in 2015. Chronic Obstructive Pulmonary Disease (COPD) is the third leading cause of death worldwide, causing 3.23 million deaths in 2019.	60	0.9
Socio-sphere	Discipline	Worldwide obesity rate: Worldwide obesity has nearly tripled since 1975.	100	0.9
Socio-sphere	Discipline	Diabetes has entered the top 10 causes of death, following a significant percentage increase of 70% since 2000. Diabetes is also responsible for the largest rise in male deaths among the top 10, with an 80% increase since 2000.	100	0.8
Socio-sphere	Discipline	The world's biggest killer is ischemic heart disease, responsible for 16% of the world's total deaths. Since 2000, the largest increase in deaths has been for this disease, rising by more than 2 million to 8.9 million deaths in 2019.	60	0.8
Socio-sphere	Discipline	Worldwide, 3 million deaths every year result from harmful use of alcohol, this represent 5.3 % of all deaths.	60	0.9
Eco-sphere	Harmony	Record-breaking 2020 Antarctic ozone hole finally closed at the end of December.	60	0.9
Eco-sphere	Harmony	China wildlife crime prosecutions up sharply after COVID-19 outbreak. China prosecuted more than 15,000 people for wildlife-related crimes in the first nine months of the year, up 66% from 2019.	10	0.7

(continued)

Table 11.1 (continued)

Sphere	Quality	Indicator	Degree	Length
Eco-sphere	Harmony	Marine ecosystem resilience as observed by experts: 80% of experts observed resilience in all ecosystem types.	100	0.5
Eco-sphere	Harmony	4 billion: people who rely primarily on natural medicines.	60	0.8
Eco-sphere	Excitement	The Food and Agriculture Organization of the United Nations reports that 800 million people worldwide grow vegetables or fruits or raise animals in cities, producing an astonishing 15–20% of the world's food.	110	0.7
Eco-sphere	Excitement	Thirty percent of the drugs sold worldwide contain compounds derived from plant material.	110	0.5
Eco-sphere	Excitement	Plants have globally increased their water use efficiency at the leaf level in proportion to the rise in atmospheric CO_2.	20	0.6
Eco-sphere	Excitement	On average, the researchers found 20 microplastic particles per 10 g of stool.	10	0.8
Eco-sphere	Discipline	Contribution of the healthcare sector to air pollution: In 2013, the healthcare sector was also responsible for acid rain (12%), green-house gas emissions (10%), smog formation (10%) criteria air pollutants (9%), stratospheric ozone depletion (1%), and carcinogenic and non-carcinogenic air toxics (1–2%).	100	0.5
Eco-sphere	Discipline	Prevalence of pathogen pollution in streams in different world regions: Severe pathogen pollution is estimated to affect around a quarter of Latin American river stretches, around 10–25% of African river stretches and about a third to one-half of Asian river stretches.	60	0.8
Eco-sphere	Discipline	Increase in particulate matter pollution: Particular Matter concentrations increased by 11.2% from 1990 to 2015.	60	0.7
Eco-sphere	Discipline	Land degradation has reduced the productivity of 23% of the global land surface.	60	0.7
Eco-sphere	Discipline	75%: terrestrial environment "severely altered" to date by human actions (marine environments 66%).	60	0.8
Eco-sphere	Discipline	85%: of wetlands present in 1700 had been lost by 2000 – loss of wetlands is currently three times faster, in percentage terms, than forest loss.	60	0.9
Eco-sphere	Discipline	Ocean acidification increased 30% since Industrial Revolution.	60	0.8

Note that references for the data were given in Sect. 11.5

11.7 Compass Results

Following the methodology by Dr. Friend thoroughly explained in previous chapters, indicators were aggregated and calibrated with the resulting compasses. We find several types of compasses. First, two compasses per sphere, one reflecting the aggregated indicators per quality (Figs. 11.1, 11.3, and 11.5) and one with all the indicators and qualities aggregated with one final arrow (Figs. 11.2, 11.4, and 11.6). Figure 11.1 depicts the three quality arrows for the econo-sphere, with the arrows of harmony and discipline being longer but angled towards excitement. The final aggregated arrow of the econo-sphere can be found in figure two, in the excitement quality, leaning towards discipline. What these compasses tell us is that there is a great deal of movement and effort in the WHO around funding, but it is not clear that this funding translates into greater public health improvements.

Figure 11.3 depicts the three quality arrows for the socio-sphere. The arrow for discipline is long, covering two-thirds of the sphere radius and angled slightly towards excitement. The arrow for harmony also reaches around two-thirds of the radius and is slightly tilted towards excitement. The excitement arrow is somewhat

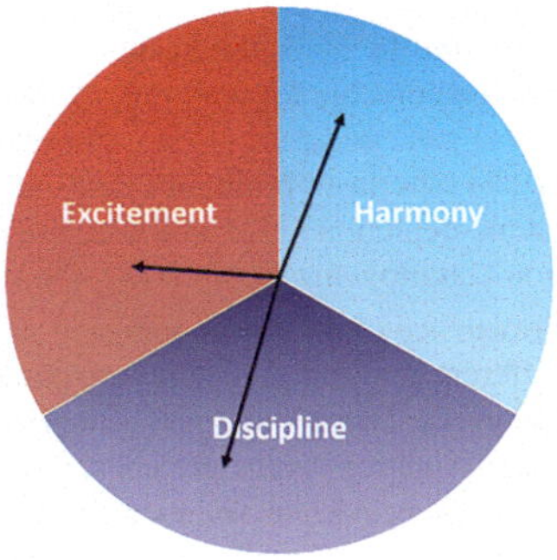

Fig. 11.1 WHO economic compass with sector arrows

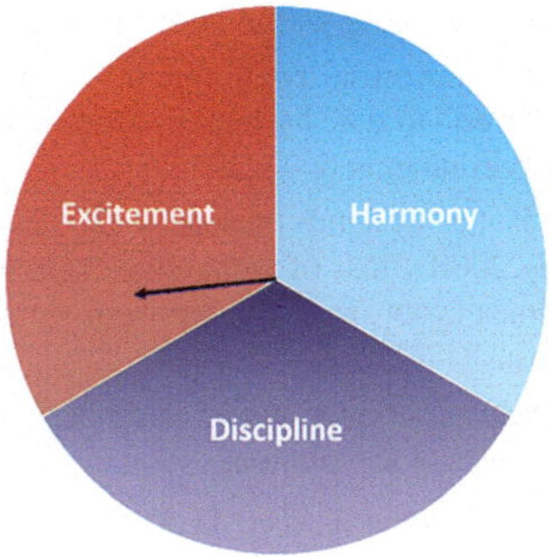

Fig. 11.2 WHO economic compass

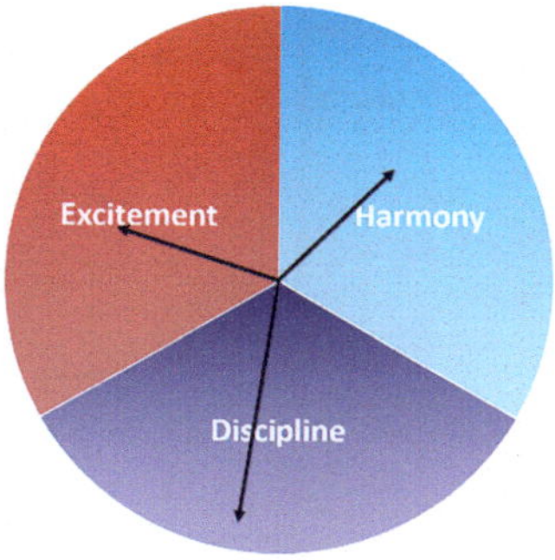

Fig. 11.3 WHO social compass with sector arrows

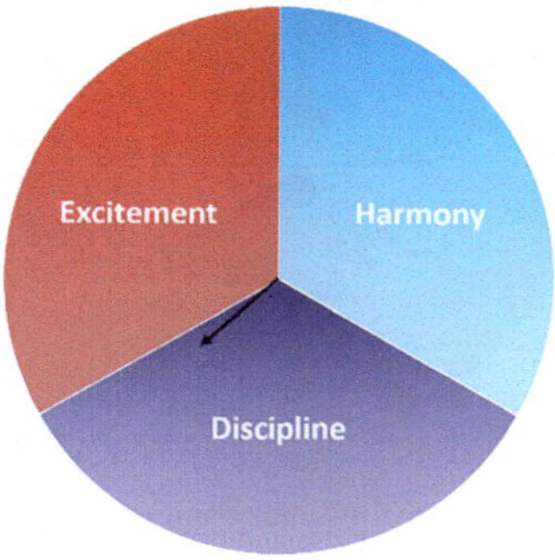

Fig. 11.4 WHO social compass

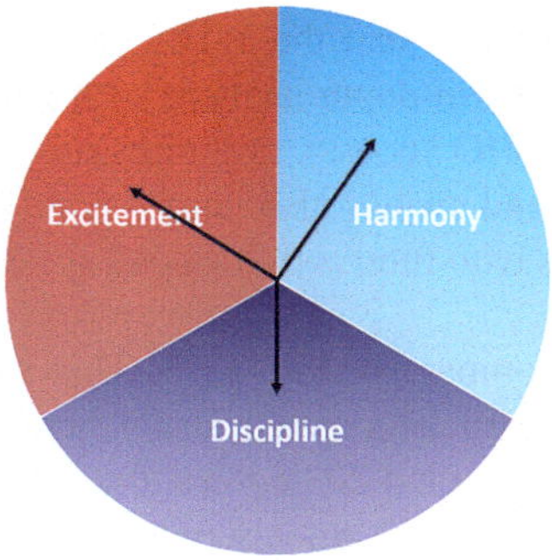

Fig. 11.5 WHO environmental compass with sector arrows

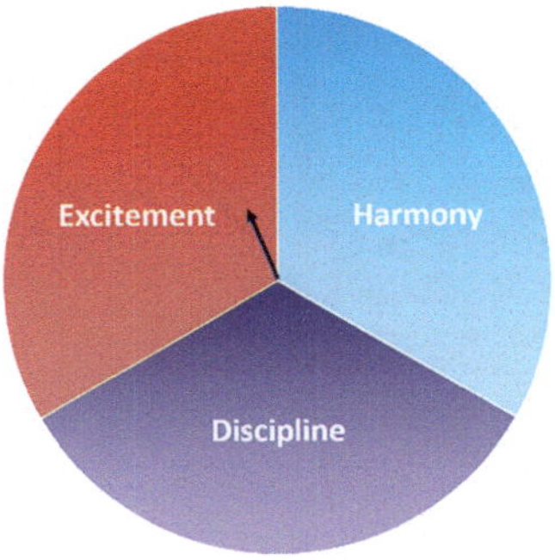

Fig. 11.6 WHO environmental compass

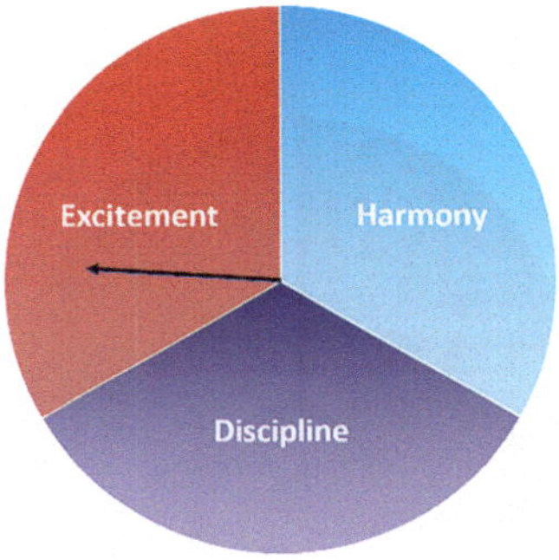

Fig. 11.7 WHO ecological economics institutional compass

angled towards discipline but of medium length. Figure 11.4 shows the final aggregated arrow of the socio-sphere, covering only one-third of the sphere radius and almost in the line between discipline and excitement, leaning around 10 degrees towards discipline.

Figures 11.2 and 11.4 indicate that the WHO seems to be failing at achieving harmony in human health. The in-depth analysis of the indicators showed intrinsic contradictions in how the WHO focuses programs and funding on some diseases over others. The indicators and arrows also demonstrate a lack of accountability to governments and companies who fund activities and systems which endanger public health (Figs. 11.5 and 11.6).

Then we find the final compass in Fig. 11.7. This is an ecological economics institutional compass. The final aggregated arrow here has a length of .6 length within the excitement quality angled 20 degrees towards discipline.

The final compasses highlights the amount of action and excitement happening at the WHO. The arrow being towards disciple can also indicate what was noted in the indicator analysis: that some areas of public health are improving greatly while others worsen rapidly.

11.8 Conclusions

This chapter has used Friend's innovative and holistic ecological economics institutional to analyze the WHO, the effectiveness of its policies and programs, and its role as the world leader in public health. This compass represents over 90 indicators that provide robustness and depth to the analysis. It is a compass worth revisiting with a large discussion group periodically with more indicators. Finding indicators for all the spheres and qualities has been a deep philosophical exercise that has required posing questions to the indicators and looking at them from all perspectives. As much as I was designing this compass, at a certain level, the compass was redesigning me, forcing me to adjust my thinking and switch paradigms, which was challenging but extremely interesting and necessary in today's polarized world.

The final institutional ecological economics compass arrow I believe is an accurate representation of the current status of global health. The arrow in the excitement quality reflects the dynamism, contradictions, and uncertainty of global health, while the angle leaning toward discipline reveals the negative impacts that human activity has on the environment and on the health of the ecosystem which in turn hurts humanity. Overall, the WHO is doing an effective job with the areas of health it addresses but it needs to widen its understanding of health to encompass ecosystem health and preventability of NDCs. The WHO is a necessary leader of public health and performs much-needed work, I hope this analysis brings some insight into how to achieve some stability so that the arrow lands in harmony, the health and lives of billions of people lie in the balance.

11.9 Policy Recommendations

I believe the result of this compass shows that the policies of the WHO are working but a new approach is needed. While health has increased in many parts of the world, many others are lagging behind. The majority of the world's population does not have access to basic health services while they also breathe polluted air, drink contaminated water, and live in ecosystems that are slowly dying and with them the ecosystem services they provide and that we mistakenly take for granted.

A recurring issue I have repeated throughout the data analysis is the contradiction of the system which makes us sick and then tries to treat or cure us. I also have identified two main problems with the paradigm in which the WHO functions. First, the predominant Western economic model has cost the world both ecosystem and human health. Until we do not change the priorities of the system, ecosystems will keep getting ill and with them, the humans that live in them. In developed nations we might get a false sense of ecosystem improvement as we have exported most polluting and destructive practices abroad, removing us from the harmful activities and leaving those in the developing states to deal with the consequences of our consumer choices. Second, although we know that humans are animals that exist within an ecosystem, we do not act as if we truly understood this. We ignore the fact that we depend on the ecosphere just like any other animal: we might have been able to overcome some environmental obstacles and manipulate some aspects of nature for our own benefit, but these are simply temporary fixes that will eventually catch up to us. We cannot control nature and we definitely cannot replace nature's services such as clean water and fertile soil over the long term.

My policy recommendation is to reconsider these two points. Any policies that deal with treating conditions such as obesity or diarrheal diseases are great in the short term, but if we do not create systems that provide people with healthy and affordable food and water, in the long term they will be a waste of resources. The WHO should divide its resources to deal with both short-term and long-term solutions. Above all, repairing ecosystem health by ending harmful industrial practices and other activities that, as I have discussed create more harm than good, would be a top priority. Because the eco-sphere encompasses all other spheres a healthy ecosystem would inevitably lead to a healthy socio-sphere, fulfilling the number one mission of the WHO. Moreover, I ask that the WHO reconsider that economic development is always positive and that more money will make everyone better off. In the case of health, many times it's the opposite: less industrial production due to less consumption leads to less pollution. In contrast, economic sanctions and taxes on polluting activities may benefit public health in the long term. The WHO should not keep improving the lives of some in the short term by hurting the health of everyone in the future. I encourage its leadership to take on ecosystem health in order to achieve its goals.

Chapter 12
Case-Study II: Report on Product Label Project

The idea of using the compass as a product label is a good way of introducing compass concepts to non-experts. It's an idea that is easily recognised by people living in modern economies.

Here is a description of the project. The project was for a new shop that was specialising in "ethical and sustainable" products – dry food goods, cosmetics and cleaning products. The owner was careful to select goods to sell that had a short transportation circuit, so "local" products, coming from small businesses. All packaging is re-usable and a client is encouraged to bring his, or her, own container. Since the food is sold in bulk, one only buys the quantity that one wants.

I proposed to the owner that my ex-student Quinn Samouilidis, should construct an entirely intuitive compass reading for each product, using an ecological economics compass. This would then be included on the label for each product, along with the name of the product and the price. The compass would be an impressionistic holistic evaluation of each item.

The owner and I, as a compass constructor, ascertained that, in light of the ideological orientation of the shop, the favoured colour is a light green, and that it would bleed towards red on one side and towards a dark grey/purple on the other. See Fig. 12.1. This is the same as the colour sensitive compass in Fig. 9.2, except that there is a sixty-degree rotation anti-clockwise. The idea was to put the "favoured" colour on top. What was counted as favoured came from the ideological orientation of the shop owner.

Over one summer, Samouilidis developed data tables and compass labels for each product. The data tables were meant to be kept under the front counter for consultation (and eventual amendment). We also produced a poster explaining very briefly what the circle was meant to represent, and how to interpret the arrow. We made a leaflet available that gave a longer description, which was also meant to be available on the website of the shop.

We hoped for three reactions – that clients would prefer, *ceteris paribus* products with the arrow pointing upwards – indicating harmony and ecological sustainability. As a second reaction, we hoped to arouse curiosity about the products and awareness

M. I. Friend, *The Institutional Compass: Method, Use and Scope*, Methodos Series 18, https://doi.org/10.1007/978-3-031-05453-2_12

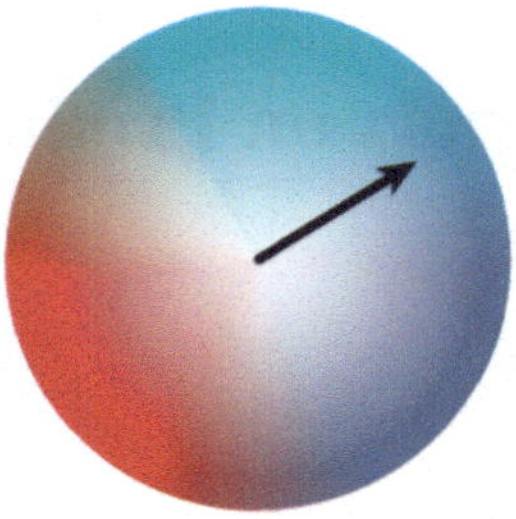

Fig. 12.1 The compass as a product label

of the many considerations that can be made concerning the product, inviting criticism and debate about the indicator arrows. We hoped that producers would learn from each other to improve their products and to co-ordinate the small producers, and small agricultural community.

Unfortunately, the shop owner decided not to include the compasses on the labels. He found that as it was, the concept of selling goods in bulk was already demanding for his clients. Also, we were too late. Before Samouilidis had finished, the shop owner had developed his own labelling system: blue stickers to indicate close circuit and green to indicate organic. The stickers he used led to confusion for his clients. He took them away after a few weeks.

What can we learn from this experience? Not all seeds fall on fertile ground. The setting up of the exercise is key. I think that his own experiment was not well thought through – the colours blue and green being too close together, and blue not suggesting short travel distance. Separating the information is also not useful, *prima facie*. Lastly, without an explanation in the form of a poster meant that if clients did not ask about the stickers, they could only guess or wonder at the significance.

Chapter 13
Case Study III: Regional Compass Hauts-de-France, Superimposing a Biorefinery, by Ahmed Yaman Abdin and Michèle Friend

We introduce the beginning of a project to evaluate a region. The region chosen was Hauts-de-France. The choice was not strategic, but opportunistic. It is the region where we lived at the time: as part of the ERASMUS+ programme, Yaman had come over as a Ph.D. student from Saarland University to learn about the compass and philosophy of the environment.

We constructed three institutional compasses: a wish compass, a non-ideological generic compass and an ecological economics institutional compass for the region of Hauts-de-France. We then looked into a bio-conversion process and estimated the impact it would have, at the small scale of a sub-region, in the context of the greater region. The actual plant we looked at was quite small – collecting biomass from six farms and providing electricity to 500 households. So, for the total region of Hauts-de-France, this is insignificant. However, at a sufficiently large scale, or over a small enough sub-region, the common use of such a process could change the regional compass reading.

13.1 The Wish Compass for Hauts-de-France

We begin by discussing the wish compass. We start with an historical recapitulation of the recent history of the region. During the industrial revolution, the region was quite prosperous. There were coal mines providing energy, there was a lot of industry, especially textile, there were a significant number of canals and easy access to the North Sea. Manufactured goods could be shipped inland from the North Sea, by the canal system, or sent overland by train or coach. Manufactured goods could be exported by sea, rail and road.

Due to the geo-political location, the world wars destroyed much of the physical infrastructure and buildings. When the coal mines closed and the manufacturing industry moved abroad, or converted to more high-tech service "products", the region was forgotten. The region became the poorest in France. Intuitively, if we

M. I. Friend, *The Institutional Compass: Method, Use and Scope*, Methodos Series 18, https://doi.org/10.1007/978-3-031-05453-2_13

are comparing this region with others in France, the actual compass would find the arrow in discipline: high pollution, high unemployment and poverty.

The technological development of very fast trains: and the increase in air travel in the late twentieth century and early twenty-first century resulted in major investment in the tourist industry – in museums and festivals, together with investment in the transportation infrastructure: TGVs (Très Grande Vitesse) to Paris, Brussels, and to London through the channel tunnel. The three universities of Lille were combined into one, a city of science (cité scientifique) was constructed in the 1960s and 1970s to act as a bridge between industrial and academic research. In compass terms, this means that the investment was meant to bring the arrow more towards excitement.

In the twenty-first century, the regional government of Hauts-de-France and the national government took the initiative to re-invest in the region with the vision of making it the leader in France, if not Europe, for the transition to a green economy – one that aligns with the concept of a circular economy.

We interpret a real circular economy to mean that the region becomes strongly sustainable. For us, this indicates that the wish spot should be located in excitement for now because of the newness of the transition. It requires risky investment and scientific expertise. Because the transition is towards a circular economy, and since we interpret this to mean strong sustainability, the purpose of the investment is to bring the region to a wish spot in harmony, maybe in 30–50 years. The wish spot will rotate over time. Moreover, it should be a wish spot in harmony for an ecological economics institutional compass, indicating that the long-term wish has matured and that the region is in alignment with the natural flows of air, water and soil nutrients. See the wish compass depicted in Fig. 13.1 for the year 2021.

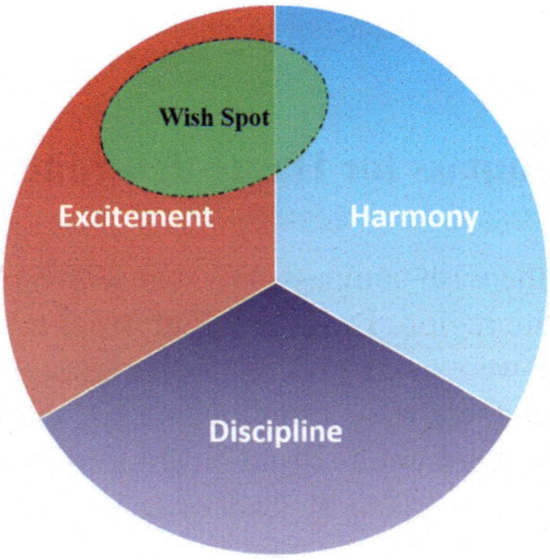

Fig. 13.1 Wish compass for the region: Hauts-de-France

13.2 The Actual Compasses for Hauts-de-France

Since we were after both a generic compass and an ecological economics compass, we looked for data in each of the nine sectors: environment-harmony, environment-discipline, environment-excitement; society-harmony, society-discipline, society-excitement, economy-harmony, economy-discipline and economy-excitement. The three sphere compasses can be seen in Figs. 13.2, 13.3 and 13.4.

Note that in Table 13.3, for the eco-sphere, there is no significant data in the harmony sector. This can happen. There is not enough significant wild territory – not enough to really sustain a healthy ecosystem without important human intervention and management. What we do find in the region is unhealthy "wild" areas (polluted waterways, for example), a lot of industrial agriculture and the rest is built up or is heavily managed park area. This is not the case everywhere in France. Other regions, where there are more mountains, for example, have more wild spaces. In terms of

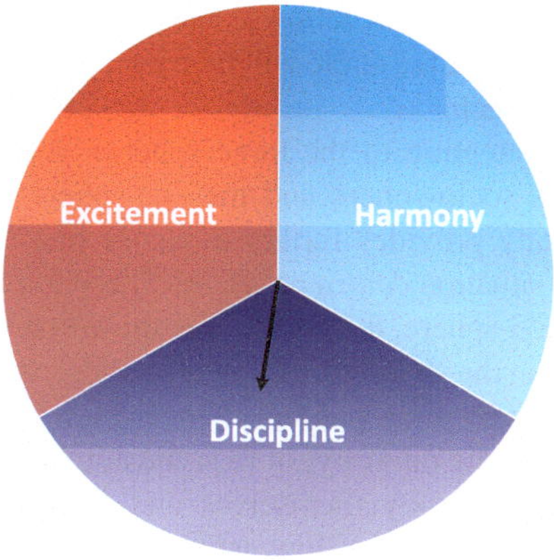

Fig. 13.2 Econo-sphere Hauts-de-France

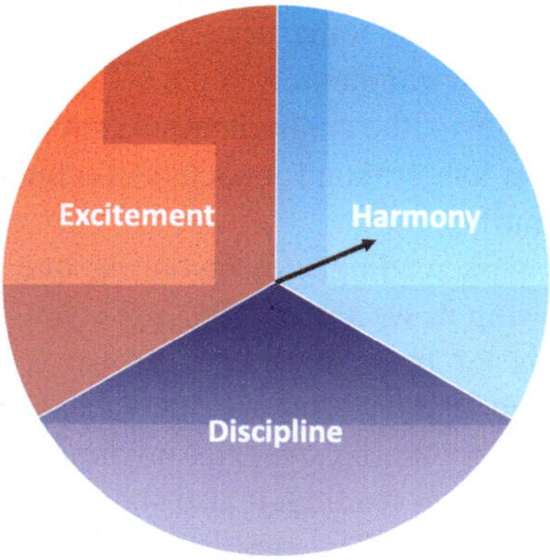

Fig. 13.3 Socio-sphere Hauts-de-France

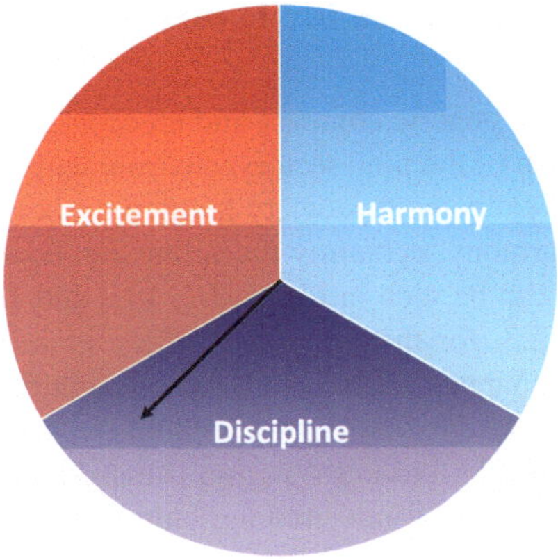

Fig. 13.4 Eco-sphere Hauts-de-France

compass construction, we proceed as follows. The harmony sector arrow will have a length of zero, and the centre of the circle will then be a point of the triangle – the one representing the harmony sector.

Let us now turn our attention to the three spheres. It is interesting to see the discrepancy between the socio-sphere and the eco-sphere. They pull in opposite directions. This case study provides further evidence that the economic situation does not track the social situation *contra* neoclassical economic *doxa*. If we compare the socio-sphere to the eco-sphere, the compasses show that we can insulate society from nature successfully in the short term. Of course, there are some organic farmers, and nature lovers, people who track and feel changes in nature, and this affects them socio-politically, but this is the minority. In fact, the number is insignificant. By and large, people in the region enjoy themselves and feel healthy despite nature's suffering. Since Lille has a major university and research campus, the cité scientifique, this adds to the social well-being of the region, but not much directly to the environment. The campus efforts towards sustainability are too small geographically to have much of an impact on the whole region.

In Sect. 7.1 we mentioned that some people believe that the health of society depends on the health of the environment. And the compasses in this case study seem to contradict the claim. However, the contradiction is temporary. Recall that the time scale for the environment is longer than for society. Technology shields us from the vagaries of nature temporarily.

The final generic compass reading, not favouring one sphere over another, is found in Fig. 13.5. Analysing it, we see that the arrow lies in discipline, but is very close to harmony. This is far from the wish spot we see in Fig. 13.1. There is something heavy and dull about the region – the flat landscape, industrial agriculture, the unpleasant weather, the economic struggle, unemployment, air, water and soil pollution, all support the compass reading. It also shows us that national government were not wrong in their diagnosis. The area is depressed and needs attention. The investment in museums, art, culture, education should be continued, since they will

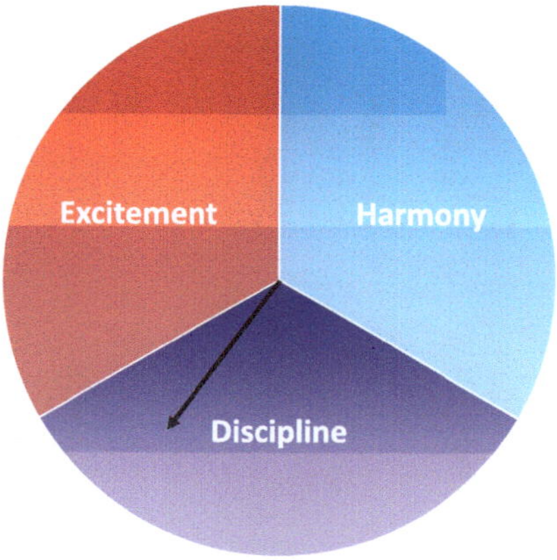

Fig. 13.5 Generic institutional compass Hauts-de-France

help to orient the arrow towards the wish spot and compensate for the poor quality of the natural environment. This is the reason economics ends up being the deciding factor between them! This does not mean that the "solution" to getting the arrow in the wish spot lies solely with the economy, rather we are interested in shifting the direction of the socio-sphere arrow and the eco-sphere arrow towards excitement.

The recommendations, then are to continue with investment, and direct it towards ecological improvement. More green spaces are needed, especially ones that are minimally controlled by humans. We need less built-up area and more organic farming with attention to water and soil quality.

We decided to also add an ecological economics institutional compass. We favoured the environment sphere over the society sphere and favoured the society sphere over the economic sphere. The reading is suitable for an ecological economist's conception of the world. That compass is depicted in Fig. 13.6.

With this reading we are even further from the wish spot. The "green" in the green transition will require a major effort. Looking after the environment becomes pressing, and not only in an indirect or superficial way – by encouraging industries that say they are "green" or are only relatively helpful, but by really taking care to directly prevent biodiversity loss, to legislate against polluted waterways, and clean them up, to ensure adequate water levels for aquatic species to thrive, to increase wild park land, to significantly reduce the use of pesticides, especially in agriculture, since, by killing the insects, they deprive birds of food stressing the eco-system. Since the land surface is mainly industrial agriculture, one suggestion would be to encourage farmers away from industrial agriculture towards more traditional farming practices, to plant hedge-rows or implement a system of set-aside fields – compensating the farmers with incentives they can use towards increasing organic food production. This is not the recent tradition in the area, and might encounter considerable social resistance, even if there is economic compensation. The monetary compensation, and monitoring of the programme (for choices of hedge species, and management of the hedge-rows) would have to be significant. Hedges encourage bio-diversity and reduce soil erosion. This in turn reduces the need for fertiliser, and

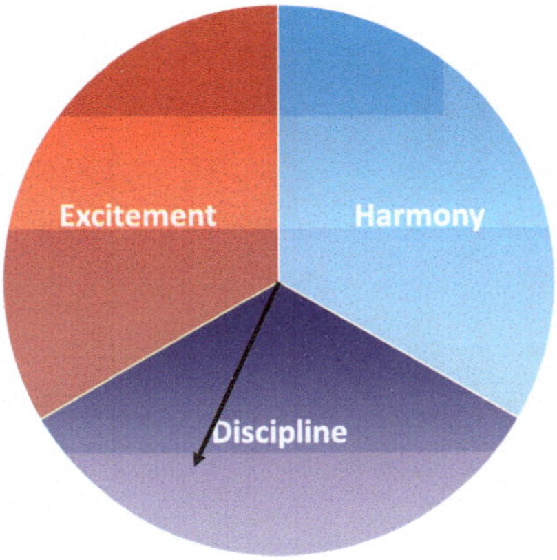

Fig. 13.6 Ecological economics institutional compass Hauts-de-France

irrigation, it reduces the quantity of soil particles in the air. This type of suggestion comes from looking at other regions, of longer traditions and at underlying causes of several data points that we want altered, as opposed to addressing particular data in policy decision making.

Another suggestion is to re-establish or re-emphasise the traditional water-ditches around the fields. Since this was a traditional practice and one that is still common in Belgium and the Netherlands, it should meet with less social resistance. Such ditches are current, but are not always well maintained. The advantage is water management. It decreases the pressure on the larger water systems to absorb the run-off from fields. It helps with irrigation when the rainfall is less predictable, it helps prevent soil erosion and promotes biodiversity. The inconvenience is that they have to be maintained – some re-digging, careful choice of hedge plants (if the two ideas are combined), and access to fields is restricted to one or two entrances for tractors – where a bridge might have to be constructed and managed. Of course, if the water-ditch and hedges are well managed they function as fencing for cattle, cows, horses and possibly sheep, thus reducing the cost of building more artificial fences – post and barbed-wire or electrical fences (wood or stone fences are not feasible in the region due to scarcity of lumber and stone quarries).

Lastly, for the environment, we suggest preventing further urban development of the coastal areas. The present development is destroying fragile coastal ecological systems. They need further protection through legislation.

Society is doing quite well, although some emphasis could be put on reducing crime, alcoholism, unemployment and political conflict. The economy needs attention, and this is reflected in the investment choices made by government in the hope that investment from outside will flow to the region in the near future, and that businesses within the region will prosper. As is already put in place, new business should align with the green transition, but again, in a real way that makes a difference at the regional level or even more locally. See the continuation of the study where we model the biofuel industry within its regional context. Before this stage, we add more detail to the analysis.

13.3 Tables, Notes and References (Tables 13.1, 13.2 and 13.3)

A more detailed examination of the data tables will show which data (or the underlying causes of the data) are pulling the final arrow away, and which data are to be encouraged. We include the data table with the ones to be encouraged shaded in green, and the ones to discourage shaded in red (to echo the idea of a green light and

Table 13.1 Economic data Hauts-de-France

General Quality	Name of indicator	Degree	Length
Harmony	GDP per capita 27823 Euro per year (2018) [1]	60	0.4
~~Harmony~~	~~GDP per capita second worst in France (2018) [1]~~	~~60~~	~~0.15~~
Harmony	20110 Euro Median of disposable income per consumption unit in 2018, in euros [2,3]	60	0.3
Harmony	3454 Total expenditure per inhabitant of local authorities in 2018 [4]	80	0.55
Harmony	-0.9% Growth rate of operating expenditure by authorities in 2018 [4]	70	0.5
Harmony	4.9% Gross savings per capita DGF of local authorities (average between 2014 and 2018)	45	0.5
Harmony	Contribution to France's GDP as compared to the regional average [5]	60	0.4
Discipline	An exceptional aid package compensating for COVID-19 [6]	130	0.5
Discipline	The solidarity fund is more than € 7 billion	130	0.7
Discipline	18,0% poverty rate in 2018, [2,7,8]	150	0.7
Discipline	18,0% poverty the second highest 2018, [2,7,8]	150	0.8
Discipline	Households declaring bankruptcy in 2020 [9] 7	190	0.6
~~Discipline~~	~~Number of businesses declaring bankruptcy declined in 2020 [10]~~	~~200~~	~~0.2~~
Excitement	foreign investment 2019 (high, above the average) [5]	270	0.7
Excitement	The number of new companies created in 2019 [11]	280	0.75
Excitement	fourth most important exporting region in France [5]	320	0.75

Table 13.2 Social data Hauts-de-France

General Quality	Name of indicator	Degree	Length
Harmony	12.9% Birth-rate in 2017 [13]	30	0.5
~~Harmony~~	~~Number of frost days: a rapid decrease~~	~~45~~	~~0.2~~
Harmony	More than a third of high school students study professionally, i.e. the highest proportion in the regions of mainland France [14]	50	0.3
Harmony	25.4% of the population over 15 is in the retirees category in 2017 [13,15–19]	60	0.55
Harmony	The number of students will drop between 2019 and 2040 [14]	60	0.4
Harmony	71.2% activity rate of people aged between 15 and 64 (2017)	75	0.4
Discipline	Unemployment rate 9.7% (2020)	140	0.8
Discipline	19.7% people without professional activity 2017	130	0.5
Discipline	19.7% people without professional activity 2017 (the highest regional standing)	130	0.8
Discipline	9.1% mortality rate in 2017 [13]	150	0.4
Discipline	Death by cancer (346.6 thousands deaths in 2016) [20,21]	165	0.75
Discipline	Per 1000 people who died from coronavirus in the Hauts de France (May 2021) total number is 8419 [22]	195	0.5
Discipline	1.2 Homicide rate in 100000 people (2000s) [23]	200	0.55
Discipline	Alcohol consumption leading to hospital emergency visits because of alcohol [24] (1,86%)	200	0.6
Excitement	Ranked second (in terms of jobs) for foreign investment projects [5]	280	0.9
Excitement	6.9% were managers and higher intellectual professions 2017	300	0.35
Excitement	Number of festivals in July 2019 (25 events) [25]	320	0.8
Excitement	Number of museums in Hauts de France is 88 [26,27]	340	0.4

Table 13.3 Environmental data Hauts-de-France

General Quality	Name of indicator	Degree	Length
~~Harmony~~	~~Forest area: 446 ± 19 (total forest thousands of hectare) (0.14 hectare/km2) [29]~~	~~60~~	~~0.2~~
Discipline	Direct GHG emissions: recent increase; general downward trend [30]	180	0.75
Discipline	Floods: first natural risk in Hauts-de-France [30]	180	0.8
Discipline	Carbon storage and destocking in soils [30]	180	0.9
~~Discipline~~	~~Heating networks: a growing share of renewable heat [31]~~	~~180~~	~~0.1~~
Discipline	Percentage of surface water in a critical state (2015) [32]	180	0.8
Discipline	Coastal urbanization increasing 40% is urbanized in the coastal area	180	0.5
Discipline	15.2 Level of air pollution in PM 2.5 (μg/m3) [23]	185	0.6
Discipline	Number of frost days: a rapid decrease	200	0.7
Discipline	+0.29°C per decade is the average increase in the region's temperature [30]	200	0.7
~~Discipline~~	~~Bird populations sensitive to climate change [33]~~	~~210~~	~~0.1~~
Discipline	Sea level: a clear evolution [33]	220	0.5
~~Discipline~~	~~10% energy consumption by renewable energies [31]~~	~~230~~	~~0.1~~
Excitement	Agricultural use of the land 10km away from the coast (60%) [33]	260	0.75

a red light for traffic). The green ones point towards the wish spot and the red ones away. These are obvious targets for specific policy recommendations.

Another strategy is to concentrate on the arrows with length >.5. If we concentrate on these, then we see that the general suggestions about changes in agricultural practice and better management of coastal areas is sound. Such changes will contribute indirectly to health of the human population. If we can use the changes to increase employment, then we will have taken care of many of the pressing issues.

13.4 Small Industry Conversion of Biomass into Electricity

We now add to the data table, for only a small industrial plant that converts farm waste into electricity. Notice two peculiarities: (i) there is not much data, (ii) we have only one datum in the harmony sector. This gives that datum "undue" influence. The reason for the disproportion in data is that the industry is new, therefore exciting, requiring investment and it does not contribute significantly on directly to economic, social or environmental harmony. See data Table 13.4.

Table 13.4 Table of biomass-electricity industry in the subregion of Hauts de France

Sphere	General Quality	Name of indicator	Degree	Length
Economic	Excitement	Spirulina investment 270K Euro	260	0.3
Economic	Excitement	Initial investment 2.2 million Euro	310	0.8
Social	Harmony	Six farms with 1600 heads of Bovine and a few thousand chickens.	60	0.6
Social	Excitement	14 experts (high level of education)	320	0.2
Social	Excitement	The bio-generation of electricity for 500 households (sound business model, feel-good factor in individuals, raising awareness in people)	340	0.25
Environmental	Excitement	Six farms with 1600 heads of Bovine and a few thousand chickens.	260	0.7

To get a sense of the quality of the contribution, we could either envisage the industry being multiplied in the region, or do the opposite and consider a sub-region of Hauts-de-France, the one just around the industry, in particular, the community where the 500 households use the electricity produced by the biomass conversion site. With the first idea, there are threshold limits – geographical places where biomass might be less available or complicated to manage, such as in the centre of the city of Lille. If we were to follow the former scaling adjustment, we would imagine implanting such industry at the scale needed to supply all of the electricity consumed in the region. To make this industrial process the *only* source of electricity in Hauts-de-France we would need to multiply the number of cattle and chickens quite significantly. There would be cattle, dairy cows and chickens on the streets of Lille, in the parks, in the private gardens and in the farmer's fields. The smell of trucks passing with manure would upset the urban communities, the region would become a net exporter of meat and so on. This is unrealistic, if not silly, as a "solution" to the electrical energy supply in the whole region. Clearly a mixed approach with the existing wind mills is more likely and is more suitable. So, we considered the sub-region at a small enough scale that it is palpably affected by the industry. We construct a compass for only the data concerning the industrial plant. We can then see not exactly how much, but by what qualitative tendency, the industry changes the regional reading. See Figure 13.7.

As noted in the general discussion, there is no reason to suppose that the industry can be multiplied throughout Hauts-de-France to become the major source of electricity in the whole region. But there might be other sub-regions who could copy the industry and enjoy local success.

The ecological economics institutional compass comparison is similarly revealing. This is because the industry simply helps to close the waste and energy loop, in

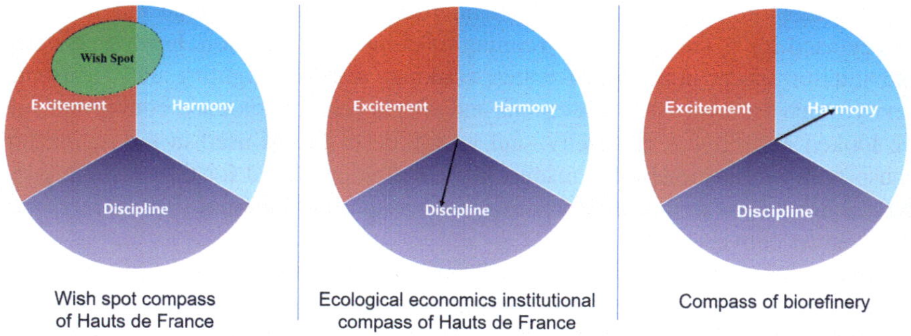

Fig. 13.7 Econo-sphere compass for sub-region with biomass-electricity industry

an effort towards a more circular economy – using (otherwise) waste (really fertiliser) to contribute to the economy, to energy needs and to reduce incinerated or material waste. The waste from the bio-electricity industry is re-used as fertiliser, so the second-waste does not go to waste. It re-enters the cattle, chicken and human food chain by fertilising plant crops. There is one advantage and one disadvantage of the second-waste. There is around the same amount in mass, but it is entropically more positive – some of the entropy having been channelled to make electricity. The advantage is that because the material is more "broken down" it is more readily available to plants, and more quickly integrated into the soil. This makes a difference in the short term, but not in the long term. The loop closing does not require a serious shift in existing agricultural practice. This is why the arrows pull in opposite directions.

In fact, if the farms supplying the bio-mass were to become organic, they might have much more difficulty, take much more labour, to collect the biomass. Therefore, while adding this industry helps to reduce the human impact on the natural environment in the region, the reduction is marginal from the point of view of the natural environment itself. The industry fits with the existing practice of industrial agriculture.

The readings of the three spheres shows us that closing the energy and waste loop, what is referred to as moving towards a more circular economy, makes only a marginal difference to the region, even on a very local level. This makes sense for reasons of entropy. Such processes marginally reduce our rate of entropy production.

This might seem obvious, or it might seem surprising. Either way, it is important information for policy makers, because really what this tells us is that the technical "solution" to energy production promised by bio-mass conversion processes, is helpful, since it moves the final compass reading *closer* towards the wish spot, by shortening the arrow. But it is worth knowing that it not enough to make any real difference. In other words, this technical solution to the green transition is not enough on its own, and other investments might be more promising. It is also quite clear that a mix of technical solutions – bio-mass conversion, wind mills, solar panels and nuclear energy will have to be accompanied by a cultural change; a real reduction in our dependence on energy in absolute terms – not only relative, that is, in *per capita* terms.

Looking more deeply, we can ask the question: "What is household and industrial energy used for?" The answer is: running machines, refrigeration, heating of water and interior space, pumping of water, cooking, washing, lighting and electronic devices such as: computers, televisions and telephones. The biomass conversion site we looked at produces electricity, and very little of this is used in the region for transportation. Non-renewable resources are still widely used for this, including by the machines used in industrial farming and transporting biomass waste material to the biomass conversion site.

To make a change that is significant with respect to the compass, we have to change our habits, life-styles and expectations as well. It is better to face this fact head-on and find creative solutions that will change travel and transportation expectations and reduce significantly our use of "free" energy, that is, our fund of low entropy.

Chapter 14
Concluding Philosophical Remarks

This chapter concludes the book, not the part of the book.

As noted in the introduction, we can construct several compasses, representing change in an institution over time, or for comparing institutions to each other. The construction is sensitive work due to our making qualitative decisions, as indicated in Sect. 5.4.2. But it is not impossible.

Remark 1: The first philosophical remark is that our analysis can be shallow or deep.

Prima facie, when we make our analysis, we focus on outliers. An 'outlier' statistic is one that influences the length and direction of the final arrow disproportionately to the others. It has a long length, and maybe a degree that is outwith the other indicator arrows in that sector. If the degree is very different, then it is qualitatively independent of the others. To be shallow in our analysis, we simply erase it and replace it with a 'better behaved' statistic, or we can change degree and length *directly on the table*, and hope that no one notices.

If we are manipulating the spheres, we can also change the relative proportions of the three spheres. Of course, with such gerrymandering, objectivity is compromised, since rather than deciding on the direction and length *independently* of the other indicator arrows, we do so *with respect to* the other indicator arrows and in particular, with respect to the final arrow and its representation on the compass. This is trickery, but might be enough to justify a policy in the short term or to a gullible audience. The robustness checks counter the gerrymandering, so it is with a less robust compass that gerrymandering is easier. Remember that if we have been careful in gathering data, and have made the data gathering and analysis inclusive of the wider public, then there should be no surprise outlier arrows missing in a robust compass.

A deeper analysis can be made by working out how to change the reality behind the length and direction of particular indicator arrows. This can be done through changes in policy that address that statistic directly. For example, if an alarming number of people are dying of lung cancer, and this is statistically correlated to

M. I. Friend, *The Institutional Compass: Method, Use and Scope*, Methodos Series 18, https://doi.org/10.1007/978-3-031-05453-2_14

smoking heavily, then we design policies to encourage general lung health, and decrease smoking.

An even deeper analysis involves looking at the statistics more thoroughly: re-examining the context and culture that give weight to the decisions concerning degree and length. We can also look for the underlying causes of the statistics within the predominant or secondary sector (we look back to the sector arrows), or by looking at the whole, hence the holistic aspect of the analysis. Returning to the smoking example, we notice that smoking is considered to be 'cool' in some sub-cultures, so we can try to counter that image in the broader media. We might also notice that it is associated with rebellion or disquiet. In this case, we might want to look for means of making people feel more at ease and in accord with society.

Remark 2: The compass design is not *ad hoc* with respect to the three qualities.

We might be tempted to change the compass by changing the qualities. We can do this in two ways. One is numerical: by adding or subtracting general qualities. The other is nominal: by changing the three general qualities to another three general qualities.

Let us start with the number three. We could add more general qualities. This is counter-recommended for the following reasons. The three qualities are conceptually orthogonal to each other. That is, they were chosen to be in some sense incommensurable. A final arrow can rotate from any of the three qualities into the other two directly: clockwise from harmony to discipline, counter-clockwise from harmony to excitement, from excitement to harmony and from excitement to discipline, from discipline to harmony and from discipline to excitement. Yet every institution displays one of these predominantly. They are not strict opposites, even if they are incommensurable. Yellow is incommensurable with red, but it is not it's opposite, being a plant is incommensurable with being a mammal, but it is not its opposite.

The representation in two dimensions allows for three incommensurables but not more. If we had two or four then there would be opposites on a two-dimensional representation. We cannot make an institutional compass by dividing the circle into four since this would suggest that the two opposing quarters are opposites when we tie our sector arrows with a rhombus. Thus, to mathematically represent the orthogonality/conceptual incommensurability of four general qualities, we would need a three-dimensional representation. Our circle compass on paper would have to be a sphere. This is by no means mathematically difficult, or difficult to *represent* with computer interface, since we can show it being rotated around, but such representations are of limited use because they are difficult *for us* to see and understand, despite the computer interface. Remember that, here we are interested in making policy decisions based on a *simple* final representation, and the simplicity is what would be sacrificed. Similarly, for five general qualities, we would need four dimensions and so on. For reasons of ease of understanding, reading and communicating the representation on screen or paper, three is better than a larger number of general qualities.

What of two? We could opt, not for a circle, but a scale of bad to good. This is counter-recommended because it is too dichotomous and simplistic. There already exist decision making aides that are dichotomous, and some are quite suitable. The compass shows its worth in subtle and complex decisions, when there will be some compromise and we are looking to satisfy various stakeholders who have agendas that conflict on some points. Our relationship with the environment is a complex matter, and we should not over-simplify it. So, in decisions concerning our relationship to the environment, the compass is recommended over other decision aides. 'Good' and 'bad' are relative terms and are sensitive to context and time. Forgetting these sensitivities is what leads to *poor* policy decisions. After all, some discipline is good: some businesses need to fail to teach us lessons and encourage us to increase efficiency, some social strife is good since it makes society more resilient, it tests and sharpens our sense of democracy. Some stress on the environment is good since, in the right measure, it promotes health and resilience.

An important reason to have three unranked qualities is that it removes us from our dichotomous thinking. We return to the fox or trickster character. See Sect. 5.6.2. We can embrace the subtleties and nuances of complex situations because the complexity is resolved into a simple and intuitive representation. This is what has been missing in the past, and might be one of the reasons politicians are reluctant to make too nuanced decisions. They are difficult to communicate and justify. The compass helps with this, not only the communication, but also the appreciation of the complexity and subtlety. These are the several reasons for three qualities, as opposed to another number.

A final reason for the number three has to do with how our brains work. The numbers: one, two and three only require one part of the brain, and even very young children and many mammals can distinguish these numbers. The number four and all higher numbers require more parts of the brain.

The nominal change is to re-name the three general qualities to three others. The very strong temptation for many people will be to think in terms of good, bad and neutral, or overshoot, undershoot and tipping point. This is scalar-quality thinking. We have this implicitly in the compass when we decide on the length of an indicator arrow, we have it implicitly when we draw a wish spot. But we do not want this to be the end of the analysis. Restricting ourselves to scalar-quality thinking is discouraged because it requires only "fast" thinking. For careful decision making, we want "slow" thinking (Kahneman). The three chosen qualities impose a rational remove that slows our thinking just enough, without becoming too complicated. The doughnut representation in Fig. 5.2 and the Fig. 5.7 representation could be done in a linear way. We just cut the circle in the doughnut and present it in a line. With the representation in Fig. 5.7, we stretch out the centre of the circle and line the indicators up next to each other. We can do this because there is no reason for the *order* of the indicators, in those representations; we do not need to close the circle. The compass, in contrast, demands the circle – because of the triangle we use to tie the qualities/sector arrows together, and because the rotation of a wish spot or some of the indicator arrows can take place both clockwise and anti-clockwise. The qualities merge into each other, as represented by colours, and as degrees are associated with adjectives.

We could, of course, not use scalar qualities, but another three incompatibles. For example, in deciding on the general quality and suitability of a piece of fabric, we might want to compare durability, beauty, insulation. Durability would be indicated by how easy it is to tear or wear out the fabric; beauty by possible patterns imprinted, shininess, pliability; and insulation by togs, noise penetration, wind penetration and so on. A piece of fabric is not an institution, so we have widened the scope in terms of what the compass arrow exercise can be applied to. Moreover, the three qualities are no longer related to each other.

Changing the qualities is possible, but remember where they come from. The three qualities come from Indian and other Oriental philosophical traditions: Hinduism, Jain and Buddhism. The original words in Sanskrit are: *sattva* for harmony, and *tamas* for discipline and *raja* for excitement. A guru will assess and advise someone based on which of the three qualities predominates in that person and which needs more emphasis. While *raja* is exciting and glamourous, it can easily tip into *tamas*, as we try to hold on to the excitement and glory. The path of wisdom is to follow a more *sattvic* life, tending a little towards *raja*. According to Kumar (2007) from whom I draw inspiration, *sattva* is also the better direction for living in harmony with the environment, and better for the environment in and of itself, which is one of the reasons I chose to translate *sattva* as harmony. This was the reason for these particular three qualities, but I hold out an invitation to experiment and try others. This will be important if we are trying to make the compass relevant to people in other cultures where they might have their own trio of general qualities.

Remark 3: There is an inescapably normative component to compass construction.

This does not make the construction subjective. On the contrary, the exercise of constructing a compass turns the norm into a description at the point where we declare the norm and make it explicit. Because compass construction is partly formal the norm is acknowledged and then taken out of our hands by being put into the calculation for generating a final compass reading. One norm is weighed against other competing norms. They are all put in the mix together. Even with the generic compass, normativity enters the exercise as we decide upon a baseline for a statistic. The conception of baseline, scale and extremes is important and worth discussing. Ideological normativity is more explicit when we add the concept of sphere. We then explicitly select a category of data to treat as more important. We express our decision mathematically by making a normative normalisation. We can debate and override that decision.

For example, there might well be times when we think that it is worthwhile to compromise the eco-sphere, for example to prevent immediate war, or under political pressure from other countries. Some governments deliberately "sacrifice" certain ecological areas in order to make the standard of living higher in the whole country. In this spirit, we would then ignore that sphere and the data on the corresponding table for the sacrificed region, or more subtly, we could reduce the relative size of the eco-sphere. Recall how Mayumi (2001, 45) puts it: as a society, we decide on a culturally acceptable *rate* of entropy production. The rate at which we consume fossil fuels is balanced against other considerations. In absolute environmental terms, we decide on a rate of environmental degradation when we use fossil fuels. The beauty of deciding on such a rate, is that we take responsibility for that decision. We are responsible for the compensation or trade-off. We are responsible to our own future, to the next generation and to seven generations hence, if we follow the wisdom of the indigenous people of the Americas.

In terms of the methodology for constructing a compass, for example, rather than insist on taking pre-massive population growth and industrial agriculture as the baseline for the eco-sphere, we could decide that the baseline is after that, say, the year 2000. We decide to return to the rates of entropy production – the using up of non-renewable resources, that we enjoyed in 2000. We can do this in absolute terms for the world, and then decide on mechanisms for distribution for the license to use up non-renewable resources. We could decide to do this for a country or other administrative boundary, or we could do this in more relative terms, such as making it a *per capita* measure.

Following Friend (2017, 101), if we add "per unit of consumption", then we have a culturally acceptable measure of ecological *efficiency*. Both are important for the purposes of ecological economics. We might also allow some institutions more leeway in compromising the environment than others. These are trade-off decisions it is better to make consciously rather than unconsciously. This only adds transparency and depth to the analysis. A deep analysis is used to make a solid justification for a policy.

The normative considerations will also be important as priorities change in a culture. It is clear that more of the public in many countries are more concerned about the environment than they used to be. This is partly because the damage is increasing, and so more people have become aware it. In contrast, in the past, not everyone could see for themselves the effects of our collective burning of fossil fuels. But it is also due to our communication with each other, with education in schools or with becoming more open to listening to the voice of indigenous people. The shift in general awareness is due to many things happening in concert. Norms change. Keeping track of changes should be part of policy, and it should be part of economics, insofar as economics is supposed to be about the management of resources.

Remark 4: There are checks for robustness of the sector arrows.

By 'robustness' we mean that the sector arrows are quite stable (at a time) – adding more indicators does not alter the degree or length of the sector arrow very significantly, instead they re-enforce the sector reading. This means that there are no *undiscovered* 'outlier indicator arrows': ones that significantly change the direction or length of the sector arrow, and therefore the final arrow. This does not mean stability over time, since the outside context can change, especially if we pass a number of tipping points, such as when ecosystems collapse. Policy decisions take place at a time, given the state of the context at that time. This is the best we can do at that time, except to anticipate future changes. Equivalently, we can be careful to adjust policy as the arrow shifts. This means that rather than staying with one policy decision, we match policy to a changing compass situation, we have a policy programme or policy system, as opposed to fixed policies. See the accountancy compass in Chap. 10.

To ensure robustness, or accuracy of the information, we have two checks. (a) We add indicators until we reach convergence on the length and position of the sector arrows, (b) we consult more people involved with the institution when we make the table. We ask them if there is an indicator that we have overlooked, and consult them for assessment of length and position. It might turn out that there is a strong disagreement. We then make two separate indicators. The idea behind wide consultation is that the sector arrows will be more robust if we consult more people who are affected by the institution than only a few people. Different people notice different things. A further advantage of wide consultation is that through participation in data inclusion and in the exercise of determining quality and length of indicator arrows, participants will understand and better accept policy decisions made on the basis of an institutional compass. The decisions being made in a complex situation are not easy, and will not please everyone. Acceptable compromise is reached through understanding the higher purpose.

Some politicians and decision makers sense that their power is compromised by participation. The decisions are no longer exclusively in their hands. For this reason, they would forgo the inclusive part of the compass construction. This omission is counter-indicated. The sense of threat and of loss of power is an illusion. The decision maker who uses the compass method will still have his, or her, name associated with the decision. After all it is him, or her, who decided to use the compass, and who leads the exercise. If the policy is in keeping with the wishes of the people served by the decision maker, then it will enjoy acceptance and longevity. In other words, the fame of the decision maker will be greater, not lesser. He, or she, will be judged favourably by history. This is why robustness and objectivity in the reading are important.

Another way of thinking about robustness is to consider the question: "Under what circumstances would different compass constructors end up with different final compass readings?" This is a question about subjectivity in construction.

There are three reasons why the same institution might have different compass readings. One is that the compass constructors included different data. The recommendation is to include all of the data that is deemed significant – so, amalgamate the data tables.

The second reason is that the analysis of particular data is different – in length or degree. If it is different in length, then other extremes of maximal and minimal are being used and that what is "normal" is also different. These issues bear discussion, and the discussion is important for consensus and mutual understanding.

The third reason is that the normative-normalisation is done with a different calculation. In this case, we confront different world-views. This is difficult to deal with on a decision-making level, since the differences tend to be philosophically fundamental. However, what we can do is try to negotiate a compromise, or take responsibility for holding a view when an alternative has been presented. After all, one of the views might be a more accurate portrayal of reality. We can only test this in the long run, as our choice in world-view and the decisions made in light of that view are played out. The point is to take responsibility towards ourselves and others for our metaphysical conceptions of reality.

It remains that it is not always possible to ensure robustness. The quality of the data might not be high, there might be few participants, there might be very little numerical data. If we lack robustness, then we make policy decisions that address the shortcoming: improve the quality of the data, improve participation. In this way we address the *limitations* of the compass exercise.

Remark 5: Even when we do not have a robust compass, and enough data, we still learn valuable lessons from the exercise of constructing the compass.

It is not always straightforward or possible to construct a compass that meets the robustness checks. In these cases, we develop policy recommendations to get *better statistics*. We can choose them, and name them very carefully in advance. It is with the material we have, and under constraints, that we do the best we can. We then have *an* explanation as to why we made a particular policy decision, and a *partial* justification for the policies, but the explanation *includes* discussing the quantity and quality of the indicators, so it is a more abstract and technical explanation and justification.

More important, we make our policy recommendations with a degree of humility. By trying to make an institutional compass we have a good sense of why we are hesitating, and we can share this information with those concerned. They can then be vigilant about the success of the policy and understand the importance of having a good suite of reliable statistics. Moreover, we have a pretty good idea as to how to change the policy if we later add new statistics that influence the position or length of the non-robust arrow. So, we can anticipate. After all, when we make policy decisions, we know in advance that we do so with imperfect information, that the context changes, that values change, but we make the decisions despite this. With the use of an institutional compass, even a non-robust one, we do *better* than just take a guess, trusting our instinct, making the decision on the basis of a monetary calculation to maximise profit or by using alternative multi-criteria decision aides. Again, the latter are entirely appropriate in the right setting and in making certain sorts of decision. The compass shows its worth in truly complex situations.

At the end of the day, compass construction, like modelling, is an art. This is so for two reasons. One is that there is an element of normativity that is inescapable. This is to be expected, since we are normative creatures. We notice only what we can notice, and what we *can* notice, depends on our education, language, experiences, open-mindedness, desires and the varying capacities of our very senses and instruments. Even when we make a compass exercise widely democratic, we collectively cannot notice every detail. We are not in the position of Laplace's Demon. What we can do, is make the evaluation as objective as possible, and this includes not omitting or trying to hide our inevitable normative leanings.

The other reason compass construction is an art is that there is a feed-back loop that changes the outcome. In creating a compass, as scientists, we learn more about the institution we study. If we advise on policy, then that policy will, hopefully, change the institution, and this change will be reflected in the final arrow of the compass. This is why it is interesting to try to keep the information as up to date as possible. At the same time as we construct a compass, the final arrow changes. We use the term "in real time". Of course, the term is disingenuous here. The best we can do is have *some* of the data be updated, as and when, instruments track a change and it is only then that the arrow can be adjusted. After all, the method of aggregation is an algorithm. It can be written as a computer program. What cannot be left to a computer is cultural changes in quality-attitudes towards facts and data. *Some* such changes can be noticed indirectly by looking at people's behaviour, but not all. This is the stuff of consumer profiling. We can use this sort of information for the compass too. But, again, not all of the data analysis can be left to computer programs. The compass engenders a feedback loop when it is used for communication, since it is a representation of where our institution is heading. It acts as a mirror. The mirror is informative, and we react to that information. We react to the representation, to then make or influence policy, and that will over time change the final compass reading, to which we react a new. This feedback-communication loop is an example of data that a computer program cannot handle well.

To extend the compass to work as a non-linear accounting method, we draw an oval in the area to which we hold ourselves accountable. As policy makers, we are then held accountable insofar as the final reading deviates from the oval. There might be perfectly good external reasons for the discrepancy, after all, even the climate is changing, which means that 'baselines' also change, pathological behaviours in climate or society become 'normalised'. Here, we should be aware of the distinction between a statistical norm or mean, and a norm of health or well-being (of an eco-system or of society). The first is a reading of where we happen to be and reflects what we collectively experience as "normal". The second is scientific. The scientific norms are removed from our experience of them. They are measured. The two norms might not coincide. In fact, increasingly they diverge since we replace awareness of our surroundings with an awareness of a virtual "reality" that is presented to us through a screen. Open discussion and increased awareness of the divergence between reality and virtual reality is necessary for finding a way towards sustainable living.

The management of scarce resources is what economics is supposed to be about. Determining that natural resources are scarce, and managing them has revealed itself to be calamitous when left to organisations or businesses that use neoclassical economics to determine policy. The institutional compass can replace neoclassical economic calculations, but it is not perfect. It is imperfect because we cannot include the trees, the birds or the rivers directly as stakeholders. In lieu, we can ask scientists, farmers and indigenous people for information about the natural environment. They are the best experts we have for evaluating and managing scarce and fragile natural resources.

References

Friend, A. (2017). System of accounts for global entropy production (SAGE-P): The accounting in the topological domain space (TDS) of the econosphere, sociosphere an ecosphere. In S. Shmelev (Ed.), *Green economy reader* (pp. 99–137). Springer.

Kumar, S. (2007). *Spiritual compass; Three qualities of life*. Green Books Ltd. Foxhole.

Mayumi, K. (2001). *The origins of ecological economics; The biomechanics of Georgescu-Roegen*. Routledge.

Appendices

Appendix 1: Argument Against the Supposed Value-Neutrality of Neoclassical Economics

The following argument is originally due to Söderbaum (2000, 53–56). I summarise and modify it here.

A popular answer to the question: "What is economics about?" is "It is about money" or "It is about making profits". This is not completely right, but it is not completely wrong either. Almost all present-day economics textbooks will give the more conceptually basic answer that economics is about the allocation of scarce resources. I prefer the term 'management', since 'allocation' has a connotation of immediate distribution, whereas 'management' conceptually, psychologically, linguistically, more easily includes the idea of not touching, or storing, a scarce resource. So, for reasons of preparing the conceptual ground, let us settle on the definition that economics is about the *management* of scarce resources.

The question then is why is it that money is a partly correct answer to the question "What is economics about?" The argument goes like this. There are many resources, enjoying different levels of scarcity. Under the concept of 'resources' we find very different *types* of thing, since resources could include: potatoes, labour, gas, knowledge, land, gold, money itself, factories, chickens, paintings, skills, a legal service, family ties, patent rights, algorithms and so on. Comparing these to each other directly is impossible because it is too complex. There is no basis of comparison. "Some kind of common 'yardstick' is needed and money is normally suggested as the 'natural' solution to this problem." (Söderbaum, 2000, 55). This is why 'money' or 'making profits' is a good answer. It is the agreed upon *solution* to the very complex problem of resource management.

As a solution, it belongs to neoclassical economic theory. With some variation, it is this theory that has been most widely used by decision makers in the so called "developed world", excluding the communist countries, during the twentieth century. It was meant as a microeconomic theory but was promoted to macroeconomics.

M. I. Friend, *The Institutional Compass: Method, Use and Scope*, Methodos Series 18, https://doi.org/10.1007/978-3-031-05453-2

This is because it turns the very difficult problem of resource management into a simple calculation left up to individuals or purchasing organisations on a self-organising free market. It also has other merits. What are they?

On the free market, we exchange resources using money. If I have a surplus of a resource, I sell it for money so that I can use that money to purchase a resource that is scarce for me. A painting is worth a certain amount of money; or rather, someone is willing to pay, at a particular moment and in a particular transaction, a certain amount of money, and the seller agrees. That same amount of money could have been used to buy potatoes or legal services. Ideally, the market is a self-regulating system. So, if the government is meant to ensure the good management of the scarce resources of the country, then it can step aside and let the market take care of the problem, and so not worry about the complexity at all. The simplicity, at the government level is a merit. Government steps in only when there is an important enough market failure. It is not always clear what, if anything, is to be counted as a market failure, as we shall see shortly.

Economists make calculations about credit and debit, the convergence of supply and demand, costs of production and so on.[1] Business people also make calculations to work out what they can supply, if there is a demand that already exists for what they can supply or how to create demand artificially through advertising.

The second merit of the free market is that the calculations are (meant to be) value neutral, and this in two ways: one is that they are numerical, so mathematical, and so, objective and independent of our emotions or sentiments. The second is that, *qua* monetary transactions, they are independent of the (political or moral) values held by those carrying out the transaction. The price does not vary with moral worth or political position, only with *whether* you are willing to pay.

Why is value-neutrality a merit? It makes the theory independent of politics, morals, and religion. It is, therefore, applicable everywhere, in any community. This makes the theory simpler, more amenable to mathematical treatment and universal. Therefore, so the argument goes, the theory is objective, scientific, true and natural. The conclusion follows only if we disregard the wider context.

The argument for the value-neutrality of neoclassical economics is quite convincing. However, to *exclude* other considerations from *economics* (resource management) has political repercussions and is a political choice at a more general level or at a higher level (the wider context). Why? Because to maximise our utility (a term of art which is supposed to mean that we maximise our enjoyment of life) we want to do two things at once: increase our purchase power, and purchase goods or services that make us happy. The two are at odds with each other. For, we cannot spend and gain money in the same market transaction. In fact, we do not really want to maximise our utility always in the present. This is because doing so might mean suffering in the future. As rational agents, we maximise our utility over our supposed life time. What does not matter in neoclassical theory is what the particular

[1] Of course, we can trick demand. That is, we create demand through advertising. After all, most advertising is not meant simply to inform us of the existence of a product or resource on the market, it is meant to make us feel inadequate for not having the product or resource. Creating the feeling is trickery. It creates an artificial demand.

preferences are that are sought by an individual. However, it remains that some of us can buy the things -objects or services- that make us enjoy our lives. But there is still a tension between satisfying immediate desires and saving money for the future. The tension can be perfectly resolved.

For some people, the gaining and securing of money itself increases their utility. For example, some people have stock-shares, or an investment portfolio. Amongst them are those who report feeling happy when the shares go up in value or when their portfolio is making them wealthier. They feel sad when the opposite happens. And yet, there is no direct pleasurable sensation. There might not even be a particular item that they wish to purchase in the future. That is, the increase in monetary wealth is not bringing the time closer to when they can fulfil a particular non-monetary goal – the experience of a service or the owning of a material good. For such rational agents, the gaining of money has become an end in itself, as opposed to a means towards some non-monetary goal attained by purchasing.

Claim 20: It is *only* in neoclassical economic theory that maximising wealth can be an end in itself. In fact, according to the theory, it is the *most rational* goal to have, since the conceptual and emotional tension between immediate satisfaction of desires for particular goods or services does not compete against the gaining of money, instead they align and merge into one.

Now, we can see that the theory is *not* value-neutral. Valuing money is a value. Moreover, lacking, ignoring or suppressing other values is a *value*. It is a value at a higher level, a meta-value. It tells us which other values to value, and which (other) values to dis-regard – in this case, *all others* in the name of rationality.

According to some, this meta-value is a destructive and perverse value. It is destructive of other people. Anyone who cannot provide a scarce service, or good, cannot accumulate money, and cannot, by definition, increase his, or her, utility. This is why we did not traditionally pay for housework. It was not a rare service. We do not pay for the air we breathe because it is abundant. In some countries we do not pay for household water, because it is abundant; although we do pay for the pumping and heating of water. Abundant goods and services have no market value, and therefore, according to the theory, no value at all. The latter is the perversion, since air and water are necessary for our short-term survival.

The theory encourages monopolies. These are nothing more than devices for making a resource scarce because the owner can then charge what he, or she, likes for the resource, by restricting its abundance on the market. It is scarce, not in the material sense of there not being enough, but it is scare on the market. If one charges a lot, then it becomes, not scarce, but non-existent, for the poor. Some people consider monopolies to be a market failure, and typically, legislation is put in place to prevent monopolies so that competition can make the resource available again at a more affordable price, that better reflects the material availability of the good or service.

Another perversion, because immoral, is that the unemployed and unemployable have no value. What does this entail? The unemployed and unemployable include children (in most countries), but that is alright since in the future they will contribute to the market: we support them as an investment. It includes retired people. This is alright because they contributed in the past. They saved money and pay it out during their retirement. It includes prisoners. Usually, they have been removed from the market, but make no mistake, a lot of money is spent by the state to maintain them, so indirectly they contribute to the economy, to GDP (gross domestic product), but not directly or individually out of choice. It includes the severely mentally and physically disabled. However, like prisoners, they contribute indirectly to the economy. It is because of their indirect contribution to the economy that we support them financially. It includes the homeless and the (often) young people who simply cannot find work. That all of these people are *without direct value* has a very strong moral repercussion, and should not rest smugly behind a pretence of value neutrality.[2]

The perversion is exposed when we consider income distribution. The simulations that are best supported by data, show us that if everyone starts with the same initial amount of money, and each makes exchanges on the free market, the distribution follows a Boltzmann-Gibbs exponential curve (Yakovenko, pp. 3–4). More important, the concentration of data points is towards the bottom income level. "...random transfers of money in economic transactions between otherwise equal economic agents [over a series of market transactions] produce a broad and highly unequal probability distribution of money among the agents." (Yakovenko, 8). We end up with a few very wealthy people and an overwhelming mass of very poor. It then takes government intervention, a tax system, laws setting ceilings on debt and bankruptcy, laws to re-equalise the distribution to re-adjust the market, to support a middle class, to break monopolies and so on. The pure economic theory, a truly free market, destroys the middle class. Some might consider this to be a market failure, because immoral, and therefore, favour government intervention, as advocated by Keynes. Since the calculations are known, and since in many countries, the destruction of a middle class is considered to be a market failure, the societies of those countries clearly do not fully believe in the value-neutrality of neoclassical economics. Real value-neutrality means that we would be indifferent to the distribution where a very few are very wealthy and the overwhelming majority are very poor – since this is where the income distribution settles objectively (mathematically) when left alone. It turns out that *de facto* very few people are indifferent in this way, and so such people have (non-monetary) values – the ones that allow us to recognise a market failure.

Therefore, pure neoclassical economic theory is not value neutral. It follows that it is not an objective or universal economic theory. It is a perfect theory in a limited context, not a global context.

Aglietta (2020, 30) puts it nicely:

> This [neo-liberal] ideology starts with the idea of a self-regulating market, where the state government is an impediment. The role of government is reduced to protecting private property. The order of the day is to increase competition by any means in global chains of production and distribution. The sole objective is to increase monetary wealth by concentrating capital gain through rent. The corollary is the fragmentation of work contracts, and the weakening of collective or individual negotiating power vis-à-vis an enterprise, thus lowering the salaries of employees and increasing inequality in society. (Translation, mine).

We can now face the fact that our attitude towards money itself is cultural, and therefore, value laden and political. In some cultures, money is a means to an end, in

[2]This zero-value attribution to the unemployed does explain the resistance in some cultures to guaranteed income schemes.

others it is an end in itself. In some cultures, it is very important to have more money than one needs, because this brings security, prestige and political power, as well as surplus purchase power. This is more strongly the case where there is no social net to take care of people at the bottom.

In some cultures, it is the inverse. In such cultures, other sorts of value compete strongly with valuing monetary wealth. This counters the claim that neoclassical economic theory is universal or natural, in the sense of aligned with human nature. Other values include: use value, practical value, sentimental value or intrinsic value. Since many readers will be less familiar with the inverse of valuing money, let me provide an example.

This is a story told by Marchand. One day, Marchand's grandfather, chairman of the Colville Tribes, pointed out the place where Chief Silcosasket's teepee had been. Marchand recounts that he wondered

> if the Chief's teepee was the best one in the village since he was the leader, but my Grandfather just laughed at me. He said actually that the Chief's teepee was the poorest one in the whole village. He said the Chief gave everything he had to the elders and to the widows and to the orphans and to the poor. A man's place was based on how generous he was and by how much he helped his people. Owning materials (sic!) goods and riches and being greedy were not important things to the Entiat people. Chief Silcosasket was famous for being wise and honest. (Marchand et al., p. 228)

Similar stories can be found especially in Oriental cultures, but even in Europe, reform movements and religious orders were sometimes fashioned on vows of poverty and modesty. Since some people of some cultures value generosity over money and material wealth, greed for material wealth cannot be universal. Contra to the evidence from "other" cultures, according to neoclassical economic theory, a rational *homo economicus* is one who maximises his, or her, utility. If being rich makes him, or her, happy, then he, or she, is the most rational of all, because there are no competing desires. However, it turns out that we make choices as to how it is that we view money, even in a society permeated with a neoclassical ideology.

There are, at least, two types of neoclassical economist: one who believes *a priori* that it is a free market that makes us better off in aggregate. So, a free market *necessarily* makes the best of all possible worlds. The other sort of neoclassical economist believes in the free market and neoclassical economic theory *a posteriori*. That is, he, or she, has found convincing evidence of the theory by observation.

The difference between the two is that the first cannot recognise any evidence as being counter to the theory. The second is willing to revise his, or her, attitude towards the theory upon observing counter-evidence. The second, also holds other values, such as equitable distribution, and when other values are too much compromised, we have market failure. It is then appropriate for government to intervene and curtail the freedom of the market.

The first type of neoclassical economist wins the argument against the second because, he, or she, accuses the second of not being fully rational. The win depends on the logical trick of holding a sufficiently tight and seemingly comprehensive *a prioristic* theory. In such a theory, there is always a get-out clause, some device for dismissing any purported counter-evidence. Here, it was the definition of rationality. The reasoning is circular. Whenever someone points to a supposed market failure, the *a prioristic* neoclassical economist implores us to have faith, it actually is the best outcome, it is only temporarily bad, but in the long term it will turn out to be best to leave the market to her own devices. The fact that it looks bad, is an illusion, and the people who suffer now will bring about a better future in aggregate, and future generations will thank us for the austerity cure. Upon further pressure, the *a prioristic* neoclassical economist will accuse the other of irrationality (dressed in the guise of sentimentality). If then questioned as to the definition of rationality being used, the answer is that an agent is rational if and only if he, or she, seeks to maximise his, or her, utility. And the most efficient (rational) way to do this is to enjoy the accumulation of money itself. Therefore, there can be no real counter-evidence to the theory on pain of irrationality; making the argument circular or *a prioristic*. We can see that there is a confusion between the individual seeking to maximise his or her utility and the aggregate maximisation. This does not forbid the individual rational agent to use other-than-market mechanisms to maximise his, or her, utility, and asking government to intervene.

Apart from the confusion over who benefits, since the reasoning is circular, it is flawed. The flaw is not in the logic itself, which is impeccable. The flaw lies at a higher level of analysis.

Circular reasoning, which is what we find in all tight and seemingly comprehensive *a prioristic* theories, can be defeated in the following way. Come up with an equally tight *a prioristic* theory that contradicts the first somewhere. Then ask *on what basis* would one chose one theory over the other. There is no non-circular way of making the choice from *within* one of the theories. Circular theories are chosen from *outside* the theory. This is why they only seem to be comprehensive.

To thwart the argument of the *a priositic* neoclassical economist, let me propose an *a prioristic* non-neoclassical theory.

In this theory, *homo economicus* is rational if and only if it[3] maximises the utility of the community; community first, individual self, second. A holder of this theory, if rational, will display economic behaviour that *contradicts* the behaviour of the rational follower of neoclassical theory.

How do we choose between the two? We step outside the theory and decide whether we favour individual selfishness or community. Neoclassical economic theory itself cannot logically *compel* us to choose it. There is the supposition that humans are naturally selfish and infinitely greedy, but this is debatable too. Selfishness and greed are not universal values. We see them as vices in many cultures.

This is not to say that neoclassical economic theory is *wrong*. It has its place – when the values that accompany it are the ones held, or are most important. However, it is an error to think that it is universally applicable. For example, it is not suitable for all macroeconomic decisions. This is why Söderbaum is a pluralist about economics. There are several economic theories, and they each harbour values and have their place. It might not always be clear which is the better for a particular situation.

[3] *Homo economicus* is a construct. It has no gender. "*Homo economicus*" is grammatically singular and therefore "it" is the preferred pronoun over "them".

In conclusion, we see that neoclassical economics is not value neutral. It is therefore, not objective or scientific in the sense of value-neutral. It is also not universal, since it is not always the appropriate theory to use in resource management. In agreement with Söderbaum and Myrdal it is safe to assume that all economic theories either implicitly or explicitly *include* non-monetary values. Otherwise, we are missing too much.

Appendix 2: Compass Construction Steps

Step 1: Our first task is to find some quantitative data on the institution.
Step 2: Verify that the quality of the data is reasonably high.
Step 3a: Classify the data in terms of the three general qualities.
Step 4: Assign a precise *degree* to each indicator arrow.
Step 5: Assign a length to each indicator arrow.
Step 6: Enter the statistics on a table with four columns: the general quality, the name and any qualifiers, the degree and the length.
Step 7: Normalise the length for the purposes of aggregation.
Step 8: Plot each not-crossed out indicator arrow in its particular sector with the corrected/mechanically normalised length. Plot them head to tail. The first has its tail at the centre of the circle. The second has its tail at the head of the first and so on. The order does not matter.
Step 9: Within each sector, draw a 'sector arrow' from the centre of the circle to the head of the last arrow in that sector. A sector arrow gives us an overall-reading of that general quality for the institution.
Step 10: Draw a triangle linking the three heads of the sector arrows.
Step 11: Erase the sector arrows.
Step 12: Find the centroid of the triangle.
Step 13: Draw an arrow from the centre of the circle to the centroid of the triangle.
Step 14a: Erase the lines used to find the centroid of the triangle.
Step 15: Normalise the arrow by adding 1/3 the radius to the arrow.
Step 3b: Classify data in terms of whether it is economic data, social data or ecological data.
Step 14b: We place the compasses concentrically in the following proportions: the radius of the ecological compass is the longest. The radius of the economics compass is half the length of the ecological compass, and the length of the radius of the social compass is exactly half way between the two.
Step 16: We draw our three 'final' sphere arrows, head to tail as in step 8 with the first one's tail starting at the centre of the circle.
Step 17: Erase the circumference of the social compass and the economics compass. Return to the general qualities.
Step 18: Add the three 'final' arrows tail to head, and draw an arrow from the centre of the circle to the head of the last arrow.
Step 19: Erase the sphere arrows. This is the final arrow for the institution, from the perspective of ecological economics.

Appendix 3: Collection of Claims

1. The deeper the analysis of the compass reading, *ceteris paribus,* the greater the longevity of the policy.
2. The compass can be used as a "common measure" for comparing institutions. The comparison is qualitative, quantitative and holistic.
3. The turn from normative to descriptive in considering our ideological orientations, has two roles. It makes the construction of the compass more objective, and it elicits philosophical debate that should not be avoided. These roles are a strength of the compass construction, not a weakness.
4. One importance of the three general qualities is that, on considered reflection, almost every object, event, institution or society will have one that predominates.
5. Outward appearances and first associations might be deceptive.
6. We see institutions, events and statistics from a perspective.
7. One of the virtues of compass construction is to draw out debates about qualities and perspectives.
8. The general qualities of an institution can change over time.
9. The arrows rotate in both directions.
10. Keeping an institutional arrow in the same place on the compass requires vigilance and constant adaptation.
11. High quality data with sensitive analysis makes for a more objective indicator arrow.
12. The representation of statistics can be objective if we sensibly decide on a baseline and the extremes, or it can be political.
13. When we have stability in a sector arrow in terms of length and degree, we have weak objectivity. This is desired and "best possible" because this is a qualitative and culturally sensitive analysis.
14. Consultation, inclusiveness and participation increase the objectivity of the compass and longevity of policy based on the compass.
15. (made by some ecological economists): The health of the economy depends on the health of society, and the health of society depends on the health of the ecosystem.
16. For the ecological economist, an institution is sustainable if and only if the ecological-economics institutional compass's final arrow is in the harmony sector. Degree of sustainability is shown by the length of the arrow. The longer the arrow the more sustainable and the more resilient the institution.
17. The compasses can be used as a basis for mediation between differently oriented groups.
18. The more artificial and unrealistic meta-choices of worldviews are, the more limited the value of the compass reading.
19. The play of the spheres is equivalent to a normalisation of the length in the data points.
20. It is *only* in neoclassical economic theory that maximising wealth can be an end in itself. In fact, according to the theory, it is the *most rational* goal to have, since the conceptual and emotional tension between immediate satisfaction of desires for particular goods or services does not compete against the gaining of money, instead they align and merge into one.

Appendix 4: Chart of Compass Construction

CONSTRUCTING A STANDARD INSTITUTIONAL COMPASS

1. Plot the data points as vector arrows, added to each other in each quality sector.

2. Draw the sector arrows.

3. Draw a triangle uniting the tips of the sector arrows.

4. Erase the sector arrows.

5. Find the centroid of the triangle.

6. Draw an arrow from the centre of the circle to the centroid of the triangle.

7. Erase the triangle.

8. Normalise the length of the arrow. **This is the constructed institutional compass.**

Appendix 5: Chart of Compass Adaptations and Extensions

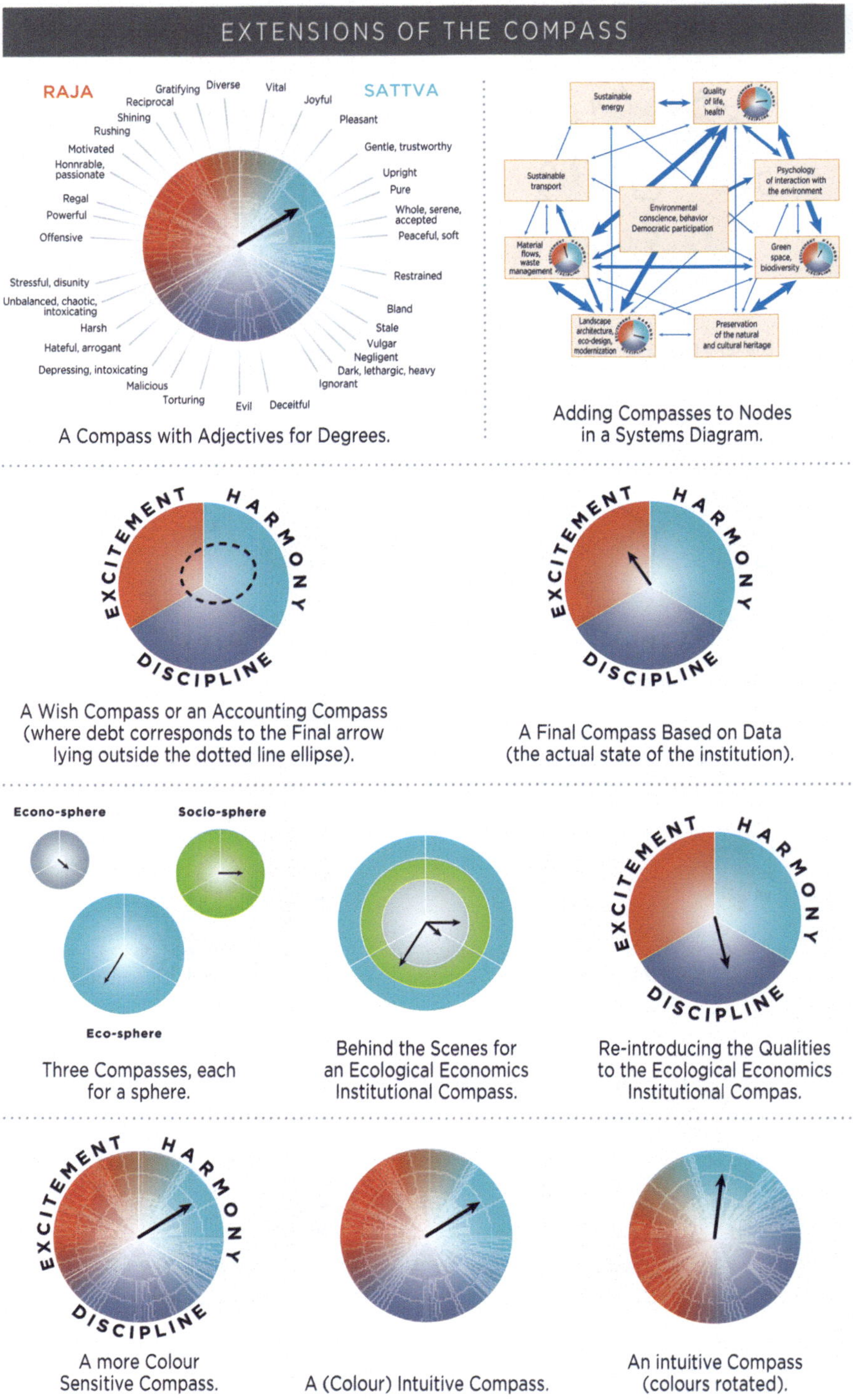

Adapted from Shmelev (2012), Shmelev & Shmeleva (2009)

Bibliography

Abdin, A. Y., & Friend, M. (Forthcoming). *Doughnuts and compasses: How to decide.*
Aglietta, M. (2020). La raie richesse des nations est leur capital publique. *Le Monde*. Dimanche 17 – Lundi 18 Mai. 30.
Alemany, M. (2020). Uruguay. Visite d'une prison modèle. *Courrier International* N°1533, 19–25 Mars 2020. pp. 32–33.
Boulding, K. (1949). Income or wealth. *Review of Economic Studies, 17*, 77–86.
Calude, C. S., & Longo, G. (2017). The deluge of spurious correlations in big data. *Foundations of Science, 33*(3), 595–612.
Costanza, R. (1992). Towards an operational definition of ecosystem health. In R. Costanza (Ed.), *Ecosystem health: New goals for environmental management* (pp. 237–256). Island Press.
Davies, W. (2018). *Nervous states; Democracy and the decline of reason.* Norton and Company.
Fitoussi, Sen, & Stiglitz. (2010). *Mis-measuring our lives.* Earthspan.
Friend, M. (2014). *Pluralism in mathematics: A new position in philosophy of mathematics* (Logic, Epistemology and the Unity of Science 32). Springer.
Friend, A. (2017). System of accounts for global entropy production (SAGE-P): The accounting in the topological domain space (TDS) of the econosphere, sociosphere an ecosphere. In S. Shmelev (Ed.), *Green economy reader* (pp. 99–137). Springer.
Georgescu-Roegen, N. (1971). *The entropy law and the economic process.* Harvard University Press.
Inglehart, R. (2015). *World values survey.* http://www.worldvaluessurvey.org/wvs.jsp
Jackson, T. (2009). *Prosperity without growth; Economics for a finite planet.* Earthscan.
Jorgensen, S. E., Fu-Liu, X., & Costanza, R. (2010). *Handbook of indicators for assessment of ecosystem health* (2nd ed.). Taylor and Francis.
Kahneman, D. (2011). *Thinking, fast and slow.* Doubleday.
Kauffman, L. H. (2018). Cybernetics, reflexivity and second-order science. In A. Riegler, K. H. Müller, & S. Umpleby (Eds.), *New horizons for second-order cybernetics* (Series on Knots and Everything Vol. 60). World Scientific.
Keen, S. (2000). The non-linear economics of debt deflation. In W. A. Barnett et al. (Eds.), *Commerce complexity and evolution* (pp. 87–117). Cambridge University Press.
Kumar, S. (2007). *Spiritual compass; Three qualities of life.* Green Books Ltd. Foxhole.
Lambert, R. (2020). La droite latino-américaine dans l'impasse. *Le Monde Diplomatique*. Mars 2020 8–9.
Larousserie, D. (2020). Comment sont élaborées les modélisations épidémiologiques. *Le Monde.* Vendredi 8 au Samedi 9 mai 2020. p. 2.

M. I. Friend, *The Institutional Compass: Method, Use and Scope*, Methodos Series 18, https://doi.org/10.1007/978-3-031-05453-2

Leyva-Lopez, J. C., & Fernández-González, E. R. (2003). A new method for group decision support based on Electra III methodology. *European Journal of Operational Research, 148*(1), 14–27.

Mageau, M. T., Costanza, R., & Ulanowicz, R. E. (1995). The development and initial testing of a quantitative assessment of ecosystem health. *Health, 1*, 201–213.

Mancuso, S., & Viola, A. (2018). *L'intelligence des Plantes. Traduit de l'italien par Renaud Temperini*. Albin Michel pour la production française.

Marchand, M. E., Vogt, K. A., Suntana, A. S., Cawston, R., Gordon, J. C., Siscawati, M., Vogt, D. J., Tovey, J. D., Sigurdardottir, R., & Roads, P. A. (2014). *The river of life; Sustainable practices of native americans and indigenous peoples*. Michigan State University Press.

Mayumi, K. (2001). *The origins of ecological economics; The biomechanics of Georgescu-Roegen*. Routledge.

Molinini, D. (2019). The weak objectivity of mathematics and its reasonable effectiveness in science. In *Axiomathes; Where science meets philosophy*. Springer.

Müller, K. H. (2016). *Second-order science; the revolution of scientific structures* (21 of the Series: Complexity | Design | Society). Edition Echoraum.

Nobbs, D. (1975). *The death of Reginald Perrin*. Gollancz.

Pani, N. (2009). Hinduism. In J. Peil & I. van Staveren (Eds.), *Handbook of economics and ethics* (pp. 216–222). Edward Elgar.

Peil, J., & van Staveren, I. (Eds.). (2009). *Handbook of economics and ethics*. Edward Elgar.

Pierson, M. (2020). *Organising ourselves as neighborhoods and watersheds against present and future threats*. Draft Copy.

Quammen, D. (2012). *Spillover; Animal infections and the next human pandemic*. W.W. Norton and Company.

Rapport, D. J. (2012). Ecosystem health indicators. In *The Berkshire encyclopedia of sustainability, measurements, indicators, and research methods for sustainability* (Vol. 6, pp. 103–107).

Rapport, D. J. (2013). Ecosystem health. In *Achieving sustainability: Visions, principles and practices* (pp. 251–260). Cengage Learning.

Rapport, D. J., & Maffi, L. (2010). Eco-cultural health, global health and sustainability. *Ecological Research, Special Feature: Environmental Change, Pathogens and Human Linkages, 26*(6), 1039–1049.

Rapport, D., Costanza, R., Epstein, P. R., Gaudet, C., & Levins, R. (Eds.). (1998). *Ecosystem health*. Blackwell.

Raworth, K. (2017). *Doughnut economics: Seven ways to think like a 21st-century economist*. Random House.

Roy, B. (1978). Electre III: Un algorithme de classements fondé sur une représentation flou des préférences en présence de critères multiples. *Cahiers du CERO, 201*(1), 3–27.

Roy, B., & Bouyssou, D. (1993). *Aide Multicritère à la Décision: Méthode et Cas*. Economica.

Shmelev, S. (2012). *Ecological economics; Sustainability in practice*. Springer.

Shmelev, S. E. (Ed.). (2017). *The green economy reader; Lectures in ecological economics and sustainable development*, Springer.

Shmelev, S. E., & Shmeleva, I. A. (2009). Sustainable cities: Problems of integrated interdisciplinary research. *International Journal of Sustainable Development, 12*(1), 4–24.

Shmeleva, I. (2017). Human values and sustainable development. In S. E. Shmelev (Ed.), *The green economy reader; Lectures in ecological economics and sustainable development* (pp. 333–366). Springer.

Smith, W. E. (2008). *The creative power: Transforming ourselves, our organisations and our world*. Routledge.

Söderbaum, P. (2000). *Ecological economics*. Earthscan Publications.

Söderbaum, P. (2016). *Economics, ideological oreintation and democracy for sustainable development* (2nd ed.). World Economics Association, Bristol, UK.

Söderbaum, P. (2017). How economics can become compatible with democracy. In S. Shmelev (Ed.), *Green economy reader; Lectures in ecological economics and sustainability* (pp. 22–38). Springer.

Varoufakis, Y. (2017). *And the weak suffer what they must? Europe, austerity and the threat to global stability*. Vintage (Penguin Random House).
Vatn, A. (2005). *Institutions and the environment*. Edward Elgar.
Vester, F. (1999). *The art of interconnected thinking; Ideas and tools for a new approach to tackling complexity*. Report for the Club of Rome.
Wright, C. (1992). *Truth and objectivity*. Harvard University Press.
Yakovenko, V. (2010). *Statistical mechanics approach to the distribution of money*. Routledge.
Yonglong, L., Wang, R., Zhang, Y., Hongqiao, S., Wang, P., Jenkins, A., Ferrier, R. C., Bailey, M., & Squire, G. (2017). *Ecosystem health towards sustainability*. Taylor & Francis.

Index

M. I. Friend, *The Institutional Compass: Method, Use and Scope*, Methodos Series 18, https://doi.org/10.1007/978-3-031-05453-2

D

E

The manufacturer's authorised representative in the EU is Springer Nature Customer Service Centre GmbH, Europaplatz 3, 69115 Heidelberg, Germany. If you have any concerns regarding our products, please contact ProductSafety@springernature.com

Printed and bound by CPI Group (UK) Ltd, Croydon, CR0 4YY
30/09/2026
02225496-0003